LABORATORY INVESTIGATIONS
IN BIOLOGY

James H. Otto
Albert Towle
W. David Otto
Myra E. Madnick

HOLT, RINEHART AND WINSTON, PUBLISHERS
New York   London   Toronto   Sydney

James H. Otto was a biology teacher and head of the Science Department at George Washington High School, Indianapolis, Indiana.

Albert Towle is a professor of biology and supervisor of biology student teachers at San Francisco State University, San Francisco, California.

W. David Otto is a teacher of biology at John Marshall High School, Indianapolis, Indiana.

Myra E. Madnick is a writer specializing in the biological sciences.

ISBN: 0-03-020266-3

78901 140 987654321

Preface

This edition of LABORATORY INVESTIGATIONS IN BIOLOGY offers a laboratory program which supports all of the major areas of biology included in the text MODERN BIOLOGY. The organization and the Investigation numbers in LABORATORY INVESTIGATIONS correlate to the chapters in MODERN BIOLOGY. Yet, LABORATORY INVESTIGATIONS is broad enough in scope to be used with any biology program. When used in conjunction with a text, LABORATORY INVESTIGATIONS presents the subject of biology as a complete laboratory science.

The Investigations in this book employ an inquiry approach which provides the students with the opportunity to add their own experiences and discoveries to the body of knowledge contained in the textbook. This involvement in the discovery of answers acts as a motivational force that gives the students the "feel" for science. In inquiring, hypothesizing, experimenting, observing, and collecting data, the student makes use of the methods of scientific investigation. By writing a laboratory report, the student develops techniques for communicating the findings of a scientific investigation.

The student investigators are guided through their inquiry in several ways. The *Objectives* help the student determine what should be learned in answering the question being investigated. The questions within the procedure guide the students in making observations and interpreting data. As they follow the procedure, they should record data, observations, and answers in a laboratory notebook. Instructions on preparing a laboratory report are given in the *Working As a Biologist* section of this book.

Data may be recorded in various ways. Charts and graphs completed by the students aid in the understanding of some relationships. Diagrams and illustrations may be drawn in notebooks or on separate pieces of paper during observations or at the end as a summary.

The *Summary* section asks questions which the student should be able to answer after completing the *Procedure and Observations*. There are also a variety of test questions which can be used to check what the student has learned. The *Investigations on Your Own* section provides suggestions for further research. These may be assigned by the teacher or used by the interested student for independent projects.

The organization of the Investigations provides for a maximum degree of flexibility. Each Investigation is an independent laboratory unit. Most of the Investigations are divided into Parts of varying difficulty. This organization provides alternatives in adjusting the laboratory program to the time available, equipment and supplies on hand, and degree of emphasis of each area of the course.

Some use is made of living materials. At the same time, LABORATORY INVESTIGATIONS remains basically teachable. Each Investigation has been classroom tested. Each one is workable in the high school biology laboratory with supplies and equipment usually at hand or readily available. Directions are detailed enough to permit students to obtain meaningful results through their own efforts, with a minimum of teacher supervision.

It is hoped that the laboratory program as presented in LABORATORY INVESTIGATIONS will give students a *personal* experience to make their endeavors meaningful and their learning permanent.

Contents

HUMAN BIOLOGY

ECOLOGICAL RELATIONSHIPS

APPENDIX

Working As a Biologist

Biology students generally spend much of their time in the laboratory. It is here that you will discover the structures and functions of living things and their relationships to one another. You will learn to use some of the methods employed by scientists: experimentation, observation, collection and interpretation of data, and drawing of conclusions.

Your techniques and ability to use laboratory apparatus should improve with each investigation you perform. At the same time, your knowledge of living things should increase.

Conducting a Biological Investigation

Each Investigation asks a question. By fulfilling the stated objectives you should be able to answer that question. The Investigations are divided into related parts. Your teacher will tell you whether you will be expected to do all of the parts or only certain ones. The length of time required to complete each part will vary. In addition to the assigned Parts, you may also use the *Investigations on Your Own* for special projects or independent research.

Recording Biological Data

Biological data include all observations you make during an investigation. The data you record will be in several forms. In dealing with *structure* (the parts of living things), you may record your observations by drawing them and labeling your drawing. Labels should always be *printed* and have a straight guideline running to the structure being named. The guidelines should be clear and should not cross each other as this would cause confusion. Names of parts are always printed horizontally.

Most of the drawings you will be asked to make are representative drawings. These show the size, shape, and location of structures found in an organism. The drawings you make need not be artistic; few of us are artists. But *drawings must always be neat and accurate or they have no scientific value.*

Data are often interpreted in graphs. *Bar graphs* may be used to illustrate relative quantities of various trials. For example, an experiment was done in which the effects of various solutions on the heartbeat of a

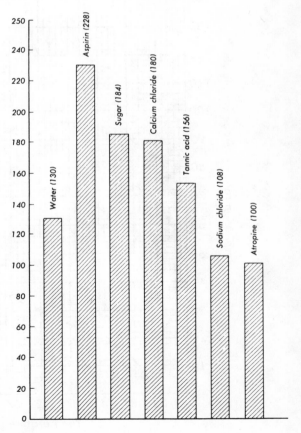

1

water flea were studied. The natural habitat of the water flea was used as a control. In its normal aquatic habitat the heart of the water flea beat at a rate of 130 times per minute. Data relating to the heartbeat rate when the water flea was placed in other solutions are shown on page 1.

Line graphs are used to show relationships between variables. For example, the relationship between temperature and breathing rate can be illustrated with a line graph. (See Investigation 34-2.) A class studied the effect of temperature on the respiration rate of the goldfish as indicated by movements of the gill cover. After studying several goldfish and tabulating the movements of the gill cover per minute in a number of goldfish, the class had the following results:

Temperature, F°	32°	37°	42°	47°	52°	57°	62°	67°	72°	77°	82°	87°	92°
Av. movement of gill cover/min.	0	13	20	25	30	35	43	49	58	81	104	120	133

Respiration rate – average per minute (vertical axis)

Temperature – degrees Fahrenheit (horizontal axis)

2

In this experiment, there were two variables, temperature and movements of the gill cover per minute. A line graph of the results shows the effect of temperature on the respiration rate of the goldfish. (See page 2.)

The subject of an Investigation may deal with the *behavior* of an organism (how it reacts and what it does). Sometimes the Investigation will deal with the *function* of an organ. Your observations will usually be in the form of answers to direct questions, data to record, or tables to complete. These answers should be based on facts gained from observation and research (including reading). Guesswork must never appear as scientific data. Although the results of your own experiment are not always what you expect, remember that the experiment that does not work is often just as important to research as the one that does.

Preparing a Laboratory Report
Writing a lab report is very different from making observations and recording data in your laboratory manual. In doing a lab report, your teacher may give you an outline or you may develop one yourself. In general, however, it should include:

 I. *Title*—This should be specific. "Growing Plants" or "Plant Nutrition" are too vague as titles. The title should tell exactly what you are studying. A good title might be: "The Effect of Mineral Deficiency on the Growth of Coleus Plants."

 II. *Purpose*—This section should state the problem you are investigating. The statement should be simple. For example, "How does the lack of certain minerals in the soil affect the growth of Coleus plants?" Your entire report must relate to this problem.

 III. *Materials and methods*—You must tell exactly what you did to prove or disprove the hypothesis. Be sure to have a control for your experiment. In this one, the control plant should be identical except for the mineral content of the soil. Describe the exact experimental procedures and use of minerals in the sequence in which you did them.

 IV. *Observations and results*—This part forms the basis of support for your analysis and conclusions. It is purely objective. *Do not* include your interpretation as an observation. You must be sure that what you observe and measure is actually there. Do not overlook any result. Record *all* experimental data and observations you make. Give complete description of what happened. Illustrations, drawings, graphs, sketches, and data tables should be used to support the information whenever possible.

 V. *Analysis and conclusions*—These are subjective in nature. Here you can interpret your results. Tell how your results prove or disprove your original hypothesis. Make each conclusion positive and distinct. You should leave no doubt in the mind of the reader as to why you feel justified in making your conclusions on the basis of the evidence you have collected.

1-1
The Microscope: How Is It Used?

OBJECTIVES
- To become familiar with the parts of a microscope
- To learn how to use the microscope

MATERIALS

MICROSCOPE
LENS PAPER
CHEESECLOTH
SLIDE
COVER GLASS
MEDICINE DROPPER
CLEAN CLOTH
TAP WATER
NEWSPRINT (PART 2)
DISSECTING NEEDLE (PART 3)
COTTON THREAD (2 DIFFERENT COLORS) (PART 3)

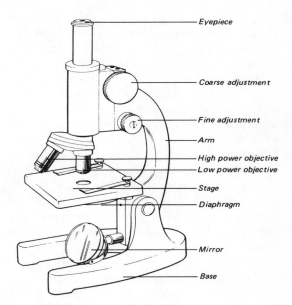

Standard compound microscope

PART 1 / PREPARING TO USE THE MICROSCOPE

You are about to discover the fascinating world that lies within reach of your microscope. Once you have learned how to use the microscope, there are many living and nonliving things that you will be able to examine in detail.

Procedure and Observations

You are now ready to set up and use the microscope. Be sure that the arm of the microscope is facing you. The base should be at least five centimeters from the edge of the table. This will keep the microscope from tipping.

Refer to the figure of the microscope as you proceed with this Investigation.

Use a piece of cheesecloth or other soft cloth to wipe off the *stage* and *frame* of the microscope. The stage is where the slide to be viewed is placed. **Do not use a cloth to wipe the lenses.**

Locate the *mirror* of the microscope. Wipe it with the cheesecloth. Turn the mirror so that the curved surface is facing a good light source. A microscope lamp, ceiling fixture, or daylight will provide sufficient light. Lighting is extremely important to a clear field of view. Some microscopes may have substage lighting. If this is so, the mirror is not needed. **Never use direct sunlight as a source of light.** This can be harmful to the eyes.

The *eyepiece* is the lens at the top of the microscope. The *objective* lenses are located on a revolving *nosepiece* at the bottom of the microscope tube. Use only special *lens paper* to clean the lenses.

Locate the *high-power* and *low-power objectives*. The low-power objective is shorter than the high-power objective. (a) In what other way do you think they differ? Turn the low-power objective until it is directly over the opening of the *stage*. (b) What magnification is printed on the lens? (c) What power is the eyepiece? Multiply the powers of the two lenses through which you are looking. (d) What is the total low-power magnification?

Locate the *diaphragm* of your microscope. The diaphragm regulates the amount of light passing through the specimen. (e) What type of diaphragm does your microscope have? Open the diaphragm or turn the disk to the largest opening so that the greatest amount of light is admitted. Now you are ready to look through the eyepiece. It is easier to use if both eyes are kept open. (f) What do you see through the eyepiece?

Adjust the mirror and/or diaphragm if you do not see a clear circle of bright light.

You are now prepared to examine something under the microscope. Before you go on to Part 2 of this Investigation, be sure that you are familiar with all of the parts of the microscope.

PART 2 / USING THE MICROSCOPE

In this Part, you will learn how to prepare a wet mount slide. You will then examine it with your microscope. Wet mount slides are slides that *you* prepare for temporary use. Prepared slides are for permanent use. Your teacher may use prepared slides to illustrate certain subjects that you will study.

Procedure and Observations

Wet mount slides are simple to prepare if you follow the steps outlined below. You will be mounting a newsprint lower case "e."

Rinse a microscope slide with water and wipe both sides with a clean soft cloth. Hold the slide by the edges. (a) Why should you do so?

Rinse and dry a cover glass as you did the slide.

Cut out a small piece of newsprint which contains a lower case "e."

Using a medicine dropper, place a drop of tap water in the center of the slide.

Place the newsprint in the drop of water. Lower the cover glass as shown below. This will prevent formation of air bubbles.

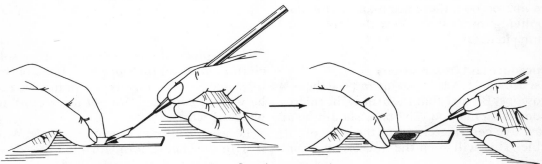

Preparing a wet mount

6

Place your temporary wet mount on the stage of the microscope and position it so that the letter "e" is facing you as you would read it. Clip it into place.

Using the *coarse adjustment*, lower the low-power objective as far as it will go *without* hitting the slide. Be sure to watch the bottom lens as you do this. *Never* lower the objective while looking through the eyepiece. (b) Why should this not be done?

Look through the eyepiece. Adjust the low-power objective by turning the *coarse adjustment* toward you. The letter "e" will soon come into view. Sharp focus can be achieved by using the *fine adjustment*. If you are having difficulty seeing the "e" clearly, check the positions of the low-power objective and the slide. (c) How would you describe the position of the "e"? Draw a picture of what you see under the microscope.

(d) What happens if you move the slide to the right? (e) What happens if you push the slide away from you? Move the "e" into the exact center of the low-power field. Focus and turn the high-power objective into position. Use the fine adjustment to correct the sharpness of the focus. (f) What is the total magnification of the high-power lens? (g) About how many times was the magnification increased when you changed from low power to high power? (h) How does this change the area of the slide included in the high-power field?

PART 3 / THE RESOLVING POWER OF THE MICROSCOPE

You will find that the materials you study have depth as well as length and width and that you need to shift your focus as you view in order to see details at various depths. Resolving power is how clear and sharp the magnified image can be made. Both light and resolving power are reduced as magnification is increased.

Procedure and Observations

Mount 2 different colored cotton fibers across each other in a drop of water on a microscope slide. Cover the slide with a cover glass. Be careful not to trap air under the cover glass. Adjust the diaphragm and bring a fiber into sharp focus with the low power of your microscope. (a) Do the fibers appear uniform in color?

As you examine the fibers, shift the focus by turning the fine adjustment back and forth slowly. (b) Describe any changes in the appearance of the fibers. (c) Explain why these changes occur. (d) How can you determine which fiber is on top when you look through the microscope?

Move the fibers to the center of the low-power field and shift to the high-power magnification. (e) Compare the brightness of the low-power and high-power fields. Bring the fiber into the sharpest possible focus with the fine adjustment. (f) Is the depth of focus as great with high power as with low power?

Summary

(a) Give the function of each of the following parts of the microscope:

Eyepiece	Low-power
Stage	objective
Stage clips	High-power
Diaphragm	objective
Mirror	Coarse adjustment
	Fine adjustment

(b) Why is good lighting so important?
(c) How should you focus the low-power objective?
(d) Which adjustment sharpens the focus?
(e) Which objective has the greater amount of magnification?
(f) If you were to purchase a microscope, what would be some features that you would look for?

INVESTIGATIONS ON YOUR OWN

1. Collect and examine many examples of textile fibers. Some of these fibers include linen, silk, wool, rayon, and nylon. Compare these fibers and observe how they differ. It is interesting to note that fiber identification is important in detection laboratories. Fibers left behind can be a clue in a crime.

2. Many simple investigations can be done using materials with which you are familiar. It is interesting to examine different types of paper. You may want to include newsprint, tissue paper, stationery, and wrapping paper in your investigation.

2-1

How Was Spontaneous Generation Disproved?

OBJECTIVES
- To appreciate the experiments of Spallanzani and Pasteur
- To become familiar with experimental procedures
- To be able to draw conclusions from scientific data

MATERIALS

MICROSCOPE
SLIDES
COVER GLASSES
6 FLASKS (250 ML)
2 SOLID STOPPERS
2 ONE-HOLE STOPPERS TO FIT FLASKS
8 CM SECTION OF STRAIGHT GLASS TUBING
S-SHAPED GLASS TUBE
6 DROPPING PIPETTES
PAN FOR PREPARING BROTH
AUTOCLAVE OR PRESSURE COOKER
GLASS-MARKING PENCIL (HEAT RESISTANT)
ALUMINUM FOIL
NUTRIENT BROTH (DEHYDRATED) OR
  BEEF BROTH
DISTILLED WATER

DEMONSTRATION OF BIOGENESIS OF MICROORGANISMS

You are about to study one of the most controversial matters in the history of biology. Theories of spontaneous generation existed long before Redi, Spallanzani, and Pasteur. In this Investigation, you will have the opportunity to repeat some of the work of these experimenters.

Procedure and Observations

To begin this Investigation, insert a section of straight glass tubing and an S-shaped glass tubing through one-hole stoppers as shown in flasks E and F on page 10.

Prepare 1,000 ml (1 liter) of nutrient broth as directed on the media bottle. Be sure that all ingredients in the broth are dissolved. Mark the 6 flasks as A through F, using a heat-resistant glass-marking pencil. Divide the broth equally among the 6 flasks. Prepare the flasks as shown in the diagram on page 10.

> Flask A will remain unsterilized and will be left open.
> Flask B will remain unsterilized and will be stoppered.
> Flask C will remain open after sterilization.
> Flask D will be stoppered after sterilization.
> Flask E will be stoppered with the straight glass tube after sterilization.
> Flask F will be stoppered with the S-shaped glass tube after sterilization.

Prepare flasks A and B and set aside. Cover the mouths of C, D, E, and F with aluminum foil. Put these flasks and the stoppers for D, E, and F in the autoclave or pressure cooker. Sterilize at 15 pounds for 15 minutes. (a) Could this Investigation be done without sterilization?

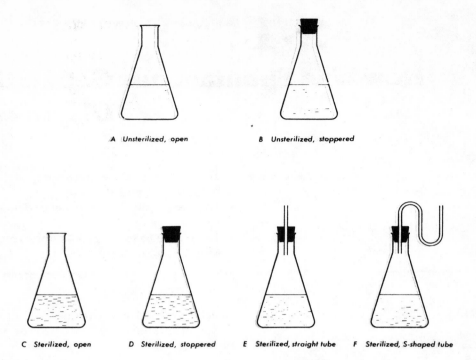

A Unsterilized, open

B Unsterilized, stoppered

C Sterilized, open

D Sterilized, stoppered

E Sterilized, straight tube

F Sterilized, S-shaped tube

After sterilization, allow the flasks and stoppers to cool in the sterilizer. Remove the aluminum foil from the flasks and insert the stoppers. (b) Why should care be taken not to touch the lower part of the stoppers?

Place all the flasks in the incubator at 35–37°C for 72 hours. (c) Why is this necessary?

Following the incubation period, examine all of the flasks. Using a clean pipette for each flask, put a drop of broth on a microscope slide. Add a cover glass and examine under high power. (d) Why should high power be used?

If microorganisms are present, they will appear as small moving bodies. In some cases, it may be necessary to darken the field by closing down the diaphragm. (e) What do you see when the material from flask A is examined?

In a table like the one shown, fill in your observations for each of the 6 flasks. DO NOT WRITE IN THIS BOOK. Each of the changes in the table indicates activity of microorganisms in the broth.

Flask	A	B	C	D	E	F
Presence of microorganisms						
Color						
Degree of turbidity (cloudiness)						
Odor						
Surface pellicle (film)						
Sediment						

Supporters of spontaneous generation and of biogenesis would interpret the results of this experiment differently. (f) How would the "spontaneous generationists" explain the presence of microorganisms? (g) How would Pasteur have viewed the same data? (h) What was meant by an "active principle"?

Summary
On a separate piece of paper, construct a table like the one below. DO NOT WRITE IN THIS BOOK.

In your table, summarize your findings from this Investigation by evaluating each of the following theories. Use the following key to interpret your findings.

+ evidence exists to prove
? possibility, but evidence is lacking
− evidence to disprove
0 does not apply

INVESTIGATIONS ON YOUR OWN

1. Construct an original investigation that disproves the theory of spontaneous generation. This investigation should be simple and should be done with easily available materials.

2. Another theory related to the theory of spontaneous generation was plant growth through the conversion of soil into plant substances. One of the most famous experiments to disprove this theory was conducted by J. B. van Helmont in the 17th century. You may want to re-create this experiment by substituting a sunflower seedling for the willow tree. Draw your own conclusions after completing the experiment.

Flasks	A	B	C	D	E	F
Living organisms were in the broth before incubation						
Broth substances were changed to living organisms by spontaneous generation						
Heat destroyed an "active principle" necessary for spontaneous generation						
Air is necessary for the growth of organisms						
Organisms present in the broth came from the air						
Organisms will not appear if neither the broth nor the air entering the flask contains organisms						

3-1
How Do We Test for Organic Compounds?

OBJECTIVES
- To identify the presence of carbohydrates in carbon
- To use chemical tests to determine the presence of various organic molecules

MATERIALS

CRUCIBLE
TRIPOD
BUNSEN BURNER
TEST TUBES
TEST-TUBE HOLDER
TEST-TUBE RACK
WHITE SUGAR
BROWN PAPER (PART 2)
BENEDICT'S SOLUTION OR FEHLING'S A AND
  B (PART 2)
SUDAN III (PART 2)
BIURET REAGENT (PART 2)
PREPARED SOLUTIONS OF:
  CORN SYRUP
  1% STARCH
  VEGETABLE OIL OR FAT
  1% GELATIN
VARIOUS FOODS SUCH AS MEATS,
  FRUITS, VEGETABLES, AND EGGS

PART 1 / IS THERE CARBON IN CARBOHYDRATE?

Both sugars and starches are carbohydrates. Have you ever noticed that when potatoes (starch) are burned, they turn black? This is a chemical property of carbon in the starch. In this Investigation, you will determine whether carbon is also present in sugar crystals.

Procedure and Observations
Place a small amount of sugar crystals in a crucible. Put the crucible on a tripod and heat with a Bunsen burner. Watch the sugar as you heat it. (a) What do you see happening to the sugar crystals?

Using a test-tube holder, hold an inverted test tube over the crucible. Let the tube cool in an upright position. (b) What do you observe? (c) What other substance do you think was present in the vapor?

Continue to heat the crucible until you observe a black residue on the bottom. (d) What do you think this substance is? (e) What has happened to the hydrogen and oxygen atoms that were present in the sugar molecules? (f) What type of change occurred in the sugar? (g) Was there an energy change? (h) Explain your answer.

PART 2 / TESTS FOR THE PRESENCE OF ORGANIC NUTRIENTS

You can determine whether sugar, starch, fat, or protein molecules are present in a substance by using certain chemical tests.

Procedure and Observations
Test for simple sugar:
Label test tubes *1* and *2*. Put 5 drops of water into tube *1* and 5 drops of corn syrup into tube *2*. Add 5 ml of Benedict's solution

to each. (a) What color appears in each tube?

Heat the tubes by placing them in a boiling water bath for at least 5 minutes. Observe any color changes. (b) What color changes occurred in tube *1*? (c) What color changes occurred in tube *2*? (d) What color finally appears in tube *2*? This color indicates the presence of simple sugar. This is said to be a *positive* test. (e) What was the purpose of tube *1*, which was a *negative* test?

Test for starch:

Using 2 marked test tubes, put 5 drops of water into tube *1* and 5 drops of starch solution into tube *2*. Add 2 drops of iodine to each tube. (f) What color change occurred in tube *1*? (g) What color change occurred in tube *2*? What you have observed in tube *2* is a positive test for starch.

Test for fats and oils:

Spread 2 drops of olive oil on a piece of brown wrapping paper. Hold the paper up to the light. (h) Can you detect a translucent "grease spot" on the paper? On another section of the brown paper, spread 2 drops of water. (i) After allowing time to dry, compare the spots.

There is another test which is more accurate. Put about one centimeter of the substance to be tested in a *dry* test tube and add 10 drops of Sudan III. Set the tube aside for 30 minutes. (j) Examine and describe the results.

Test for proteins:

Using 2 marked test tubes, put 20 drops of water into tube *1* and 20 drops of gelatin into tube *2*. Add 2 drops of Biuret reagent to each tube. **CAUTION: Use care in handling Biuret reagent. It may burn skin or clothing.**

(k) What color change occurred in tube *1*? (l) What color change occurred in tube *2*? Gelatin solution is a protein. (m) What color change in Biuret reagent indicates the presence of protein?

PART 3 / IDENTIFYING UNKNOWN ORGANIC NUTRIENTS

The foods you eat are made up of carbohydrates, fats, and proteins. These nutrients are necessary for the maintenance of cellular activities in all plants and animals. The chemical tests you learned in Part 2 may be used to identify the composition of foods.

Procedure and Observations

Test the foods you are given for the presence of simple sugar, starch, fats and oils, and protein. Construct a table like the one shown on the next page. DO NOT WRITE IN THIS BOOK. Record a plus (+) if the test is positive and a minus (−) if it is negative.

Summary

(a) Can the sugar be tested for the presence of carbon?
(b) What is sugar composed of?
(c) Does an energy change take place when sugar is heated? Explain your answer.
(d) What color does iodine turn when put on starch?
(e) What indicator reacts by turning from blue to brown or orange when heated with certain sugars?
(f) How does Biuret reagent react with protein?
(g) What does Sudan III do to fat?

INVESTIGATIONS ON YOUR OWN

1. Test foods for the presence of carbon by heating them as you did the sugar crystals. Suggested foods may include: cereals, fruits, maple syrup, candy, and cookies. Evaluate the findings. Do some foods seem to contain more carbon than others?

2. You may wish to test other common foods for the presence of sugar, starch, fat, or protein molecules.

FOOD TESTED	ORGANIC NUTRIENTS			
	Simple Sugar	Starch	Fats and Oils	Protein
Lean beef				
Raisins				
Dried beans				
Peanuts				
Apple				
Onion				
Popcorn				
Banana				
Skim milk				
Whole milk				
Egg yolk				
Egg white				

3-2
What Are Enzymes? What Factors Affect Them?

OBJECTIVES
- **To become familiar with the action of enzymes**
- **To observe the speed of enzyme activity**
- **To observe the effect of temperature on enzyme activity**

MATERIALS

2% DIASTASE
1% STARCH SOLUTION
TEST TUBES
IODINE
DROPPER
WHITE PLATE

PART 1 / DEMONSTRATION OF ENZYME ACTION

In this Investigation, you will study the digestion of a starch by the enzyme diastase.

Procedure and Observations

Place 10 drops of starch solution in a test tube. Add 5 drops of diastase solution. Place a drop of this mixture on the white plate. To this drop, add a drop of iodine solution. (a) What happens when the iodine solution is added?

On a clean area of the plate, again add a drop of iodine to a drop of the mixture. Repeat every 5 minutes. (b) What happens to the indicator color as you continue this procedure? (c) What is the function of the iodine here?

Construct a table like the one below. Fill it in with your results at 5-minute intervals. DO NOT WRITE IN THIS BOOK.

Time Elapsed	Color When Iodine Added
5 min.	
10 min.	
15 min.	
20 min.	
25 min.	

(d) Why does this change in color take place? (e) What action has the diastase had on the starch? (f) What do you conclude is the function of diastase?

PART 2 / SPEED OF ENZYME ACTION

The speed of enzyme action is dependent upon the amounts of enzyme and material or *substrate* that is being acted upon. In this Part, you will observe how certain enzyme reactions can be speeded up.

Procedure and Observations

Prepare 5 test tubes each containing 5 drops of diastase. Increase the amount of starch in each test tube by adding 1, 5, 10,

15

15, and 20 drops of starch respectively to each test tube. Test each test tube with iodine. Fill in a table like the one below with the results observed. DO NOT WRITE IN THIS BOOK.

Amount of Starch	Results Observed
1 drop	
5 drops	
10 drops	
15 drops	
20 drops	

(a) How has the increase in starch affected the rate of enzyme action? (b) Would you expect the same results if the amount of enzyme was increased and the amount of starch was kept constant? (c) Explain your answer.

To find out if your conclusion was correct, do the same as you did previously, but increase the enzyme and leave the starch constant at 10 drops. Test each test tube with iodine. Record your results in a table like the one used above for the varying amounts of starch. (d) What can you conclude from this section of the Investigation?

PART 3 / EFFECT OF HEAT ON ENZYMES

How does heat affect the action of enzymes?

Procedure and Observations
Heat 3 test tubes (each containing 5 drops of diastase solution). Heat one for only a few minutes; bring the second just to a boil; and fully boil the third for a few minutes. Test the action of each on 10 drops of starch. Use iodine as an indicator. Record your results for each of the 3 test tubes.

(a) What happens to an enzyme when it is heated? (b) Does boiling have a greater effect on enzyme activity than heating? (c) What conclusions can you draw from this Part of the Investigation?

Summary
(a) What is one of the functions of the enzyme diastase?
(b) Why are enzymes important in the digestive process?
(c) What is the function of iodine in testing the effect of diastase on starch?
(d) What effect does an increase in the amount of starch have on diastase?
(e) What effect does an increase in the amount of enzyme have on the starch substrate?
(f) Does heating an enzyme affect it in any way? If so, how?
(g) What happens when an enzyme is boiled?
(h) What conclusions can you draw about the factors that affect the action of enzymes?

INVESTIGATIONS ON YOUR OWN

1. Different enzymes react with various types of food in the digestive process. For example, certain enzymes digest protein. You can test this by making a small amount of gelatin (protein) and adding pineapple juice to it. Put it in the refrigerator to jell. What happens? Pineapple contains a protein-digesting enzyme called bromelain. This enzyme can be tested on other proteins.

2. Most meat tenderizers contain an enzyme called papain. This enzyme is extracted from the papaya melon. Test its activity on boiled egg white or other protein foods. A solution of the tenderizer can be made by dissolving a teaspoon of the substance in 100 ml of distilled water. Why do you think papain is used in meat tenderizers?

4-1

What Are Cells?

- **To identify and observe cork cells**
- **To identify and observe the epidermal cells of an onion**
- **To become familiar with the structure of plant cells**

MATERIALS

MICROSCOPE
SLIDES
COVER GLASSES
FORCEPS
BOTTLE CORK (PART 1)
RAZOR BLADE
ONION (PART 2)
SCALPEL (PART 2)
IODINE STAIN (PART 2)

PART 1 / OBSERVING CORK CELLS

More than 300 years have passed since Robert Hooke first described cork cells in his book *Micrographia*. In this Investigation, you will repeat Hooke's early experiment with cork cells.

Procedure and Observations
Carefully, shave a very thin section from a bottle cork with a razor blade. Prepare a wet mount slide of the cork slice. Examine the specimen under low power, studying it in different positions. Draw a sketch of what you observe.

Now examine the specimen under high power. Draw the cells as you see them under high power. Make the drawing about 5 cm in diameter. (a) How would you describe the units that compose the cork? (b) Are these units of similar shape? (c) Are they of similar size? (d) Are they filled with any material? (e) If so, explain what that content appears to be. (f) Are there spaces between the cells? (g) Do you think that these cells are alive?

PART 2 / ONION CELLS

The epidermis of the onion is ideal for cell study because it is composed of a single layer of cells. As you study these cells, you are looking into functioning units of living material.

Procedure and Observations
Cut an onion lengthwise. Remove a thick scale. Peel the delicate, transparent tissue from the *inner surface* as shown in the figure on the next page.

Cut a square of the tissue and mount it on a slide in a drop of water. (NOTE: Avoid wrinkling the tissue.) Add a cover glass. Examine the living cells under low power. (a) What is the shape of the cells? (b) Are they similar in shape? (c) What color is the living cytoplasm?

Carefully raise one side of the cover glass and add a drop of iodine stain. (d) What effect does iodine have on the cells?

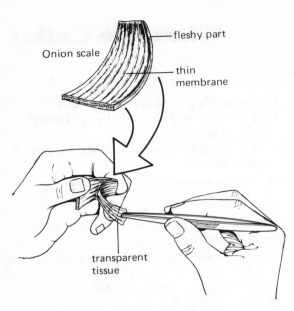

Onion scale

fleshy part

thin membrane

transparent tissue

1. Observe many different types of nonliving and living cells. Compare your findings to the cork and onion cells that you observed in this Investigation. Draw sketches of the cells and their organelles.

2. It is possible to observe the mitochrondria of some cells under the light microscope. Cut a strip of celery stalk containing "strings." Place this strip, with the inner surface up, in a 5% sucrose solution. Cut a thin strip from between the "strings." Observe the mitochondria. If you add a few drops of 0.001% Janus Green B solution, the mitochondria will stain a blue color. However, this color will quickly fade because of enzyme action.

Study the cells carefully under low power. Draw a small group of cells making each cell about 3 cm long.

Select one cell that shows the contents clearly. Move it to the center of the microscopic field. Using high power, examine all the parts of the cell. (e) What is the appearance of the cytoplasm? (f) What is the appearance of the nuclei? (g) Are the nuclei always in the same position in the cell? (h) Does the onion epidermal cell have depth? (i) Explain your answer.

Make a drawing of a single cell as it appears under high power. Label: **cell wall, cytoplasm, nucleus,** and **nucleolus.**

Summary
(a) What are the units of cork seen under the microscope?
(b) How did the cork units differ from those of the onion epidermis?
(c) Why is an iodine stain used in this Investigation?
(d) Identify and give the function of the nucleus.

4-2
Do Animal Cells Differ from Plant Cells?

OBJECTIVES
- To observe plant cell structures
- To identify the plasma membrane of cells
- To recognize the differences in structure between plant and animal cells

MATERIALS

ELODEA LEAVES (*ANACHARIS*)
MICROSCOPE
SLIDES
COVER GLASSES
MEDICINE DROPPER
COLORED PENCILS
HUMAN CHEEK CELLS (PART 2)
TOOTHPICK (FLAT TYPE) (PART 2)
METHYLENE BLUE (PART 2)

PART 1 / CELLS OF A LEAF

Although most cells of plants and animals are similar in structure, there are a few major differences. In this Investigation, you will observe these differences under the microscope.

Procedure and Observations

Prepare a wet mount of an *Elodea* leaf. The whole leaf should be used. Examine the leaf under the low power of the microscope. Then select a portion of the leaf where the cells are particularly distinct. Center this portion in the microscope field. Bring it into focus under high power. Use the fine adjustment to observe the cells at various depths. (a) In which layer are the widest cells located?

Observe the small, oval, green bodies that appear in the cells. These are the chloroplasts. (b) Are any of the chloroplasts moving? (c) If you see movement, are all the chloroplasts moving in the same direction? (d) Are they all moving at the same speed? (e) Can you observe any structures for movement? (f) Explain how the chloroplasts move.

On a separate piece of paper, draw some cells of an *Elodea* leaf. Use arrows to indicate the direction of chloroplast movement. Label your drawing, indicating the **cell wall, chloroplasts, cytoplasm,** and **nucleus.**

Summary
(a) In what ways do elodea cells differ from human cheek cells?
(b) What is the function of chloroplasts?
(c) Why are chloroplasts green in color?
(d) What is the outer covering of a cheek cell called?
(e) Do cheek cells contain chloroplasts?
(f) Are both plants and animals composed of cells? Explain your answer based on observations of elodea and cheek cells.

INVESTIGATIONS ON YOUR OWN

1. You can investigate many types of plant cells and identify the cell walls as well as the organelles. You may want to include potato cells, tomato pulp cells, and beet cells in your investigation.

2. There are many interesting investigations that one can do with human cells. Some skin taken from under the fingernails can be studied. These cells can be compared with those from the cheek. Identify the structures that you observe.

PART 2 / HUMAN EPITHELIAL CELLS

In this Part, you will examine the cell structure of human epithelial (cheek) cells, and you will note the absence of the cell wall that was present in the elodea cells.

Procedure and Observations
Gently scrape the inside of your cheek with a clean toothpick. You probably will not be able to see any material on the toothpick. Prepare a wet mount of this material by stirring the toothpick in a drop of water on a slide.

Add a drop of methylene blue and a cover glass. Examine the cells under low power of the microscope. Switch to high power. Carefully look for the outer edge of the cytoplasm. (a) How does it compare with the outer edge of the elodea cells? (b) What is this outer edge called? (c) Describe the shape of cheek cells. (d) In what ways do the cheek cells differ from the elodea cells? (e) Why did you use methylene blue in this Investigation? (f) Describe the appearance of the cytoplasm.

Draw a single cheek cell (high power) and label the **plasma membrane, cytoplasm,** and **nucleus.**

5-1

What Is a Selectively Permeable Membrane?

OBJECTIVES
- To observe the functioning of a selectively permeable membrane
- To demonstrate how molecules enter and leave cell membranes
- To understand the importance of selectively permeable membranes to cell life

MATERIALS

STARCH SUSPENSION
80% GLUCOSE SOLUTION
IODINE SOLUTION
DISTILLED WATER
MEDICINE DROPPERS
BENEDICT'S SOLUTION
STRING
1.5 CM CELLOPHANE DIALYSIS
   TUBING (20 CM LONG)
2 BEAKERS

A SELECTIVELY PERMEABLE MEMBRANE

In this Investigation, you will see how certain molecules pass in and out of cells. The cell membrane is a selectively permeable membrane. Selectively permeable membranes allow some substances to pass through them while preventing the passage of other substances.

Procedure and Observations

Soak a 20-cm section of cellophane dialysis tubing in water for a few minutes. Gently rub the ends between your thumb and index finger until the ends separate. Carefully push a pencil or a glass rod through the opening to hold it open. Twist one end of the tubing and tie it tightly with string. Remove the glass rod or pencil. Fill this dialysis bag ¾ full with starch suspension and ¼ full with 80% glucose solution. Tie the top of the bag with string, as shown in the figure on page 22. Leave a loose piece of string 10-15 cm long. Rinse the bag with distilled water. (a) Why is this necessary?

Place the bag in a beaker of distilled water. Leave the string outside the beaker so that you may remove the bag from the water. After 20 minutes, withdraw a dropperful of water from the beaker. Place this in a test tube and add 10 drops of Benedict's solution. Heat in a boiling water bath for 10-15 minutes. (b) What are you testing for? (c) Is this substance present in the water? (d) What color should the water become if it is present? (e) If so, explain why it is present.

(f) Observe the level of the liquid in the dialysis bag. Do you note any changes? (g) Do you note any changes in the liquid in the beaker? (h) Can you draw any conclusions from these observations?

For every 30 drops of the liquid in the beaker, add 3 drops of iodine. Observe the

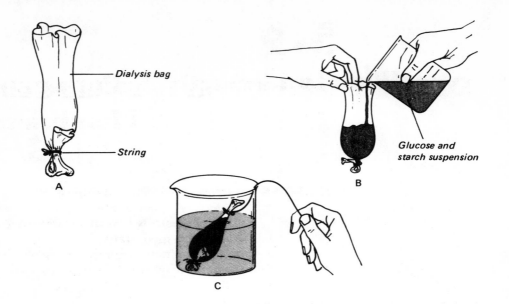

Dialysis bag

String

A

Glucose and starch suspension

B

C

color of the water after the iodine has been added. Let stand for 8-10 minutes. (i) What changes, if any, do you observe? (j) What substances passed through the membrane?

Summary
(a) Why was it important to rinse the dialysis bags before parts of this Investigation?
(b) Has osmosis been observed in either or both parts of the Investigation?
(c) Did diffusion take place in either or both parts of this Investigation? If so, explain.
(d) What substance is used to test for the presence of starch?
(e) What substance is used to test for the presence of glucose?
(f) What color occurs when the indicator is added and starch is present?
(g) What color occurs when the indicator is added and glucose is present?
(h) What evidence, if any, did you find that indicated that the dialysis bags were selectively permeable?
(i) What conclusions can you draw from this Investigation concerning the action of living plasma membranes?

INVESTIGATIONS ON YOUR OWN

1. You may be interested in studying the action of the enzyme diastase on diffusion. Prepare a dialysis bag using diastase solution: add starch solution to the diastase and tie-off the dialysis bag. Fill a beaker with distilled water. The water should be about 37° C. After about 20 minutes, take two samples of the water from the bottom of the beaker. Test one sample for starch and the other for glucose. Record your observations and draw conclusions concerning enzyme action.

2. Design an original investigation to illustrate the process of diffusion. Include a control in your investigation.

5-2
Does Osmosis Occur in Living Cells?

OBJECTIVES
- To demonstrate turgor pressure in plant tissues
- To observe cells in various salt concentrations
- To determine if osmosis occurs in living cells

MATERIALS

POTATO SLICES
CUCUMBER SLICES
4 CULTURE DISHES
DISTILLED WATER
1% NaCl SOLUTION
15% NaCl SOLUTION
SPRIG OF ANACHARIS (ELODEA) (PART 2)
MICROSCOPE (PART 2)
GLASS SLIDES (PART 2)
COVER GLASS (PART 2)
DROPPER (PART 2)
FILTER PAPER (PART 2)

PART 1 / TURGOR IN PLANT TISSUES

Turgor is the rigidity or stiffness of plants due to the water present in their cells. In this Part, you will observe the presence and loss of turgor pressure.

Procedure and Observations
Fill 2 culture dishes with distilled water and 2 with 15% NaCl solution. Place some of the slices of potato in one of the dishes with distilled water and in one dish with 15% NaCl solution. Place cucumber slices in the remaining 2 dishes. Leave the dishes for about one-half hour. Observe the fresh vegetables that had not been placed in any

of the dishes. (a) How would you describe their stiffness and texture?

Remove some of the vegetables from the distilled water. (b) How would you describe their stiffness and texture? (c) Has the turgidity of the cells in the distilled water increased or decreased? (d) What conclusions can you draw from this observation?

Remove some of the slices from the 15% salt solution. (e) How would you describe their stiffness and texture? (f) Do these slices have greater or lesser turgidity than the slices that were not in any of the dishes? (g) Draw conclusions concerning the turgidity of the slices in the NaCl solution. (h) Did osmosis occur in this Part of the Investigation?

PART 2 / OSMOSIS IN PLANT CELLS

In this part, you will observe microscopically what happens to cells placed in solutions of varying salt concentrations.

Procedure and Observations
Remove one leaf from a sprig of *Anacharis* and prepare a wet mount slide with tap water. Examine under high power. (a) What do you see? (b) Describe the position of the cell membrane and chloroplasts. Draw the cell that you observed.

Place one drop of 15% NaCl solution at the edge of the cover glass. About every 30 seconds, add another drop of NaCl solution until you observe a change in appearance of the cell. (c) How many drops of NaCl were added before a change was noticed? (d) Do you think that water moved in or out of the cell? (e) Why do you think this change occurred? Draw the cell that you observed after the NaCl was added.

Place a piece of filter paper at the edge of the cover glass and absorb as much of the salt solution as possible. Add distilled water at the edge of the cover glass, a drop at a time, watching the cells closely. (f) Do you observe any changes in the cells? Draw the cell that you observed after the distilled water was added.

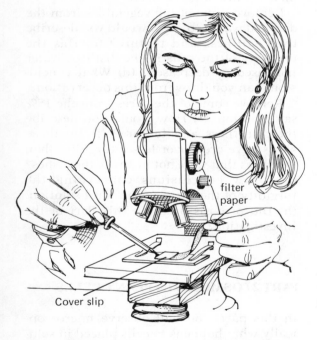

filter paper

Cover slip

Compare your drawings of the *Anacharis* cells in tap water, 15% NaCl, and in distilled water.

Summary
(a) Did diffusion take place when NaCl solution was added to the *Anacharis* cells?
(b) If so, explain why it took place.

(c) How would you explain the condition of the vegetable slices that were in the salt solution?
(d) How would you define turgidity?
(e) Of what value is turgidity to a plant?
(f) What purpose did the freshly cut vegetables (not placed in any culture dishes) serve in this Investigation?

INVESTIGATIONS ON YOUR OWN

1. The permeability of cell membranes can be tested effectively by using red blood cells. In this investigation, you can test the effect of temperature (as you did in Part 3) on the cell membrane. Prepare four test tubes of tap water. One should be 0°C; one at 25°C; one at 50°C; and one at 65°C. Mix each test tube of water with three drops of blood. Place a stopper in each tube and invert a few times. The bursting of red blood cells is called hemolysis. You will know that this has occurred in your test tubes when the cloudiness in a test tube becomes clear. Draw conclusions from this investigation.

2. Design your own investigation that tests the effects of one factor on the diffusion process. It might be interesting to use acids and bases in testing the effect of pH on diffusion.

6-1
How Does Light Affect Photosynthesis?

OBJECTIVES
- To determine the effect of light on photosynthesis
- To observe the rate of photosynthesis under different light conditions
- To determine which wavelengths of light affect the rate of photosynthesis

MATERIALS

ANACHARIS (ELODEA)
6 PYREX TEST TUBES
4 PIECES OF GLASS ROD (5 CM)
150-WATT REFLECTOR LAMP
SODIUM BICARBONATE
DILUTE BROM THYMOL BLUE SOLUTION (PART 2)
0.1% HYDROCHLORIC ACID SOLUTION (PART 2)
6 TEST-TUBE STOPPERS (PARTS 2, 3)
MEDICINE DROPPER (PART 2)
FORCEPS (PART 2)
TEST-TUBE RACK (PART 2)
250-ML BEAKER (PARTS 2, 3)
6 SHEETS OF CELLOPHANE; 7 CM BY 15 CM; RED, YELLOW, GREEN, BLUE, AND 2 CLEAR (PART 2)
SODA STRAW (PART 2)
RUBBER BANDS (PART 2)
RING STAND (PART 3)
FUNNEL, SHORT STEM (PART 3)
2.5 CM DIAM. GLASS TUBING (PART 3)
WOOD SPLINT (PART 3)

PART 1 / THE RATE OF PHOTOSYNTHESIS

The rate at which photosynthesis takes place can be determined by recording the number of oxygen bubbles that escape from the cut end of a sprig of *Anacharis*. In this Part, you will observe the effect of light on the rate of photosynthesis.

Procedure and Observations

Fill 4 test tubes with water to within 3 cm of the top. Select 4 sprigs of *Anacharis* that have been growing in bright light. Each sprig should be about 7 cm. Wind each sprig around a glass rod and immerse in one of the test tubes. Sodium bicarbonate forms carbon dioxide in water. Add a small amount of sodium bicarbonate to each test tube. (a) Why should this be done?

Place one test tube under bright sunlight or a reflector lamp; the second should be in daylight; the third in diffuse light; and the fourth in total darkness. Allow the plants to remain in these light conditions for 15 minutes.

Observe the cut ends of each plant. Use a timer or a watch with a second hand and count the number of oxygen bubbles given off by each plant in 1 minute. (b) What do the bubbles tell you about the rate of photosynthesis? (c) Under which condition is the bubble count the greatest? (d) Under which light condition is the bubble count the least? (e) What conclusions can you draw from this Investigation?

Continue to record the results of the Investigation by counting the bubbles for 5 minutes. Record your observations in a table like the one below. DO NOT WRITE IN THIS BOOK.

Environmental Condition	Rate per Minute	Rate per 5 Minutes	Average Rate per Minute
Sunlight or reflector lamp			
Daylight			
Diffuse light			
Darkness			

(f) How do you account for the variation in the rate of bubbles in the 4 plants?

PART 2 / THE EFFECT OF WAVELENGTHS OF LIGHT ON PHOTOSYNTHESIS

In Part 1, the effect of light on photosynthesis was clearly indicated. In this Part, you will examine the effect of the different wavelengths (colors) of light on photosynthesis. Different wavelengths of light contain varying amounts of energy.

Procedure and Observations

Fill a beaker with 100 ml of water. Add brom thymol blue to color the water a pale blue. Using a soda straw, blow into the solution. This will cause a change in color. (a) What color does the solution become? (b) What causes this color change?

Place 5 test tubes in a test-tube holder and insert a sprig of *Anacharis* in each. Add the solution from the beaker to cover the sprigs of *Anacharis* in the test tubes. Place a stopper in each test tube. Fill a sixth test

tube with the same solution, but do not place an *Anacharis* sprig in it. Stopper this tube. (c) What function does this tube perform?

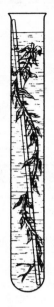

Wrap a cellophane sheet of a different color around each test tube. Wrap one tube containing *Anacharis* and one without the plant with clear cellophane. Use rubber bands to secure the cellophane sheets. Expose the test tubes in the rack to the light of the lamp for about 20 minutes. Examine each test tube and record your results in a table like the one below. DO NOT WRITE IN THIS BOOK.

Test Tube	Color of Indicator after 20 Minutes	Number of Drops of Hydrochloric Acid to Restore Color
Red		
Yellow		
Green		
Blue		
Clear		

(d) How do you account for the changes in the test tubes? (e) What substance were the *Anacharis* sprigs absorbing? (f) Which wavelength (color) was most effective in increasing the rate of photosynthesis? (g) Which color was least effective in increasing the rate of photosynthesis?

Remove the *Anacharis* from the 5 test tubes. Add 0.1% hydrochloric acid drop by drop to each test tube until the original color' returns. Count the number of drops necessary for each to change color. Record your findings in the second column of your table.

(h) Why does the hydrochloric acid return the color to the original? (i) What was the color of the liquid in the tube without the *Anacharis*? (j) What was the purpose of this test tube?

PART 3 / WHAT IS THE BY-PRODUCT OF PHOTOSYNTHESIS?

Biologists have found that a gas is released during the light phase of photosynthesis. Water plants are used in this Part because any gas given off appears as bubbles in the water.

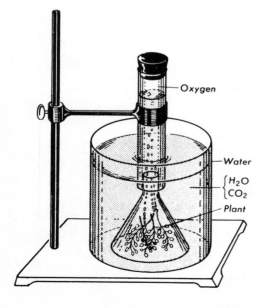

Oxygen
Water
$\begin{cases} H_2O \\ CO_2 \end{cases}$
Plant

Procedure and Observations
Place some healthy *Anacharis* in a beaker filled with water. Cover the plants with a funnel. Obtain a 15 cm long piece of glass tubing, 2.5 cm in diameter. Plug one end of the tubing with a rubber stopper. Fill the tubing with water. Carefully invert it over the funnel stem below the surface of the water as shown in the figure. Be careful not to leave any air in the tube.

Set the experiment in a sunny place and observe for several days. The light will provide energy for chemical reactions within the plant to occur.

When the tube is partially filled with gas, you can test to see whether it is carbon dioxide or oxygen. Light a splint of wood and gently blow it out. The splint should be gently glowing. Remove the stopper and test the gas with the glowing splint. If the gas is oxygen, the splint will glow more brightly or even ignite. If the gas is carbon dioxide, the glow will be put out. (a) Which gas did you discover?

Summary
(a) How can the rate at which photosynthesis takes place be determined?
(b) Why was sodium bicarbonate added to the test tubes in Part 1 of this Investigation?
(c) Under which condition of light was the bubble count the greatest?
(d) Under which condition of light was the bubble count the least?
(e) What conclusions did you draw from Part 1 of this Investigation?
(f) What substance was absorbed by the *Anacharis* sprigs in Part 2 of the Investigation?
(g) Which wavelength was more effective in speeding up the rate of photosynthesis?
(h) How do you know this is so?

INVESTIGATIONS ON YOUR OWN

1. The effect of temperature on the rate of photosynthesis can also be determined. Prepare 4 sprigs of *Anacharis* as you did for Part 1. Place one test tube in a water bath and using ice chips reduce the temperature to 10°C. Record the oxygen bubbles given off after 1 minute and after 5 minutes. Add hot water to the water bath and separately raise the temperature to 20°C, 30°C, and 40°C. Use a separate test tube of *Anacharis* at each temperature and record the number of oxygen bubbles released. Draw conclusions from your investigation concerning the effect of temperature on the rate of photosynthesis.

2. Design an original investigation that will show how different concentrations of carbon dioxide affect the rate of photosynthesis.

6-2
What Factors Affect Respiration?

OBJECTIVES
- To demonstrate that carbon dioxide is produced during respiration
- To observe the release of energy during respiration

MATERIALS

ANACHARIS
8 TEST TUBES
2 TEST TUBE RACKS
GRADUATED CYLINDER
BROM THYMOL BLUE
AMMONIUM HYDROXIDE
AQUARIUM WATER
FRESH APPLE CIDER (PART 2)
DRY YEAST (PART 2)
2 THERMOS BOTTLES (PART 2)
2 GAS BOTTLES (PART 2)
THERMOMETER (PART 2)
RUBBER TUBING (PART 2)
2 TWO-HOLE STOPPERS TO FIT
   THERMOS BOTTLES (PART 2)
2 ONE-HOLE STOPPERS TO FIT
   GAS BOTTLES (PART 2)
4 PIECES OF GLASS TUBING (PART 2)

PART 1 / PRODUCTION OF CARBON DIOXIDE BY ANACHARIS

Plant cells as well as animal cells respire. In this Investigation, you will demonstrate that carbon dioxide and energy are produced during respiration.

Procedures and Observations

In this Part, you will demonstrate that plants respire by testing for the presence of carbon dioxide.

Brom thymol blue is blue in an alkaline environment, but turns yellow in an acid environment. Carbon dioxide in the presence of water forms a weak acid.

Prepare a solution containing 50 ml of aquarium water and 20 ml of brom thymol solution. Fill 8 test tubes to within 3 cm of the top with this solution. Add a sprig of *Anacharis* to 4 of the test tubes. (a) Why did you leave 4 test tubes without *Anacharis?*

Place 2 test tubes with the *Anacharis* and 2 without plants in the dark. Put the other test tubes in bright sunlight. Observe the tubes the next day. (b) Which of the tubes showed a change in color? (c) Why did this happen? (d) What process has taken place?

PART 2 / ENERGY RELEASE DURING RESPIRATION

In this Part, you will use the process of fermentation. Fermentation is a type of respiration in which glucose is oxidized and carbon dioxide and ethyl alcohol are formed. You will determine how much energy is released as heat during this process.

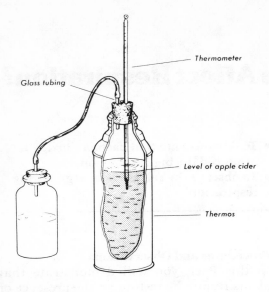

Thermometer

Glass tubing

Level of apple cider

Thermos

Procedure and Observations

Fill a thermos bottle two thirds full with fresh apple cider. Add 2 g of dried yeast. Insert a piece of glass tubing, as shown, into one of the holes of a two-hole stopper. Then insert a thermometer into the apple cider when the stopper is placed in the thermos bottle. Fill a gas bottle one half full of brom thymol blue. Now put the stopper in the thermos bottle and insert the long end of the glass tubing into the one-hole stopper of the gas bottle, as shown. Identify this thermos bottle as the experimental bottle. As a control, set up a similar apparatus but omit the yeast. Observe the experiment carefully. Record the temperature of both the experimental and control bottles at the beginning and at 24-hour intervals for 3 days. This record should be made in a table like the one shown here. DO NOT WRITE IN THIS BOOK.

Thermos bottle	Temperature			
	Start	24 hours	48 hours	72 hours
Control				
Experimental				

(a) Was energy produced in either of the thermos bottles? (b) If so, why did this oc-

cur? (c) Describe the contents of both bottles. (d) Did you notice any change in the gas bottle? (e) If so, why was there a change?

(f) Was there any product other than carbon dioxide produced during fermentation? (g) What type of respiration is being performed by the yeast cells?

Summary
(a) What evidence did you find that respiration occurs in *Anacharis*?
(b) Why must a control be used in the *Anacharis*-respiration Investigation?
(c) Why did fermentation take place in one thermos and not in the other?
(d) How can you prove that a product other than carbon dioxide is produced during fermentation?

INVESTIGATIONS ON YOUR OWN

1. You may be interested in finding out whether germinating seeds release carbon dioxide. To do this, soak some seeds (wheat, corn, peas) in 5% formalin solution for about 20 minutes. Wash the seeds in cold water and soak overnight. Fill a gas bottle one third full with the seeds. Fill a second bottle about one third full with brom thymol blue. Use a U-tube to connect the two gas bottles. Set up a similar apparatus as a control. However, destroy the seeds in the control by soaking them in 10% formalin for an hour. Observe what occurs in the demonstration bottle and in the control. Draw conclusions from your observations.

2. Design an original experiment that involves the influence of different foods on yeast respiration rates. Draw conclusions from your observations.

7-1
What Is the Structure of DNA?

OBJECTIVES

- To understand the basic structure of the DNA molecule
- To construct a model of the DNA molecule
- To identify and label the molecular structure of a DNA molecule

MATERIALS

CONSTRUCTION PAPER
CARDBOARD
PIPE CLEANERS OR SMALL STICKS
GLUE OR TAPE
COLORED BEADS OR GUM DROPS
GLASS-MARKING PENCIL

BUILDING A DNA MODEL

DNA has been referred to as the most exciting biological discovery of this century. DNA (deoxyribonucleic acid) is found in the chromosomes of all living things. In this Investigation, you will examine the structure of DNA by building your own DNA model.

Procedure and Observations

The DNA molecule is in the shape of a double helix. A helix is a spiral shape. The double helix forms the sides of the molecule or "twisted ladder." The sides are composed of alternating units of deoxyribose sugar and phosphate. The internal building blocks of the molecule or rungs of the ladder are composed of nitrogen-containing bases that are joined to the sides. The basic unit of DNA is called a *nucleotide* and consists of a deoxyribose molecule, a phosphate, and a base.

There are four types of bases in DNA. Two of the bases are *purines*. The purines are *adenine* and *guanine*. The other two bases are *pyrimidines*, called *thymine* or *cytosine*. The bases are known by their code letters A, G, T, and C. These bases always bond in a certain way. Adenine bonds only to thymine and guanine bonds only to cytosine.

(a) Given the following code letters, predict to which base each would be bonded: A, T, G, C.

Consider a base sequence in one DNA chain. (b) How would you fill in the corresponding portion of the other chain?

A G T C T T C G A G T A C G G

A DNA model can be constructed by using simple materials. This model will enable you to see the structure of the DNA molecule. To make the sides of the DNA ladder, cut 2 strips of heavy construction paper. They should be about 38 cm long and 3 cm wide. Color the strips with alternating colored boxes to indicate the phosphate and sugar units. Attach the strips of construction paper to a piece of cardboard (glue or tape can be used). Criss-cross the strips to form the spiral of the double-helix.

Use 4 different colored beads, gum drops, or jelly beans to illustrate the bases. Write the base code letters on this material using

31

a glass-marking pencil. Attach the beads (or other material) to pipe cleaners (or toothpicks) to form a "nucleotide" by attaching units to the side of the ladder. Be sure the bases are paired correctly as you complete both sides of the ladder.

Redraw the diagram below on a separate piece of paper. Label each part of the helix and fill in the base code letters that correspond to the correct nucleotide. Be sure to label: **phosphate unit, deoxyribose, hydrogen bond, guanine, cytosine, thymine,** and **adenine.**

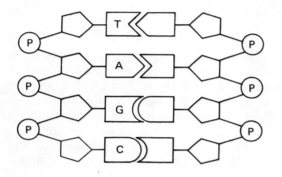

Summary
(a) What is the general structure of the DNA molecule?
(b) What composes the backbone or side piece of the DNA molecule?
(c) Of what is each three-part unit of DNA composed?
(d) What is this three-part unit called?
(e) What are the purine bases of DNA?
(f) What are pyrimidine bases of DNA?
(g) What are the code letters of the bases?
(h) In what sequence do these bases bond together?
(i) How are the strands of the DNA molecule held together?

INVESTIGATIONS ON YOUR OWN

1. In this Investigation, you made one simple type of model of the DNA molecule. You may be interested in using other materials such as plastic, metals, and ceramics to make an original model.

2. An interesting non-laboratory investigation would be a study of the history of the discovery of DNA. Though Watson and Crick proposed the DNA model, as we know it, many other people were involved in this discovery. One interesting book on the subject is *The New Genetics*, by Leonard Engel (Doubleday and Co., Garden City, New York).

8-1

What Are the Phases of Mitosis and Meiosis?

OBJECTIVES
- To recognize the different stages of mitosis
- To examine the mitotic phases in plant and animal cells
- To diagram chromosome changes in meiosis
- To differentiate spermatogenesis from oogenesis

MATERIALS

PREPARED SLIDES OF ONION ROOT TIP
MICROSCOPE
PREPARED SLIDE OF WHITEFISH
 BLASTULA (PART 2)
FRESH ONION (PART 3)
SLIDES (PART 3)
COVER GLASSES (PART 3)
RAZOR BLADE (PART 3)
BEAKER (PART 3)
TOOTHPICKS (PART 3)
COLORED PENCILS (PART 4)

PART 1 / MITOSIS IN PLANT CELLS

In this Part, you will observe the phases of cell division known as mitosis. The genetic materials are replicated and distributed through the process of mitosis.

Procedure and Observations
Observe the stages of mitosis by examining the cells of an onion root tip with the microscope. The phases of mitosis are: *prophase, metaphase, anaphase,* and *telophase. Interphase* is the phase when a cell is preparing for mitosis.

Observe the onion root tip under low power of your microscope. Locate an area of the root tip where mitotic changes can be observed. These changes are best observed in the region between the tip of the root and where the cells are beginning to elongate. Turn to high power to observe the cells more closely. How many stages can you locate? Refer to the diagram on the next page to help you identify the phases. (a) What role does the spindle play in the dividing cell? (b) Where does the cellulose wall form in the mother cell? (c) What is its function? (d) How can you differentiate prophase from metaphase? (e) What occurs during interphase?

PART 2 / MITOSIS IN ANIMAL CELLS

In this Part, you will observe the mitotic phases in animal cells. You will observe certain structures that were not present during mitosis in plant cells.

Procedure and Observations
Locate as many phases of mitosis as you can in the prepared slide of the whitefish blastula. Look for a cell in which the

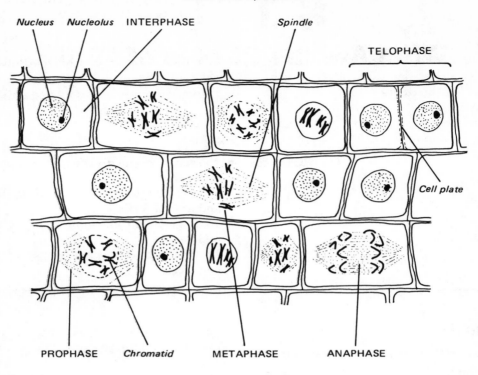

Nucleus Nucleolus INTERPHASE Spindle

TELOPHASE

Cell plate

PROPHASE *Chromatid* METAPHASE ANAPHASE

chromatids are visible. Study the poles of the spindle.

(a) How do the poles of the spindle differ from those of the onion root tip? (b) Compare the separation of daughter cells with that of the plant cell wall. (c) Are there any structures in the animal cell that were not present in the plant cell? (d) Are there any mitotic structures present in both the plant and animal cells?

On a separate piece of paper, draw an animal cell in each of the 5 stages of mitosis. To the right of the drawing, summarize the changes that occur at each stage.

PART 3 / PREPARING SMEARS OF ONION ROOT TIPS

You should now be familiar with the stages of mitosis. You are ready to prepare some slides of your own showing mitosis.

Procedure and Observations

Cut off the dried roots of a fresh onion close to the base of the bulb. Fill a beaker 2/3 full of water. Insert 3 toothpicks into the onion as shown in the figure. Place the onion in the beaker so that the bottom of the bulb is in the water. Set the beaker in a dark place.

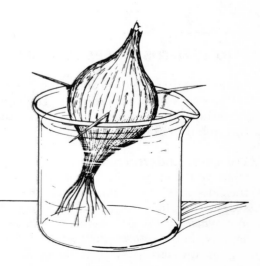

Observe the onion daily until new white root tips appear. They should grow to a length of 1-3 cm. When these have formed, fill a watch glass with acetocarmine stain. Remove the onion from the water. Using a sharp razor blade, slice off the lower, denser half of the onion root tip. Place this on the watch glass.

Heat the tips in the stain over a moderate flame for 3-5 minutes. Do not let the stain boil. Remove the tip from the watch glass and place it on a clean slide. Add a drop of fresh acetocarmine stain.

Carefully examine the root. Cut off the part of the root tip which is most deeply stained. Chop this part into fine pieces with your razor blade on a slide. Mount with a cover glass. Press firmly on the cover glass to mash the material into a thin layer. Do not break the cover glass.

Examine the slide under low power. Locate cells that have dark-stained, threadlike structures, the chromosomes. Use high power to study the cells more closely. Make a drawing of each stage of mitosis you find.

PART 4 / CHROMOSOME CHANGES DURING MEIOSIS

Meiosis is a process that occurs only in the reproductive cells. This process allows for the reduction in chromosome number during the spermatogenesis and oogenesis.

Procedure and Observations

Simplified diagrams of egg and sperm formation are given. Copy these diagrams on a separate sheet of paper. Use these diagrams to indicate changes that occur during meiosis. Refer to your text to help you identify the stages.

Draw 2 pairs of chromosomes (use a different color for each) in the first stage of egg formation, the primary oocyte. Mark one chromosome of each pair A and one B. (a) What happens in the second cell during oogenesis? Show this in your diagram. (b) What are the chromosomes called following this division?

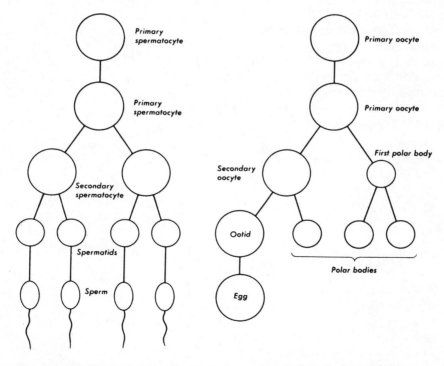

Sperm formation (spermatogenesis)

Egg formation (oogenesis)

The chromosomes form pairs, separate, and move toward opposite poles. The primary oocyte divides, forming a secondary oocyte and the first polar body. Follow these steps in your diagram. Identify the chromosomes as *A* and *B*, and use colored pencils to illustrate changes. (c) What has occurred during this phase? (d) What happens when the chromatids separate during the division of the secondary oocyte? (e) What is the chromosome number of the ootid and second polar body? (f) What happens to the ootid?

Fill in the chromosomes of the egg cell and the 3 polar bodies. (g) What is the function of the polar bodies in reproduction?

Show the chromosome changes for sperm formation just as you did in egg formation.

Summary

(a) List the stages of mitosis.
(b) What is the significance of the mitotic process?
(c) How does mitosis in plant cells differ from mitosis in animal cells?
(d) What structures are present in both plant and animal cells?
(e) In what cells does meiosis occur?
(f) How would you define meiosis?
(g) What is the significance of meiosis?
(h) During which stages of the reproductive process does meiosis occur?
(i) What would occur if there were no reduction of chromosome number?

INVESTIGATIONS ON YOUR OWN

Examine different types of animal and plant cells and observe the phases of mitosis. Many prepared slides are available for this type of observation.

9-1

How Does Chance Influence Inheritance?

OBJECTIVES
- To observe how chance affects which genes appear in gametes
- To use beans to represent the recombination of chromosomes during fertilization

MATERIALS

2 BOXES (BOTTOM HALF OF HALF-GALLON MILK CARTON)
100 RED BEANS
100 WHITE BEANS

DEMONSTRATING CHANCE

Procedure and Observations

The class should be divided into pairs for this study. Each pair of investigators should have two boxes of beans. Each box contains a mixture of 50 red beans and 50 white beans. (a) If each box represents a set of genes from one parent, what could each bean represent?

In a series of rounds that will be timed by your teacher, take one bean from each box and lay the pairs in rows: red-red, red-white, and white-white. (b) Why must a bean be chosen from each box?

After each round, count the beans in each row and record the selected combinations in a table like the one shown. DO NOT WRITE IN THIS BOOK.

(c) How many combinations are possible using two kinds of beans? (d) What accounts for the variation in offspring represented by the pairs of genes?

| Round | Number of pairs of beans in: | | | |
	Row 1 Red-Red	Row 2 Red-White	Row 3 White-White	Total Pairs
Section 1				
Section 2				
Section 3				
Section 4				
Class Totals				

Summary

Summarize your observations by calculating the ratios for each type of gene pair using the following procedure:

1) Add the total of your 3 rows and divide the sum by 4. (The 4 represents the reduction that occurs in the formation of eggs and sperm during meiosis.)
2) Divide the quotient into the total for each row.
3) The number obtained expresses a ratio. A sample calculation is given.

Sample Calculation

(1) $37 + 86 + 41 = 164$
$164 \div 4 = 41$

(2) $37 \div 41 = 0.9$
$86 \div 41 = 2.1$
$41 \div 41 = 1.0$

(3) Ratio .9 red-red;
2.1 red-white;
1.0 white-white
or 1:2:1

(a) Express the ratio in whole numbers.
(b) Why is it necessary to have so many beans in each box?
(c) Why is it necessary to select so many pairs?
(d) What are the chances of selecting the same color in a gene pair?
(e) What are the chances of selecting a different color?
(f) Explain the importance of using two different colors.
(g) What genetic principles are demonstrated by this study?
(h) How does chance selection of genes, as demonstrated with beans, provide the basis for variation in organisms?

INVESTIGATIONS ON YOUR OWN

Roll dice for 100 times and keep a tabulation of the sum of the numbers which appear on the dice. Plot the tabulations on a sheet of graph paper. Determine the probability of rolling dice to achieve a 2, 3, 4, or 5, etc. Write up your results and include a discussion of how a little knowledge of probability is useful in the study of genetics.

9-2
How Can Inheritance Be Predicted?

OBJECTIVES
- To diagram inheritance in monohybrid crosses
- To explain incomplete dominance
- To observe how inheritance demonstrates Mendel's Laws and Principles

MATERIALS

NO MATERIALS OR APPARATUS REQUIRED (PARTS 1, 2, 3)
GENETIC CORN SHOWING A 1:1 RATIO OF PURPLE-NONPURPLE (PART 4)
GENETIC CORN SHOWING A 3:1 RATIO OF PURPLE-NONPURPLE (PART 4)
STRAIGHT PINS (PART 4)

PART 1 / PREDICTING RATIOS IN A MONOHYBRID CROSS

In this Part, you will diagram the inheritance of a single trait. Flower position on pea plants is the trait to be studied here.

Procedure and Observations

The parent plants crossed by Mendel are shown in the diagram. *Axial flowers* grow along the stem. *Terminal flowers* develop only at the tip of the stem. Mendel found in pea plants that axial (A) flower position is dominant to terminal (a) flower position. Examine the genotypes of each parent.

(a) Which parent is homozygous for the dominant trait? (b) the recessive trait? (c) What gene will be contained in the gamete of the male parent? (d) the female parent? Diagram the cross in an F_1 Punnett square like the one shown. DO NOT WRITE IN THIS BOOK.

(e) What genes were inherited by the F_1 offspring? (f) When planted, what will be

flower position

axial   terminal

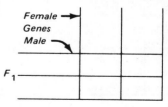

P ♂ Axial (AA) X ♀ terminal (aa)

Female Genes →
Male ⟍

F_1

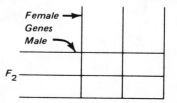

F_1 Axial (Aa) X Axial (Aa)

Female Genes →
Male ⟍

F_2

the position of the flowers produced by the F$_1$ plants? (g) How is the Principle of Unit Characters demonstrated? (h) the Principle of Dominance?

In a Punnett square, show the cross of the F$_1$ offspring with themselves to obtain the F$_2$ generation. (i) Why is this called a mono-hybrid cross? (j) What ratio do you predict for phenotype among the F^2 offspring? (k) What is the predicted ratio of genotype among the F$_2$ offspring? (l) When complete dominance is involved, would the predicted ratios obtained in this cross hold true for any monohybrid cross?

PART 2 / WHAT RATIOS ARE OBTAINED IN A DIHYBRID CROSS?

Procedure and Observations
In horses, black coats and trotting gait are dominant while the recessive alleles are white and pacing gait. If the male is homozygous for both dominant traits: (a)

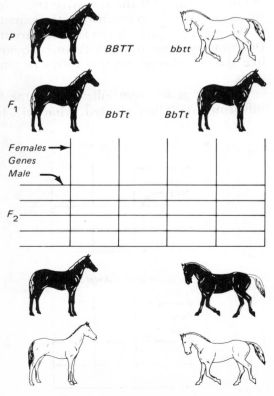

What is the genotype of the male? (b) What genes are present in the sperms?

(c) If the female is recessive for both traits, what genes are present in the eggs? (d) What is the genotype of the F$_1$ genera-tion? (e) What is the phenotype of the F$_1$ generation?

Assuming a male and female are pro-duced in the F$_1$, use these as parents to pro-duce the F$_2$ generation. Diagram the possi-ble inheritance of the offspring from such a cross in the Punnett square like the one shown. List the ratio of the following phenotypes:
  black-trotters
  black-pacers
  white-trotters
  white-pacers

(f) Would a dihybrid cross of this type al-ways produce the same phenotype ratio? Explain.

(g) Summarize the 9 possible genotypes of the F$_2$ offspring. (h) Are the ratios ob-tained from these offspring predictable? Explain.

PART 3 / HOW IS INCOMPLETE DOMINANCE SHOWN IN A PLANT AND ANIMAL?

In inheritance involving incomplete domi-nance, both alleles in a gene pair exert an equal influence on a trait.

Procedure and Observations
When a snapdragon plant bearing red flow-ers is crossed with a snapdragon plant bear-ing white flowers, plants bearing pink snapdragons are produced. (a) If the male parent is homozygous for red snapdragons, what kind of gene will be present in the sperms? (b) If the female is homozygous for white, what kind of gene will be present in each egg? (c) What is the genotype of the F$_1$?

Draw a Punnett square to show the cross between two plants producing pink snap-dragons to obtain the F$_2$ generation. (d) In-dicate the ratios of colors in the snapdragon flowers produced.

PART 4 / HOW DO GENETIC TRAITS APPEAR IN CORN?

The color of corn grains (purple or nonpurple) is an inherited characteristic that is easily observed. When pure strains of corn producing purple grains are crossed with pure strains of corn producing nonpurple grains, all of the offspring have purple grains.

Procedure and Observations

Determine what kind of cross produced your ear of corn by counting the number of purple and yellow kernels. Use a straight pin to mark your starting row. Record your count of each row in a table. *Do not pick the kernels from the ear.* (a) What percent of the seeds were purple? (b) nonpurple? (c) What is the ratio of purple to nonpurple seeds?

(d) Based on the ratios, what are the genotypes of the parents crossed to obtain your ear of corn? (e) Explain any evidence of purple color in the nonpurple grains.

Summary

(a) Briefly define each of Mendel's Law and Principles that have been demonstrated in the crosses you have completed in this Investigation: Principle of Dominance, Principle of Unit Characters, Law of Independent Assortment.
(b) In a cross of two individuals heterozygous for a single trait, what genotype and phenotype ratios would be obtained?
(c) What phenotype ratio is obtained when individuals heterozygous for two traits are crossed?
(d) Explain if the Law of Independent Assortment would apply if the genes for coat color and gait in horses were carried on the same chromosomes.
(e) On the basis of your results, explain how genetic principles yield predictable results.

INVESTIGATIONS ON YOUR OWN

Obtain an ear of corn showing a 9:3:3:1 ratio (purple-smooth-yellow-shrunken seeds) and determine the genotypes of the parents by counting the characteristics inherited on your ear of corn. Classify and record your count of the seeds. Summarize your findings by determining the genotype and phenotype ratios. Outline a cross of the F_1 and F_2 generations which were used to produce the ratios as you have determined them.

10-1
What Are Sex-Linked Traits?

OBJECTIVES
- To study how sex is determined
- To diagram the inheritance of sex-linked traits

MATERIALS

2 PENNIES
ADHESIVE TAPE
FORCEPS (PART 3)
4 TEST TUBES (15 CM) (PART 3)
2 UNTREATED WHITE PIPE CLEANERS
  (PART 3)
4 PIPE CLEANERS SOAKED IN 10% HYDRO-
  CHLORIC ACID SOLUTION (PART 3)
2 PIPE CLEANERS SOAKED IN 1% SODIUM
  HYDROXIDE SOLUTION (PART 3)
WEAK BROM THYMOL BLUE SOLUTION
  (PART 3)

PART 1 / HOW IS SEX DETERMINED?

Procedure and Observations
Each human body cell contains 23 pairs of chromosomes. One of these pairs is different in the male and female. (a) What is this 23rd pair of chromosomes called?

Examine the genotype in the figure.

♂XY   x   ♀XX

(b) What is the genotype of the female ♀? (c) Following meiosis, how many different sex chromosomes will be in the eggs? (d) What difference may be seen in the genotype of the male ♂? (e) What is the possibility of chromosomes in sperms following meiosis?

Now let's demonstrate the probability involved in sex determination. Tape an "X" on one side of a penny, and on the other side, tape a "Y." On another penny, tape an "X" on both sides. Now, flip both coins and let them land. (f) What "chromosomes" appear?

Continue the flips for at least 30 times. Record the chromosome combination that appears each time in a table. (g) What is the approximate ratio of genotypes obtained from flipping the pennies?

Now diagram the inheritance of sex chromosomes in a Punnett square. (h) What is the probability that the offspring will be male? (i) female? (j) Which gamete actually determines the sex of the offspring? (k) Why is it impossible to predict accurately the sex of offspring?

PART 2 / COLOR BLINDNESS — A SEX-LINKED TRAIT

Procedure and Observations
When a gene is carried on a sex chromosome, it is said to be sex-linked. In humans, the genes controlling color vision are

located on the X chromosome. The X chromosome carrying a gene for normal vision is represented X^C, while X^c represents a gene for color blindness. Study the following table before diagramming the inheritance of color blindness in humans.

GENOTYPES		
Female	Vision Ability	Male
$X^C X^C$	normal	$X^C Y$
$X^C X^c$	carrier	----
$X^c X^c$	color blind	$X^c Y$

Use a Punnett square to determine the color vision ability of the offspring of a couple whose genotypes are $X^c Y$ and $X^C X^c$. (a) What percent of the females are color blind? (b) What is their genotype? (c) What percent of the males are color blind? (d) How is it possible that some male offspring have normal vision when the male parent is color blind?

PART 3 / A MODEL OF SEX LINKAGE

Procedure and Observations

In this Part, you will use pipe cleaners to represent sex-linked chromosomes and test tubes to represent body cells. Obtain 4 pipe cleaners that have soaked for an hour in a 10% hydrochloric acid solution, 2 pipe cleaners soaked for an hour in a 1% sodium hydroxide solution, and 2 untreated pipe cleaners. Bend 2 untreated cleaners into a cane shape to represent the Y chromosome. Those soaked in the hydrochloric acid solution will represent the XC chromosome, while those soaked in the sodium hydroxide solution represent the X^c chromosome.

Number the test tube "cells" *1* through *4*. Fill each tube two thirds full of brom thymol blue solution. This model demonstrates the masking of the genes when a dominant and recessive gene are present in the same cell. *The color which appears in the test tube cells indicates the phenotype.* The solution turns yellow in the presence of a base (sodium hydroxide). Distribute the variously treated "chromosomes" as shown:

Set up two acid "chromosomes" in tube *1*; an acid and a base in tube *2*; an acid and an untreated cleaner in tube *3*; and a base and an untreated in tube *4*. Observe any

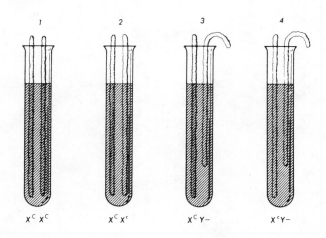

Technique for setting up the test tube "cells"
and pipe cleaner "chromosomes"

43

color change in the tubes. Record your observations and conclusions in a table like this one. DO NOT WRITE IN THIS BOOK.

Genes	Color change	Color vision	Sex
X^CX^C			
X^CX^c			
X^CY^-			
X^cY^-			

Summary
(a) Why is sex determination considered a matter of chance?
(b) Explain why males more often exhibit sex-linked traits than females.
(c) In the demonstration using pipe cleaners, what percent of the males would be color blind?
(d) females?
(e) If the male had been color blind and the female a carrier, what percent of the females would be color blind?
(f) What percent of the males would be color blind?

INVESTIGATIONS ON YOUR OWN

Hemophilia is a sex-linked trait of humans inherited in the same manner as color blindness. Because it often results in death, it is said to be lethal. Prepare a report on this sex-linked disease and other sex-linked traits not studied in this Investigation. Include in your report an analysis of where it occurs in populations and the consequences of its being inherited.

10-2

How Are Fruit Flies Used to Study Inheritance?

OBJECTIVES
- To become familiar with techniques used for culturing and examining fruit flies
- To observe certain inherited characteristics
- To study sex linkage as observed in fruit flies

MATERIALS

Cotton Plugs for Jars
Materials for Assembling
  Etherizing Jar:
    Cotton Wad
    Adhesive Tape
    Ethyl-Ether
    Caps for Jars
Petri Dishes for Re-Etherizing Device
Culture of Wild-Type Fruit Flies
Culture of Fruit Flies (Red-Eyed Males and Females) (Part 3)
Culture of Fruit Flies (White-Eyed Males and Females) (Part 3)
Hand Lens (Parts 2, 3)
Camel Hair Brush or Toothpicks (Parts 2, 3)
Grease Marking Pencil (Parts 2, 3)
2 Fresh Culture Jars (Large Baby Food Jars) (Part 3)

PART 1 / ETHERIZING FRUIT FLIES FOR EXAMINATION

Procedure and Observations

Obtain a jar in which wild-type fruit flies have been cultured. To examine these flies, it is necessary to immobilize them through the process of etherization. Before proceeding, prepare an etherization jar and a re-etherization device as shown in the figure on the next page.

Carefully read each of the following steps before beginning the procedure.

Procedure for Etherization and Examination of Fruit Flies

(1) Place several drops of ethyl-ether on the cotton wad of the etherizing jar and temporarily replace the lid. **(Warning: Ether is a highly volatile and toxic substance. USE WITH CAUTION.)**
(2) Tap the culture jar gently to dislodge the flies from near the mouth of the culture jar.
(3) Remove the cotton plug from the culture jar and the lid from the etherizer. Quickly, bring the opened mouths of the jars together. (a) Why is this necessary?
(4) Invert the jars so that the culture jar is on top. Hold the jars firmly together.

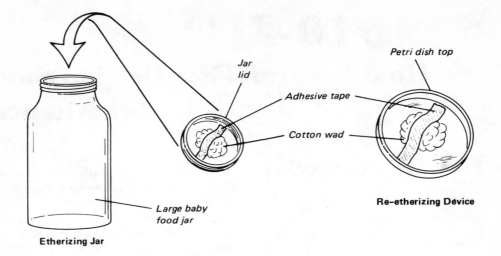

Jar lid

Petri dish top

Adhesive tape

Cotton wad

Large baby food jar

Etherizing Jar

Re-etherizing Device

(5) Tap the culture jar to cause the flies to fall into the etherizer. Recap the culture jar. (6) After about 10 seconds, pour the etherized flies out on a sheet of white paper. (b) How can you detect the flies that have been over-etherized? These may still be examined for their body characteristics. (7) Recovery of flies takes about 5 minutes. Your examination of body characteristics must be done quickly. Under-etherized flies will recover in about 1 minute. To re-etherize them, place a few drops of ethyl-ether on the small cotton wad attached to

the lid of a Petri dish. Place this re-etherizer over the awakening flies.

PART 2 / EXAMINATION OF THE CHARACTERISTICS OF FRUIT FLIES

Procedure and Observations

Examine traits shown in the figures and the chart opposite to become familiar with some of the major characteristics that may be observed in fruit flies. As you examine the flies with a hand lens, use a camel hair brush or

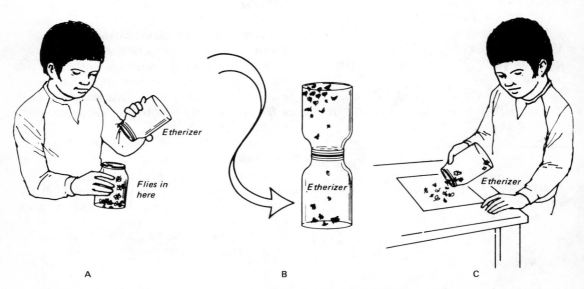

Etherizer

Flies in here

Etherizer

Etherizer

A

B

C

Characteristics	Dominant	Recessive
Size and Shape of Wings	long	vestigial, curved, miniature, bent
Color and Shading of Body	gray	black, yellow
Eye Color	red	brown (sepia), black, white

toothpick to separate and classify the flies according to the characteristics observed. As your examination proceeds, you should be able to determine that some have a broader abdomen than others. These are the females. The smaller males have a black-tipped, blunt, posterior end.

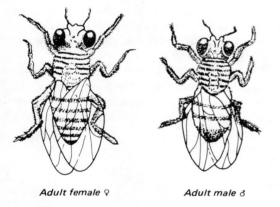

Adult female ♀   Adult male ♂

Continue your examination of the fruit flies daily for a week. On a separate piece of paper, construct a table like the one shown. Record the number of fruit flies you have observed that exhibit the trait listed. DO NOT WRITE IN THIS BOOK.

PART 3 / STUDYING SEX-LINKAGE IN FRUIT FLIES

Procedure and Observations

Experimental mating must be made with females having unfertilized eggs. (a) Why must virgin female flies be used?

Virgin female flies may be obtained by removing all adults from the cultures of the red-eyed and white-eyed flies. Examine these cultures 10-12 hours later to see if new adults have emerged. These flies should not have mated and may be used in the matings to be performed.

Etherize the new adults and select from the culture 2 or more red-eyed males, and 2 or more red-eyed virgin females. (b) What is the possible genotype of the male? (c) the female?

Do the same with the white-eyed culture. In a new culture jar, place 2 or more white-eyed males and 2 or more red-eyed virgin females. (d) What is the genotype of the male parent? (e) What are the possible genotypes of the female parent?

In another culture jar, place 2 red-eyed males and 2 white-eyed virgin females. Identify each culture bottle with the parent

Date	Sex		Body Color			Wings					Eye Color			
	M	F	Gray	Black	Yellow	Normal	Vestigial	Curved	Miniature	Bent	Red	White	Black	Brown

cross and date. Set them aside in a location at room temperature and away from bright light. After a week, examine the cultures.

Remove and discard the parent flies. Examine the cultures daily for the emergence of the F_1 generation flies. As emergence progresses, etherize and determine the sex and eye color for each of the flies. Continue etherization and examination of the F_1 generation until at least 100 flies have been classified. *Do not return the flies to the original culture.* Record your findings of the F_1 generation in a table like the one below. DO NOT WRITE IN THIS BOOK. Study the F_1 generation for 7 days.

From the F_1 generation offspring, select 2 or more red-eyed males and 2 or more red-eyed females and place them in fresh culture jars. After 7-8 days, examine the cultures. Remove the parent flies. Etherize as before and identify the eye color and sex of the F_2 offspring as they emerge. Examine at least 150 F_2 generation flies. Record your data in a table for the F_2 generation as you did for the F_1 generation.

Summary

(a) On the basis of your data, discuss the body color, wings and eye color that are dominant in the wild-type fly as indicated in the frequency of appearance in random matings.

(b) What is the purpose of the two different sets of parents in obtaining the F_1 generation?

(c) Are the virgin red-eyed female parents genetically pure for red eyes? Explain.

In the questions that follow, the numbers 1 and 2 refer to the original matings carried out in Part 3.

   (1) white-eyed male   x   red-eyed female
   (2) red-eyed male   x   white-eyed female

(d) If all the offspring in cross no. 1 were red-eyed, what is the probable genotype of the female parent?

(e) If white-eyed males and females were obtained from cross no. 2, what is the probable genotype of the female parent?

(f) In a Punnett square, diagram a cross to show how white-eyed offspring of both sexes may be obtained from a single mating. Indicate the genotypes of the parents.

F1 GENERATION OFFSPRING				
	Female		Male	
Date	Red-Eyed	White-Eyed	Red-Eyed	White-Eyed
1.				
2.				
3.				
4.				
5.				
6.				
7.				

11-1
What Are Some Human Genetic Traits?

OBJECTIVES	• To study the inheritance of some human traits
	• To determine the frequency of selected traits in a given population
	• To see the extent of genetic variability

MATERIALS

PTC (PHENYLTHIOCARBAMIDE) PAPERS

PART 1 / GENE FREQUENCIES

Procedure and Observations

Read the short description of each of the following traits. Determine which trait you have (your phenotype). Record your findings in a table like the one below. DO NOT WRITE IN THIS BOOK. In recording your genotype, use only a single symbol to indicate dominance since you do not know whether you are homozygous or heterozygous for the trait.

(1) *Attached Ear Lobe:* In most people, the ear lobes hang free. But when a person is homozygous for a certain recessive gene(e), the ear lobes are attached directly to the side of the head.

(2) *Widow's Peak:* In some people, the hair line drops downward and forms a distinct

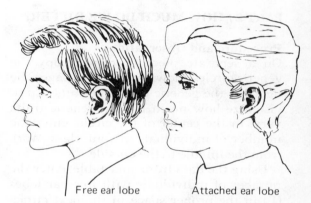

Free ear lobe   Attached ear lobe

point in the center of the forehead. This is known as a widow's peak. It results from the action of a certain dominant gene (W).

(3) *Tongue Rolling:* A dominant gene (R) gives some people the ability to roll the tongue into a U-shape when the tongue is extended from the mouth. Nonrollers (r) can do no more than produce a slight downward curve of the tongue when it is extended from the mouth.

(4) *Bent Little Finger:* A dominant gene (B) causes the last joint of the little finger to

Trait	Your Genotype	Dominant	Recessive	Ratio	Frequency (%) of Your Trait
Ear Lobes					
Widow's Peak					
Tongue Rolling					
Bent Little Finger					
PTC Tasting					

bend inward, toward the fourth finger. Lay both hands flat on the table, relax the muscles, and note whether you have a bent or a straight little finger.

(5) *PTC Tasting:* Place a piece of PTC paper on your tongue or if you detect no taste, chew the paper. If you still detect no obvious taste, you are a nontaster and are homozygous for a recessive gene (t). The tasting of this chemical results from the presence of a dominant gene (T).

Your teacher should compile the data for the entire class. Record these figures on the chart that you have made.

PART 2 / HOW MUCH DO WE DIFFER?

Procedure and Observations

On a separate piece of paper, copy the genetic circles shown on the next page. The figure of the genetic circles permits you to visualize how much human genetic traits vary. In the center of the circle, enter the number of individuals in your class. Work from the middle to the outside.

Using the data from your table, enter the number of individuals with free ear lobes (E) in the proper space in the next circle. Enter the number of students with attached ear lobes in the proper space. Continue outward, dividing the group into each trait indicating the number in each group. If any more than one person remains in the outermost section, you may extend the section by adding another trait. (a) How will this help? (b) If you had to keep extending the traits, how many more could you add? (c) Why are there always two choices as you move to each step? (d) If two people ended

up on the same outer space, would they look alike? (e) If you had 100 circles, would these two people look alike?

Summary

(a) To what extent do the ratios obtained compare to Mendelian ratios previously studied? Explain any variation.
(b) Could two parents who are tasters have a child who is a nontaster? Explain.
(c) What situation could result in less variation in a human population than what you have observed in Part 2?
(d) How do the ratios obtained for the characteristics observed compare to the national average? The national average is 65% for PTC tasting and tongue rolling and 35% for nontasters and nonrollers.
(e) Account for any variation.

INVESTIGATIONS ON YOUR OWN

Prepare one pedigree of your family's ability to roll their tongues and another on any one of the characteristics studied in this Investigation. Construct the pedigree representing two generations beginning with your parents and continuing to their offspring, which would include you. A square is used to represent a male and a circle a female. Shading of either square or circle indicates the possession of the recessive trait. Each generation is indicated by a Roman numeral. The squares and circles are joined by lines indicating relationships. Pedigrees may be expanded to include as many generations and relationships as desired. Review the pedigree shown to understand how relationships may be indicated.

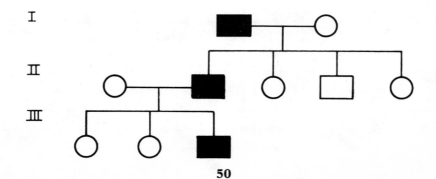

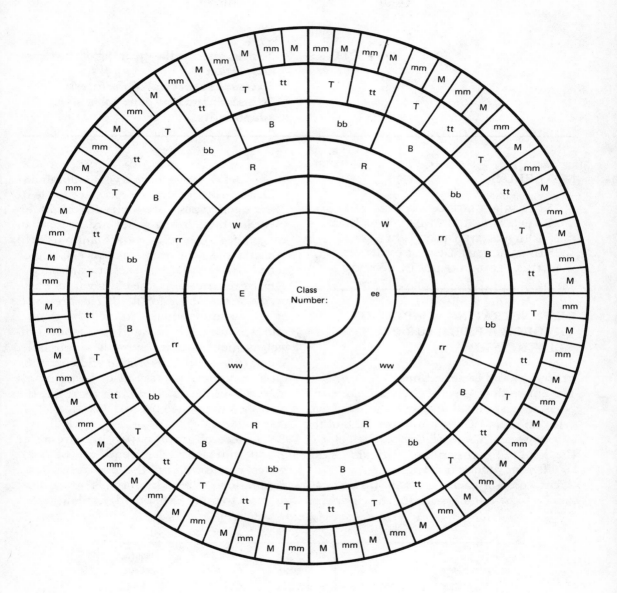

13-1
What Does Adaptation Mean?

OBJECTIVES
- **To demonstrate the meaning of the term adaptation**
- **To visualize survival of the fittest**
- **To understand how gene pools affect adaptability**

MATERIALS

25 CLEAR ACETATE DISCS, 1 CM DIAM.
25 YELLOW ACETATE DISCS, 1 CM DIAM.
25 RED ACETATE DISCS, 1 CM DIAM.
25 BLUE ACETATE DISCS, 1 CM DIAM.
ENTIRE FLOOR AREA OF CLASSROOM

DEMONSTRATING ADAPTATION THROUGH A PREDATOR-PREY RELATIONSHIP

Procedure and Observations

The entire floor area of the classroom will be used as a habitat for a population of acetate "animals." These animals are all of the same species. The variation in the color of the discs representing the "animals" is due to different genetic inheritance.

The color of each "animal" (disc) is assumed to be homozygous for the color trait with "clear" being homozygous dominant (CC). The other colors are recessive to clear. Their genotypes are rr(red), bb(blue), yy(yellow). (a) What genes are present in the gene pool of the acetate animals? (b) What is the gene frequency of each color gene in the population of acetate animals?

Each individual in the class will act as a predator searching for food. The prey will be the acetate animals. You will be given 3 minutes to search the area for "food." Collect as many acetate animals as possible. When time is up, reassemble and count the total number of acetate discs found by all members of the class. Fill in a chart like the one shown below. DO NOT WRITE IN THIS BOOK.

On a piece of graph paper, prepare a bar graph indicating the frequency of color genes remaining in the acetate animal population. (c) Which "animals" were most difficult to find? Explain. (d) Explain which

Acetate Animals	Number Originally	Number Found	Number Left on Floor	Frequency of Genes Left
Clear				
Red				
Yellow				
Blue				

acetate animals seemed to be the most fit. (e) Which acetate animals were the most poorly adapted? Why? (f) What, eventually, will happen to the genes of the most poorly adapted animals?

Assume each of the remaining clear acetate animals was mated with one of the remaining colored animals, and each mating produced one offspring and all the parents lived. (g) How many acetate animals would be added to the population in the area? (h) Explain the color of the offspring.

(i) As far as the predators(you) are concerned, which of you will live and which of you will die? (j) List several factors that make the predators better adapted for hunting these acetate animals.

Summary
(a) What genes in the gene pool allow the acetate animals to be better adapted?
(b) Explain how you have observed the concept of "survival of the fittest."
(c) How would you describe the "struggle for existence" between the predators and the acetate animals?
(d) What does it mean for an organism to be adapted to its environment?

INVESTIGATIONS ON YOUR OWN

All organisms are adapted for living in their particular environment, but some seem to exhibit a greater adaptation than others. Prepare a report on 20 organisms representing different groups of the plant and animal kingdoms. Include in your discussion why each organism is considered to be so highly adapted. Discuss what changes would have to occur in their environment to make them less adapted and unable to compete successfully with other organisms.

14-1
How Do We Classify Organisms?

OBJECTIVES
- To learn how a classification key is constructed
- To use a classification key to identify unknown organisms

MATERIALS

SCISSORS, PAPER, PENCIL

PART 1 / A STUDY OF CLASSIFICATION

Procedure and Observations

The classification categories in biology are: kingdom, phylum, class, order, family, genus, and species. A system of classification may be applied to any number of objects.

(a) Examine the figures on the next page and list some of the characteristics that you observe. (b) If considered in biological terms, what classification category would each individual figure represent? (c) What classification category would the entire group of figures represent?

Trace these figures on a separate piece of paper. Be sure to shade in the figures which are shaded here. *Do not* copy the numbers onto the figures you have drawn.

Cut apart the figures you have drawn. Each figure should be on a separate piece of paper. Assemble the figures into two groups based on common characteristics. For instance, put all the figures with curved lines into one group. The second group, then, will be figures with all straight lines. (d) By thus separating the figures into two smaller

groups, what classification category has been achieved?

You should now have in the straight-line group 12 straight-line figures: 1 rectangle and 1 triangle with lines projecting from them and 10 others being shaded or unshaded triangles, squares, or rectangles. The group of figures with curved lines, representing the other phylum, will not be used further in this Part of the Investigation.

Using the characteristic of lines projecting from the figures, divide the 12 figures into two groups. (e) In this division, what classification category has been achieved? (f) What characterizes the remaining 10 figures?

Separate the shaded figures from the unshaded figures. (Save the shaded figures for later use.) (g) What classification category has been achieved? (h) What characterizes the remaining 6 figures?

Separate the triangles from the other 4 figures. (Save the triangles for later use.) (i) What classification category does each group represent?

The remaining 4 figures can be divided into two smaller groups on the basis of being squares or rectangles. Make the separation and save the rectangles. (j) What classification category is represented by the group of squares and the group of rectangles?

The group of squares should now have in it a large square and a small square. Make the final separation on the basis of the size

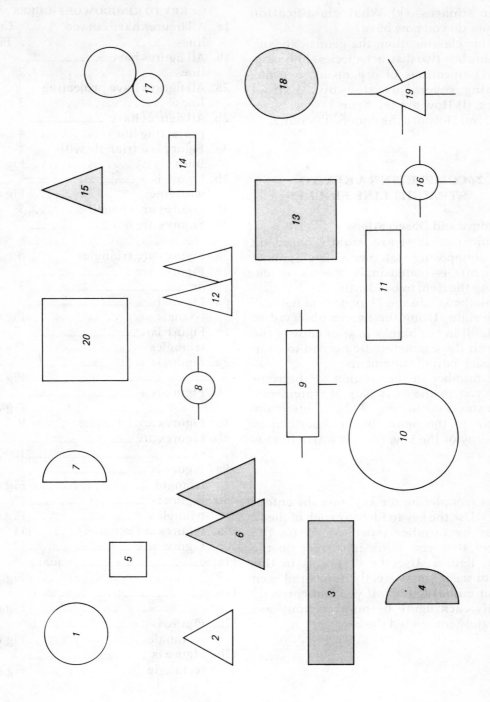

of the squares. (k) What classification category do you now have?

In this classification, the genus category contains but two distinct species. In biological classifications of organisms, a genus contains several related but distinct species. (l) How are the figures (species) related? (m) How are the figures different?

PART 2 / COMPLETING A KEY TO STRAIGHT-LINE FIGURES

Procedure and Observations

Classification keys are usually based on pairs of opposing statements. Each pair of statements is increasingly specific in describing the item to be identified.

Copy the key to the "kingdom of figures" on the right. Using the figures observed in Part 1, fill in the blanks in your copy of the key with the characteristic needed to complete each pair of statements.

The number in the column at the right refers you to the next pair of statements. When you come to "Fig. # ____," insert the number of the figure being described in your copy of the key. DO NOT WRITE IN THIS BOOK.

After completing the key, mix the cutout figures. Use the key to identify each of the 12 figures by number (species). Write the number that you think is correct on the cutout figures. Use the diagrams in this book to see if you correctly numbered each of your cutout figures. If you can correctly identify each figure by number, you have accurately completed the key.

KEY TO KINGDOM OF FIGURES

1a. All figures have curved lines . . . . Curved Figures

1b. All figures have _____ lines 2

2a. All figures have projecting lines 3

2b. All figures have _____ projecting lines 4

3a. Figure is a triangle with lines . . . . Fig.# ___

3b. Figure is a _____ with lines . . . . Fig.# ___

4a. Figures are shaded 5

4b. Figures are not _____ 8

5a. Figures are triangles 6

5b. Figures are _____ or _____ 7

6a. Figure is _____ triangle . . . . Fig.# ___

6b. Figure is _____ triangles . . . . Fig.# ___

7a. Figure is a _____ . . . . Fig.# ___

7b. Figure is a _____ . . . . Fig.# ___

8a. Figures are triangles 9

8b. Figures are _____ or _____ 10

9a. Figure is _____ triangle . . . . Fig.# ___

9b. Figure is _____ triangles . . . . Fig.# ___

10a. Figures are squares 11

10b. Figures are _____ 12

11a. _____ square . . . . Fig.# ___

11b. _____ square . . . . Fig.# ___

12a. Figure is _____ rectangle . . . . Fig.# ___

12b. Figure is _____ rectangle . . . . Fig.# ___

PART 3 / USING A CLASSIFICATION KEY TO IDENTIFY CERTAIN SPECIES OF FISH

Procedure and Observations

Study the terms defined below. All of these refer to structures of a fish.

TERMS REFERRING TO THE STRUCTURE OF FISH

barbel — a fleshy projection from the lips or head.

scales — overlapping outgrowths of the skin.

FINS

adipose — a small fin on the top mid-line of the body near the tail fin.

anal — a fin along the lower mid-line of the body near the tail fin.

caudal — tail fin.

dorsal — the fin or fins along the top mid-line of the body.

pectoral — the paired fins nearest the head, corresponding to front legs or arms.

pelvic — the paired fins nearest the tail, corresponding to hind legs.

Closely examine one of the drawings of a fish shown on the next page. Read both statements listed under number 1 in the classification key. One of these statements should describe the fish you have chosen; the other should not. Refer to the number after the statement that fits your fish and look for that number in the key. Again select the statement that describes the fish you picked. Continue through the key until you come to a name after one statement. This should be the name of the fish you picked. Practice using the key to identify several of the fish shown.

Example:

Suppose you want to find the name of fish number 2. Look at the classification key. Note that each numbered item presents two possibilities. We see that our fish has no scales, or at least we cannot see any. So we choose item 1b. This refers us to number 12. So we go down the page to number 12. Our fish is not elongated or snakelike (item 12b), so we go to number 13 of the key. The fish we are classifying has barbels growing from its lips and the top of its head (item 13a), so we go to number 14 of the key. Since our fish has a caudal fin that is rounded, and a blunt head, we see that it is the *Bullhead Cathead catfish* (also known as *horn pout* in some parts of the country).

Summary

(a) Based on what you have learned in this Investigation, discuss classification as a useful tool for a biologist.

On a separate piece of paper, write the following as complete sentences by filling in the missing words:

(b) A group of closely related species is a ___?___ .

(c) A subdivision of a family is a ___?___ .

(d) The largest of the classification categories is the ___?___ .

(e) The most specific of the classification groupings is the ___?___ .

(f) A group of closely related classes is a ___?___ .

(g) The subdivision of an order is the ___?___ .

(h) A ___?___ is composed of several closely related orders.

INVESTIGATIONS ON YOUR OWN

Select commonly seen groups of related objects (automobiles, canned goods, etc.) and classify them into the major classification categories. Construct a key to their identification. Try your classification key with some individuals in your class to see how well it works.

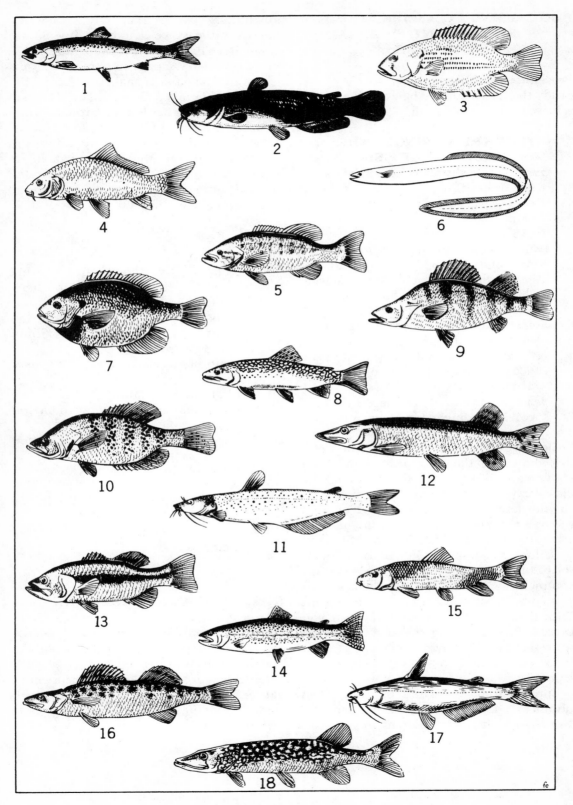

CLASSIFICATION KEY TO CERTAIN FISH

1a. Body noticeably covered with scales 2
1b. Scales not covering body or too small to be seen 12
2a. Dorsal fin single 3
2b. Dorsal fins two or more, joined or separated 6
3a. Body more than four times as long as broad (top to bottom); front edge of dorsal fin far back on body; mouth large, hinge back of eye 4
3b. Body less than four times as long as broad; front edge of dorsal fin about midway between head and tail; mouth not large, hinge in front of eye 5
4a. Dark lines forming netted design on body, fins not spotted .... *Pickerel*
4b. Body covered with yellow spots; fins spotted .... *Northern pike*
5a. Mouth turned downward; barbels absent; dorsal fin not elongated .... *White sucker*
5b. Mouth not turned downward; barbels present; dorsal fin elongated .... *Carp*
6a. Two dorsal fins separated, the anterior spiny and the posterior soft 7
6b. Two dorsal fins united, forming an anterior spiny portion and a posterior soft portion 8
7a. Top of head concave, forming a hump in front of dorsal fin; dark vertical bars on body .... *Yellow perch*
7b. Top of head not concave, body sloping to dorsal fin and not forming a hump; dark blotches on body .... *Wall-eyed pike*
8a. Body more than three times as long as broad 9
8b. Body less than three times as long as broad 10
9a. Hinge of jaws behind the eye; notch between spiny and soft dorsal fin deep and nearly separating into two fins .... *Large-mouth black bass*
9b. Hinge of jaws below the eye; notch between spiny and soft dorsal fin not nearly separating into two fins .... *Small-mouth black bass*
10a. Mouth large, hinge below or behind eye 11
10b. Mouth small, hinge in front of eye .... *Bluegill*
11a. Five to seven spines in dorsal fin; dark spots forming broad vertical bars on sides
.... *White crappie*
11b. Ten or more spines in dorsal fin; sides flecked with dark spots .... *Rock bass (Redeye)*
12a. Body much elongated and snakelike; dorsal, caudal, and anal fins continuous ... *Eel*
12b. Body not elongated and snakelike; dorsal, caudal, and anal fins separate; adipose fin present 13
13a. Barbels growing from lips and top of head; head large and broad 14
13b. Barbels lacking; head not large and broad 16
14a. Caudal fin deeply forked; head tapering 15
14b. Caudal fin rounded or slightly indented but not forked; head blunt *Bullhead catfish*
15a. Dorsal fin rounded at top; body silvery, speckled with black markings *Channel catfish*
15b. Dorsal fin long and pointed at top; body bluish-gray without speckles .. *Blue catfish*
16a. Caudal fin deeply forked; back not mottled and with few spots ...... *Atlantic salmon*
16b. Caudal fin square or slightly indented; back mottled or spotted 17
17a. Back and caudal fin spotted; broad horizontal band along sides ...... *Rainbow trout*
17b. Back mottled with dark lines; caudal fin not spotted; fins edged with white ....
.... *Brook trout*

15-1

What Is a Phage Virus?

OBJECTIVES
- To demonstrate the effects of a virulent phage virus
- To understand how a bacterial cell is destroyed in the lytic cycle

MATERIALS

STOCK CULTURE OF *ESCHERICHIA COLI* STRAIN-B
STOCK CULTURE OF *T-EVEN* BACTERIOPHAGE
INOCULATING LOOP
SEVEN 1-ML PIPETTES
4 BACTERIOLOGICAL PIPETTES GRADUATED AT 0.01 ML
ONE 10-ML PIPETTE GRADUATED IN 1 ML
FOUR 6-IN. CULTURE TUBES
8 PETRI DISHES
500-ML FLASK
GLASS ROD BENT AT 90° ANGLE (5 CM ON EACH SIDE)
INCUBATOR
REFRIGERATOR
NUTRIENT BROTH
NUTRIENT AGAR
DISTILLED WATER

EFFECT OF T-EVEN PHAGES ON ESCHERICHIA COLI

Bacteriophages are extremely small particles that multiply in living bacterial cells. These particles are too small to be seen under your light microscope. What evidence can we use to show that phages enter bacterial cells and are reproduced there?

The electron microscope is powerful enough to show what happens during the attack of a bacterial cell by a phage virus. You can demonstrate the activity of the phage particles by inoculating a bacterial culture with a phage virus.

Procedure and Observations

Transfer a loopful of *Escherichia coli*, Strain-B, to 250 ml of sterile nutrient broth. Incubate the inoculated broth for 24 hours at 35-37°C (96-98°F).

Label three culture tubes containing 9 ml sterile nutrient broth as *1*, *2*, and *3*. Transfer 1 ml of *T-even* bacteriophage culture to tube 1. Diffuse the inoculum by rotating the tube between the hands. Then transfer 1 ml of this inoculum to tube 2 and diffuse the inoculum. In the same manner, transfer 1 ml from tube 2 to tube 3.

Transfer 0.01 ml of the phage culture from tube 1 to a sterile agar plate identified as *1*. Add 1 ml of *E. coli* to this same plate. Mix and spread the inoculum over the plate with a bent glass rod. Transfer 0.01 ml of phage inoculum from tubes 2 and 3 to two additional plates. Add 1 ml of *E. coli* culture to the plates. Mix and spread with a bent glass rod. Introduce 1 ml of *E. coli* to a fourth plate to serve as a control. Incubate all plates for 24 hours at 35-37°C (96-98°F). Do not invert the plates.

After 24 hours examine the plates. Notice the film of bacteria on the control plate. Examine the other plates and look for plaques. Each plaque contains a large number of phage particles. These are descendents of a single phage particle that infected a single *E. coli* cell. They reproduced within it, causing the bacterial cell to rupture, releasing phage particles that destroyed other bacteria in the area.

Determine that the clear areas contain phage particles. Use an inoculation loop to transfer a loopful of material from one plaque to a culture tube containing 9 ml of sterile nutrient broth. Put 1 ml of *E. coli* on a sterile agar plate. Then transfer 0.01 ml of the phage culture. Mix and spread on the plate. Incubate for 24 hours at 35-37°C (96-98°F). After 24 hours, examine the plate for plaques. These are evidence that phage particles were present in the plaques on plates 1, 2, and 3.

Summary

(a) What is another name for a phage?
(b) Of what is the coat of a phage composed?
(c) Of what is the core of a phage composed?
(d) What does the phage inject into the bacterial cell?
(e) How is this accomplished?
(f) What occurs when the phage injects this material?
(g) What eventually happens to the bacterial cell?

INVESTIGATIONS ON YOUR OWN

1. Make your own model of a phage virus from materials around your home. Such materials include: pipe cleaners or paper clips, beads, buttons, cardboard, and a thimble.

2. Examine electron micrographs of phages and the lytic cycle. Compare these photos to the diagrams that you have drawn and to those in the text. What differences do you see?

16-1

How Are Bacteria Cultured and Distributed?

OBJECTIVES
- **To become familiar with bacteriological techniques**
- **To use sterile techniques**
- **To collect bacteria from objects**

MATERIALS

DEHYDRATED NUTRIENT AGAR
1000 ML ERLENMEYER FLASK
TEST TUBES
PETRI DISHES
WIRE BASKET
BALANCE
CLEAN CLOTH
PAPER TOWELS
COTTON
LARGE SPOON OR SPATULA
PAN
FUNNEL
RUBBER TUBE WITH CLAMP
RING STAND
PRESSURE COOKER OR AUTOCLAVE
HOT-AIR OVEN
DISTILLED WATER
INCUBATOR (PART 2)
HOT PLATE (PART 2)
COLONY COUNTER (PART 2)

PART 1 / PREPARATION AND STERILIZATION OF CULTURES

Many of the techniques that you will use in this Investigation are used daily in bacteriological laboratories. In order to ensure sterile technique, each step should be performed with care, and according to directions given.

In this Part, you will become familiar with the preparation of medium for culturing bacteria and with sterile technique.

Procedure and Observations

Use a commercially prepared nutrient agar to prepare medium. Prepare enough medium for a 1-liter flask. Stir the mixture and put the flask on a burner. Continue to stir *constantly* until the solution comes to a boil. Be sure that all the agar has dissolved. Pour the medium into an Erlenmeyer flask and plug the mouth of the flask with cotton. This medium should be used immediately to pour slants or culture plates, or both.

To prepare "slants":

Pour the agar into a beaker to make it easier to pour into test tubes. Fill the test tubes one third full of medium and plug them with cotton or sponge stoppers. The plugs should fit securely and should extend about 2 cm into the tube and 3 cm out of the tube. Avoid getting medium on the upper walls of the tube or around the mouth. Set them upright in a basket. Do not allow the medium to touch the plug. (a) Why should the medium not touch the plug?

Place the basket of plugged tubes in a pressure cooker or autoclave and sterilize at 15 lbs for 25 minutes. In operating the pressure cooker, be sure that you leave the valve open until a stream of steam is given off. (b) Why is it important that all the air be removed from the chamber?

After sterilization, allow the medium to cool slightly but not to gel. Remove the tubes from the sterilizer and lay them, individually, in a slanting position so that the agar extends from the bottom of the tube to a point about 3 cm below the cotton plug. The tube should not be slanted so much that the medium touches the cotton plug. (c) Why should this be done in this manner?

The entire bottom of the tube should be covered with medium. Allow the tubes to cool to room temperature. (d) Why are these tubes referred to as "slants"?

Slant

To prepare culture dishes:

Wash the Petri dishes, rinse thoroughly, and allow to dry. Wipe them with a clean cloth and place them, with covers on, in a hot-air oven at 175°C for 2 hours. Leave them in the oven or stack and cover them with paper towels until used.

Sterilize the prepared agar medium in an autoclave or pressure cooker. Arrange sterile Petri dishes in piles of about 4 each. Wash your hands thoroughly. Remove the flask of medium from the sterilizer and take out the cotton plug. Flame the mouth of the flask. Pour the dishes by raising the cover slightly and adding enough sterile medium to cover the bottom of each dish to a depth of about one half cm. Replace the cover as quickly as possible as shown below. (e) Why should this be done?

Put the dishes on a level surface and allow them to gel. To store the poured dishes, wrap in paper and place them where they will not be disturbed.

PART 2 / COLLECTING BACTERIA

In this Part, you will demonstrate the wide distribution of bacteria by collecting them from numerous objects.

Procedure and Observations
Prepare sterilized agar plates according to the directions given in Part 1. Heat a tube of sterile agar in a water bath until the agar has melted. Pour the agar into a Petri dish.

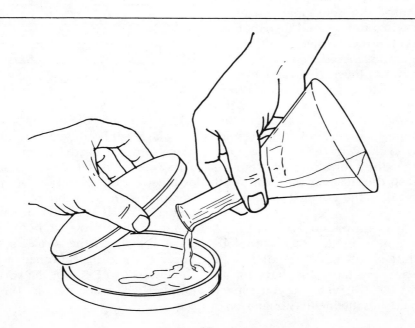

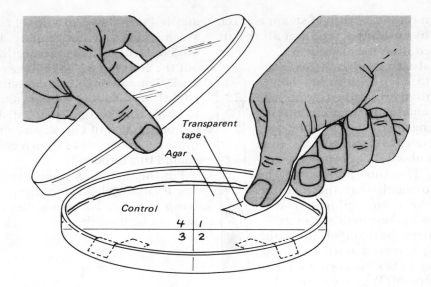

Transparent tape

Agar

Control

4 | 1
3 | 2

Try to keep the top of the dish on as much as possible. Once the agar has gelled, the contact plates are ready.

Divide the Petri dish into four parts by marking the outside of the bottom with a wax marking pencil. Number the sections 1 through 4. Leave one section untouched as a control. Many different objects can be used to demonstrate bacterial distribution. The placement of these objects on the contact plates is called *inoculation*.

There are many objects that can be tested for bacteria: lipstick, door knob, clothing, money, dishes, silverware, etc. Use cellophane tape to inoculate 3 sections. Touch a piece of tape to the object to be tested. Lift the lid over the Petri dish and place the tape on the medium for a minute. Remove the tape. Keep the lid over the dish at all times. (a) What is the advantage of doing this?

Close the dish immediately after the 3 contacts have been made. Record the objects on a data sheet. Label the dish with your name and the date. Incubate for 48 hours at 35-37°C. (b) What do you expect will happen during the incubation period?

After 48 hours, check your results and record them in a table like the one below. DO NOT WRITE IN THIS BOOK.

Petri Dish: Section	Object Tested	Number of Bacteria Colonies
1		
2		
3		
4		

(c) Do you find colonies in every section of the plate? (d) If not, explain. Study the colonies under a hard lens or a microscope. These can be observed through the bottom of the inverted plate. (e) Do you find any organisms in addition to the colonies of bacteria? (f) If so, what are they? (g) Account for their presence in the Petri dish.

(h) Which of the subjects chosen produced the greatest number of colonies? (i) the fewest? (j) Explain the variation in the number of colonies on the individual plates.

Summary

(a) Why are sterilization procedures so important in the study of bacteria?

On a separate piece of paper, complete the statements below. The missing words may be found in the list provided.

Answers

agar	sterilize
cultured	Petri
inoculate	colonies
contaminated	medium

(b) _?_ may be used as a growth medium.

(c) Heating in a pressure cooker is done to _?_ equipment and growth media.

(d) Single bacteria are not visible to the naked eye but bacterial _?_ are visible.

(e) A _?_ dish is filled with growth medium to culture bacteria.

(f) A sterile medium which becomes cultured with an undesirable organism is said to be _?_

INVESTIGATIONS ON YOUR OWN

1. There are many different methods of exposing a medium to bacteria. Inoculation can be accomplished by use of an inoculating needle or dissecting needle. Sterilize the instrument by passing it through a flame until it glows red. Streak plates can be made by inoculating a medium with a left to right movement of the inoculating needle. Exposure plates are made by exposing a Petri dish to the air.

   Slants can be inoculated in the following manner: turn the cotton plug to be sure that it will slip out easily; sterilize the inoculating needle by passing it through a flame; touch the sterilized needle to the source of bacteria; holding the slant in your left hand, remove the plug by grasping it between the bent little finger and the palm of the right hand (you are holding the needle with the thumb and forefinger of the same hand); flame the mouth of the tube; insert the needle into the tube and lay the point against the lowest part of the medium; make a zigzag line along the surface of the medium from the bottom to the top; flame the needle and the mouth of the tube and replace the cotton plug.

   You may want to inoculate one or more slants with each of the following: milk, stagnant water, and a stock culture of harmless bacteria.

2. You may want to test the bacteria count in various rooms of your home and school. This can be done by exposing Petri dish medium to the air for 15 minutes. Proceed as you did in Part 2 of this Investigaton. Draw your own conclusions from your findings.

16-2
How Are Bacteria Classified?

OBJECTIVES
- To recognize three forms of bacteria
- To study the motility of bacteria
- To stain bacteria for microscopic examination

MATERIALS

PREPARED SLIDES OF THE VARIOUS FORMS
OF BACTERIA
DISTILLED WATER
MICROSCOPE
BEAN INFUSION:
15-20 DRIED BEANS (PARTS 2, 3)
400 ML BEAKER (PARTS 2, 3)
DEPRESSION SLIDES (PART 2)
HANGING-DROP (25 MM) COVER GLASSES
(PART 2)
PETROLEUM JELLY (PART 2)
BUNSEN BURNER (PARTS 2, 3)
INOCULATING LOOP (PARTS 2, 3)
TOOTHPICKS (PART 2)
BROTH CULTURE OF A FLAGELLATED BAC-
TERIUM (PART 3)
BACTERIA CULTURES (SLANTS OR PETRI
DISH CULTURES PREPARED IN INVESTIGA-
TION 16-1) (PART 3)
PAPER TOWEL (PART 3)
COVER-GLASS HOLDER (PART 3)
SIMPLE STAIN (CRYSTAL VIOLET,
METHYLENE BLUE, OR SAFRANIN) (PART 3)
GRAM'S DIFFERENTIAL STAINS AND
REAGENTS (CRYSTAL VIOLET, 5% SODIUM
BICARBONATE SOLUTION, GRAM'S IODINE
SOLUTION, 95% ALCOHOL OR ACETONE,
CARBOL FUCHSIN OR SAFRANIN) (PART 3)

PART 1 / FORMS OF BACTERIA

In this section of the Investigation, you will study prepared slides of the three forms of bacteria: *coccus*, *bacillus*, and *spirillum*. These bacteria have characteristics that can be easily identified under the microscope.

Procedure and Observations

Examine the prepared slides under low and high power of the microscope. (a) Should you view the bacteria under high or under low power?

Clearly identify each of the three forms of bacteria. (b) Describe how each form differs from the others.

On a separate piece of paper, draw each form of bacteria that you have observed. Label your drawings.

PART 2 / MOTILITY OF BACTERIA

In this Part, you will study the motility or movement of bacteria. Movement is exhibited generally by collisions of bacteria in a medium. This movement or motion is referred to as *Brownian movement*. True movement, or motility, is exhibited by flagellated bacteria.

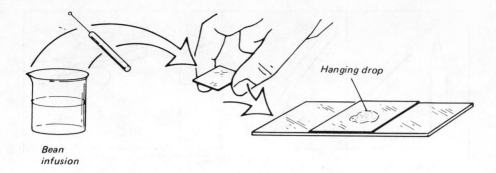

Bean
infusion

Hanging drop

Procedure and Observations

Motility can be examined by preparing a
bean infusion and examining the bacteria
in this infusion. To prepare a bean infusion,
place 15-20 beans in half a beaker of water
and boil for a few minutes. Add water to fill
the beaker. Set the infusion in a warm
place, exposed to the air, for 2 or 3 days.

Using an inoculating loop, transfer a
loopful of bean infusion to the center of a
hanging-drop cover glass. Using a toothpick, place a thin film of petroleum jelly
around the edge of the depression of the
culture slide. Hold the culture slide, hol-
lowed side facing down, over the drop.
Press the slide gently against the cover
glass so that the petroleum jelly makes contact.

Gently invert the slide and examine under high power of the microscope. The infusion should be filled with bacteria. Darken
the field by closing the diaphragm, and the
organisms will be more visible. (a) Which
forms are most common? (b) Do you find
colonies? (c) If so, what kind are they?

(d) Are motile (free-swimming) bacteria
present in the infusion? (e) What type of
motion is demonstrated in your culture?
(f) Do the cells move individually or in
groups? (g) What cell structures enable
many bacteria to move in fluid surround-
ings? (h) Can you distinguish any flagella
on the cells?

PART 3 / STAINING BACTERIA

Staining is an important part of bacteriological technique because it helps to em-
phasize cell structures and shapes. *Simple
stains* color the cells and make them more
visible. *Differential* stains identify bacteria
based on their reaction to the stain. Gram's
stain is a well-known differential stain.

Procedure and Observations
Use of simple stains.

Mount a clean cover glass in a holder.
With a flamed inoculating loop, place one
loopful of distilled water in the center of the
cover glass. Flame the loop again and transfer a small number of bacteria from an agar
slant or a colony on a Petri dish culture to
the drop of water. Spread the bacteria in
the thin film on the cover glass. If you use a
bean infusion, place one loopful of the infusion on a cover glass and spread in a thin
film. Allow the film to air-dry.

Invert the cover glass (bacteria film
down) and using forceps pass it through the
flame of a Bunsen burner 3 times. This kills
the bacteria and fixes them to the cover
glass.

Flood the smear with crystal violet (or
other simple stain). Allow it to stand 2 or 3
minutes. The staining time will vary with
the stain you use and the organism you are
staining. Wash the smear in tap water until
no more stain washes out. Air-dry or blot
all but the surface of the smear. Mount on a

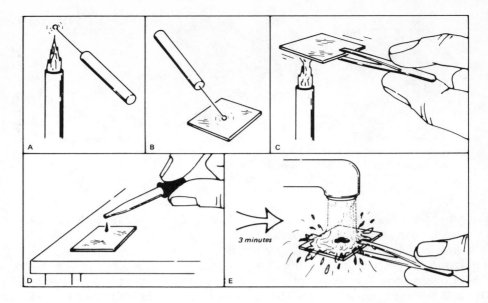

slide for examination with your microscope.

Examine all areas of the film with low power. Select a portion of the smear in which the bacteria are well distributed. They should be separated enough to see individual cells. Examine this portion under high power. You should be able to see the bacteria clearly and determine their shape and grouping with standard high-power magnification (430 or 440X). If an oil-immersion microscope is available (970 or 1,000X), you will be able to see the bacteria more clearly.

Gram's differential staining technique.

Gram's differential stain is perhaps the most widely used stain in bacteriology. Nearly all bacteria are classified as Gram-positive or Gram-negative by their reaction to this stain.

The procedure involves the use of two stains. The initial stain (you will use crystal violet) stains all bacteria. Other reagents used in the procedure cause some bacteria to retain this initial stain and remain violet in color. These organisms are classified as Gram-positive. The procedure also makes use of 95% alcohol to decolorize certain bacteria. These organisms lose their violet color and are stained red with a counter-stain, carbol fuchsin or safranin. We classify them as Gram-negative.

The determination of bacteria as Gram-positive or Gram-negative is important, not only in classification but in determining many other properties, including sensitivity to various antibiotics in the treatment of infectious diseases.

To make a Gram's stain preparation of a bacteria film, transfer bacteria from a colony in an agar slant or Petri-dish culture to a drop of distilled water on a cover glass, using a flamed inoculating loop. Air-dry the film and fix in a flame. Flood the film with crystal violet. Add 3 or 4 drops of 5% sodium bicarbonate solution. Allow to stand for 2 or 3 minutes. Quickly, rinse in water until no more stain washes out of the film.

Flood the stained film with Gram's iodine for 1 to 2 minutes. (The iodine fixes the stain in Gram-positive bacteria.) Rinse in water. Using a dropper, rinse the film with 95% alcohol until no more stain runs out. This decolorizing usually requires from 30 seconds to 1 minute.

Flood the film with carbol fuchsin or safranin (a counterstain) for 30 seconds to 1 minute. Rinse in water to remove the excess stain. Air-dry or blot the cover glass, and examine under high power. (a) What color are your bacteria? (b) Would you classify them as Gram-positive or Gram-negative? (c) Did all of the bacteria in your film produce the same staining reaction?

If other members of your class made Gram's stain preparations, examine other films to see both Gram-positive and Gram-negative organisms.

Summary
Differentiate between the following terms:
(a) true motion
    Brownian motion
(b) coccus
    bacillus
(c) bacillus
    spirillum
(d) simple stain
    differential stain
(e) Gram-positive
    Gram-negative

INVESTIGATIONS ON YOUR OWN

1. In this Investigation, you examined prepared slides of different bacterial forms. You may be interested in examining living cultures and identifying these forms in the live cultures. Do the living forms of bacteria appear different from the prepared slides?

2. There are certain *special stains* which are used by bacteriologists to identify particular structures or types of bacteria. You may wish to investigate these stains and design an experiment that would test one or more of them.

17-1
Do Antiseptics and Antibiotics Work?

OBJECTIVES
- To determine the effect of antiseptics on bacteria
- To determine the effect of various antibiotics on the growth of bacteria
- To determine sensitivity and resistance of bacteria to antibiotics

MATERIALS

COMMON ANTISEPTICS (3 SHOULD BE SUFFICIENT: YOU MAY WISH TO INCLUDE MOUTHWASHES)
5% PHENOL SOLUTION
FILTER PAPER
FORCEPS
PETRI DISHES
3 ERLENMEYER FLASKS (250 ML)
500-ML ERLENMEYER FLASK (PART 2)
NUTRIENT AGAR
NUTRIENT BROTH
COTTON PLUGS FOR FLASKS
STERILE 1-ML PIPETTES
BULB TO FIT 1-ML PIPETTE
PAPER PUNCH
METRIC SCALE
STOCK CULTURES OF *ESCHERICHIA COLI*, *BACILLUS SUBTILIS*, *PROTEUS VULGARIS*
WAXED PENCIL OR GUMMED LABELS
6 MEDIA BOTTLES (PART 2)
COTTON (PART 2)
INOCULATING LOOP (PART 2)
PRESSURE COOKER OR AUTOCLAVE (PART 2)
DRY-AIR OVEN (PART 2)
DIFCO SENSITIVITY DISCS—PENICILLIN, STREPTOMYCIN, TERRAMYCIN, CHLOROMYCETIN, AUREOMYCIN, AND TETRACYCLINE (PART 2)

You are probably familiar with antiseptics and antibiotics. However, do you know how effective these substances are and how they differ? Will different antiseptics and antibiotics affect certain bacteria and not others? These are just a few of the questions that you will answer in this Investigation.

PART 1 / EFFECT OF ANTISEPTICS ON THE GROWTH OF BACTERIA

In this Part, you will determine the bactericidal action of various antiseptics. You will compare the effectiveness of each antiseptic with that of a 5% phenol solution, which is used as a standard.

Procedure and Observations
Obtain a variety of antiseptics, including 5% phenol solution. Mark the bottoms of three Petri dishes, dividing each into quarters. Number the quarters 1 through 4. Mark one dish *A*, one *B*, and one *C*. Using a sterile 1-ml dropper, transfer 1 ml of the *Bacillus subtilis* inoculum to sterile Petri dish *A*.

Using another sterile dropper, prepare sterile Petri dish *B* with the *Escherichia coli* inoculum. Prepare sterile Petri dish *C* with *Proteus vulgaris* inoculum. Cool liquefied nutrient agar to 45°C and pour all of the dishes. Use care to diffuse the inoculum through the warm nutrient agar before it gels.

Using a notebook paper punch, punch small discs of filter paper (unless prepared discs are available). With forceps, dip 3 filter paper discs into the 5% phenol antiseptic. Drain excess liquid from the disc so as not to drip antiseptic on the surface of the poured plate. Place 1 disc in the number 1 quadrant of each culture dish. Discs should be placed 2 cm from the rim of the Petri dish. Prepare 3 discs for each antiseptic. Place 1 disc of each antiseptic in one quadrant of each culture dish. Incubate all plates for 48 hours at 35–37° C.

After incubation, examine the plates for evidence of a zone of inhibition around the discs. These will appear as clear areas and indicate destruction of bacteria or inhibition of growth. Invert the dish and lay a metric scale across each disc. Measure the width of the zone of inhibition on each side of the disc. Record the data in a table like the one below. DO NOT WRITE IN THIS BOOK.

(a) Did you expect to get the results that you did? Explain your answer. (b) Were the antiseptics that you used more or less effective than the control of 5% phenol solution? (c) Were any of the bacterial cultures greatly inhibited by a particular antiseptic? If so, which ones? (d) Were any of the bacterial cultures *not* affected by the antiseptics used? If so, which ones?

PART 2 / THE EFFECT OF ANTIBIOTICS ON BACTERIA

In this Part, you will use the disc technique to determine whether bacteria are sensitive or resistant to an antibiotic.

Procedure and Observations
Identify each of the sterile Petri dishes with the name of the bacteria you are testing. Using a pipette bulb (not your mouth), transfer 1 ml of the inoculum to the appropriate Petri dish. Then pour 20 ml of the sterile nutrient agar which has been previously liquefied and cooled to 45°C into each Petri dish. Agitate the plates so as to diffuse the inoculum. Allow it to gel.

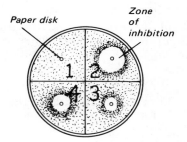

Paper disk / Zone of inhibition

After the agar has gelled, turn the Petri dish over. Use a wax pencil to divide the dish into 4 quadrants. Number each quadrant as shown.

Using sterile forceps, place the antibiotic discs (usually three levels of concentration are available) 2 cm from the edge of the dish. Place them in quadrants *2, 3,* and *4* as shown. As a control, place a filter paper disc which has been soaked in sterile distilled

Antiseptic	Inhibition Zone (diameter)		
	Bacillus subtilis (A)	Escherichia coli (B)	Proteus vulgaris (C)
1. 5% phenol			
2.			
3.			
4.			

	Bacillus subtilis (Gram-positive)	Escherichia coli (Gram-negative)	Proteus vulgaris (Gram-negative)
Penicillin			
Streptomycin			
Terramycin			
Chloromycetin			
Aureomycin			
Tetracycline			

water in quadrant *1*. Invert the plates and incubate at 37° C for 48 hours.

After 48 hours, examine the plates and look for a zone of inhibition. This is a clear area formed around the disc due to the inhibitory action of the antibiotic.

Test all of the antibiotics against all of the bacteria you have available. This will give you some interesting results for comparison of sensitivity.

There are many variables in this test such as: the amount of the inoculum, the type of organism, the diffusion rate of the antibiotic, and the rate of deterioration of the antibiotic. Therefore, sensitivity is determined by the presence of a zone around any of the discs and not by the size of the zone.

Consider the organism resistant if you find no zone on the plate. The organism is very sensitive to the antibiotic if there is a zone around the lowest level of concentration. An organism showing a zone around the disc of medium concentration, but not around that of the lowest, would be classified as sensitive or moderately sensitive. A zone around the disc of highest concentration indicates the organism is only slightly sensitive to the antibiotic.

On a separate sheet of paper, construct a table like the one shown above. Now examine the plates and record the results as *resistant*, *slightly sensitive*, *sensitive*, or *very sensitive* in the appropriate column in your table. DO NOT WRITE IN THIS BOOK.

Summary

(a) What does a clear zone around the discs indicate in both parts of this Investigation?

(b) How can the effectiveness of an antiseptic be determined?

(c) Does the strength of an antiseptic affect the zone of inhibition? If so, which antiseptics were the strongest?

(d) Are some antiseptics more effective against Gram-negative organisms than Gram-positive organisms? If so, which antiseptics were more effective against Gram-negative organisms?

(e) Why is it so important that aseptic techniques be used in both parts of this Investigation?

(f) What variable factors could affect the zones of inhibition in Part 2?

(g) Are all antibiotics equally effective against each type of bacteria? Explain.

INVESTIGATIONS ON YOUR OWN

1. Design an investigation testing various brand-name antiseptics to see which one was the most effective in the inhibition of bacterial growth. Be sure to use an antiseptic substance as a control.

2. Why are some bacteria more resistant to certain antibiotics than other bacteria? Attempt to answer this question through research and experimentation. At the beginning of the investigation, be sure to determine which bacteria are most resistant to a particular antibiotic. Then, attempt to find out why.

18-1

Which Protozoans Are Found in Fresh Water?

OBJECTIVES
- To identify microscopic life in pond water
- To observe the movement of microscopic organisms
- To identify various forms of protozoans

MATERIALS

POND WATER OR CULTURES OF
  MICROORGANISMS
SLIDES
COVER SLIPS
MICROSCOPE
METHYL CELLULOSE SOLUTION
MEDICINE DROPPERS

OBSERVING A POND-WATER COMMUNITY

In this Investigation, you will take a close look at the organisms that live in a drop of pond water. These organisms make up a community. Such a community is composed of many different types of organisms including algae, protozoans, and tiny invertebrates. In this Investigation, you will identify the types of organisms that are present in this community.

Procedures and Observations
As you do this Investigation, refer to your text and the illustrations in it to help you identify the organisms in your pond water sample. Prepare a number of wet mounts of pond water. Be sure to prepare a slide of the muddy water as well as the clear water. (a) Why is this important?

Observe the slides under both low and high power. Compare the organisms in your slide to those on page 74. See how many organisms you are able to identify.

(b) Do you see any invertebrate animals? If so, identify and draw them on a separate piece of paper.

(c) Do you see any protozoans? If so, identify and draw any protozoans that you find. (d) How can you tell the difference between protozoans and algae? (e) Describe the movement of the protozoans.

You may wish to observe the protozoans more closely. This can be done by preparing another wet mount and adding a drop of methyl cellulose solution. Examine under both low and high power. (f) What happens when the methyl cellulose is added?

Are the organisms in the pond culture producers or consumers? Producers are those organisms which produce their own food. (g) Which organisms are producers? (h) How can you determine that they are producers?

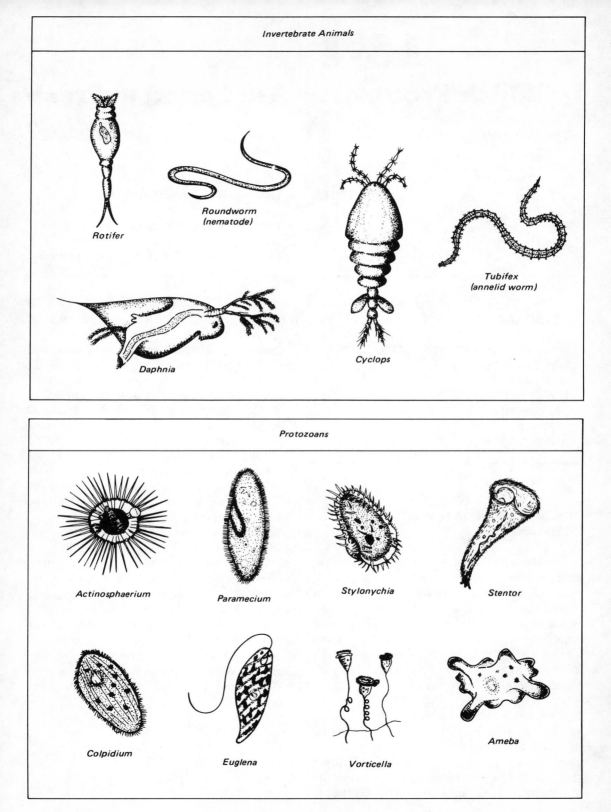

Invertebrate Animals

Rotifer

Roundworm (nematode)

Cyclops

Tubifex (annelid worm)

Daphnia

Protozoans

Actinosphaerium

Paramecium

Stylonychia

Stentor

Colpidium

Euglena

Vorticella

Ameba

Summary

(a) What types of organisms were found in the muddy water as compared to the clear water? Why do you think this is so?

(b) Name one protozoan, one alga, and one invertebrate that you identified in your pond water slide.

(c) How can you tell the difference between a producer and a consumer?

(d) What contributions does a producer make to the pond water community?

(e) What contributions does a consumer make to the pond water community?

(f) Which organisms move the fastest in your wet mount?

(g) What do you think may be the reason for this?

INVESTIGATIONS ON YOUR OWN

1. In order to obtain many organisms of the same type, you may be interested in growing a pure culture of a particular organism. Once you have done this, you can use this culture to investigate several factors. You may be interested in the effects of temperature on certain stains (such as crystal violet) on your culture.

2. Collect a number of water samples from different environments. Sea, marsh, lake, and aquarium water can be used. Prepare wet mount slides of each of these types of water and examine them for microscopic life.

18-2
Do Protozoans Respond to Stimuli?

OBJECTIVES

- To observe the specialization of the organism, paramecium
- To identify the structures of the paramecium
- To label a diagram of a paramecium
- To observe the response of paramecia to various stimuli

MATERIALS

PARAMECIA CULTURE
MICROSCOPE
TEXTBOOK OR CHARTS
CULTURE SLIDES
COVER GLASSES
CARMINE RED SOLUTION
ACETIC ACID
METHYL CELLULOSE
TEST TUBES (PART 2)
STOPPERS FOR TEST TUBES (PART 2)
DARK PAPER (PART 2)
MATCHES (PART 2)
SPUN GLASS (PART 2)
PIECES OF CARDBOARD (PART 2)
SALT CRYSTALS (PART 2)
VINEGAR (PART 2)
INK (PART 2)

PART 1 / OBSERVING PARAMECIA

In this Part, you will examine a common protozoan. The paramecium is a unique organism with specialized structures for movement. The paramecium appears to move more rapidly than it really does because of the magnification of the microscope.

Procedure and Observations

Place a drop of scum from the paramecium culture on a slide. Cover with a cover slip. Examine the movement of the paramecia under the low power of the microscope. On a separate piece of paper, diagram the shape of the paramecium. Use arrows to indicate the direction of movement of the paramecium. (a) Examine the cell carefully and determine why the cell moves in this manner.

In order to quiet the animals for further study, you may prepare traps of cotton fiber or use a drop of methyl cellulose on the slide. Now examine the paramecium under high power. Use your text or charts to identify the various parts. (b) Is the cell flexible? (c) Can it change its shape like the ameba? (d) If not, explain why.

Examine the edge of the cell and locate the cilia. (e) What is their function?

Add a drop of carmine red solution to the slide. These particles will make it easier to observe the cilia. The paramecium will ingest these particles. You should follow their path through the organism. Locate the oral groove and note that cilia also line it. (f) What is the function of these cilia?

Locate a food vacuole with carmine red particles. Observe the vacuole for a few minutes to determine movement. (g) In what

Paramecium caudatum

direction do the vacuoles move? (h) Explain your answer.

How does the paramecium live in fresh water (a hypotonic solution)? Look for clear circles with numerous canals leading to them at either end of the cell. Watch their action for a few minutes. (i) Describe what they do. (j) What are they called?

Add a drop of acetic acid at the edge of the cover glass and observe what happens. (k) Record your observations. (l) What is the function of this action?

Copy or trace the outline of the paramecium given above on a separate piece of paper. Draw in all of the organelles you can locate. Label the parts on your drawing. Show the direction of movement of the food vacuoles.

PART 2 / RESPONSE OF PARAMECIA TO STIMULI

In this Part, you will determine whether paramecia respond positively or negatively to chemicals, gravity, heat, and touch.

Procedure and Observations
Response to chemicals.

Add a drop of paramecium culture to a slide and focus under low power. Now add a few salt crystals and carefully observe a paramecium. (a) How does it react? (b) What happens to the paramecium? (c) Why does this occur?

Wash the slide and add another drop of paramecium culture. Add a drop of vinegar to the culture. (d) What response do the paramecia make to the vinegar? (e) What type of substance is vinegar? (f) Do you think that paramecia tend to live in an acid or alkaline environment? (g) On what do you base this conclusion?

Prepare another slide and cover with a cover slip. Place a drop of ink under the edge of the cover glass. (h) Observe under low power and describe what happens to the paramecia.

Response to gravity.

Pour paramecium culture into 4 test tubes. Insert stoppers into all of the tubes. In order to demonstrate that the response is due to gravity rather than light, cover 2 of the tubes with dark paper. Put a covered and uncovered tube in a vertical position. Put the remaining 2 cultures in a horizontal position. Allow the cultures to remain in their respective positions for 10 minutes. Examine each of the tubes.

(i) Where are the paramecia concentrated in the uncovered tube in the vertical position? (j) in the covered tube? (k) in the uncovered horizontal tube? (l) in the covered horizontal tube? (m) Does light have any affect on the response to gravity?

Response to heat.

Prepare a slide of paramecia and check under low power to be sure that several animals are present. Add a drop of hot water to one side of the cover glass. Examine the slide under low power at once. (n) How do the paramecia react to the heat?

Response to touch.

Put a drop of paramecium culture on a slide for microscopic study. Locate one of the organisms in the field. (o) Now gently tap the slide and observe and record the reaction of your specimen. Put a few strands of spun glass just under the cover glass of a paramecium culture. (p) Observe and record the reaction of the paramecia.

Summary

On a piece of paper, copy the list of terms in the left column below. Test what you have learned by matching the number definitions with each structure or stimulus.

(a) pellicle
(b) oral groove
(c) cilia
(d) food vacuole
(e) contractile vacuole
(f) trichocysts
(g) heat
(h) touch
(i) salt
(j) weak acid

1. positive response
2. negative response
3. ingests food
4. eliminates water
5. defense mechanism
6. for locomotion
7. transports food through cytoplasm
8. protective surface

INVESTIGATIONS ON YOUR OWN

1. There are many other interesting protozoans that you may wish to investigate. The ameba and euglena are two such protozoans which can be studied in the same manner as the paramecium.

2. Design an investigation to test the effect of light on paramecia. Be sure to include a control. Draw conclusions from your investigation.

19-1
What Are Some Forms of Fungi?

OBJECTIVES
- To observe the structure of common bread mold
- To study the nutrition of bread mold
- To investigate the reproduction of bread mold
- To examine blue-green molds

MATERIALS

CULTURE OF BREAD MOLD
MICROSCOPE
DISSECTING NEEDLES
SLIDES
COVER GLASSES
FORCEPS
STOCK CULTURE OF *PENICILLIUM NOTATUM*,
  ASPERGILLUS NIGER (PART 2)
SABOURAUD'S DEXTROSE AGAR (PART 2)
PETRI DISHES (PART 2)
INOCULATING LOOP (PART 2)
HAND LENS (PART 2)
BUNSEN BURNER (PART 2)
AUTOCLAVE OR PRESSURE COOKER (PART 2)
HOT-AIR OVEN (PART 2)

PART 1 / GROWING BREAD MOLD

Most of you are probably familiar with common bread mold. This black mold is frequently seen as a cottony growth on bread or other foods.

Procedure and Observations
In this Part, you will prepare a bread-mold culture. This can be done if there are the proper conditions of moisture, darkness, food supply, and the right temperature.

To prepare a bread-mold culture, trim a piece of bread so that it will fit into a covered dish. Pour water over the bread and then drain the excess water so that none remains in the dish. Keep the dish uncovered for about an hour. Cover the dish and place it in a dark cool place for about a week. (a) Why did you leave the dish uncovered for an hour? (b) Why do bread molds form on bread that is kept in bread boxes or covered drawers?

When the mold has formed, remove an individual mold plant from the culture. These plants can be recognized as a cluster of gray threads with black knobs at the ends. Prepare a wet mount slide of the mold plant. Examine under low power. Use your text or charts for reference. (c) What is the mass of hyphae called?

After you have identified the three types of

mold

hyphae under the microscope, describe the function of each type.

(d) How do mold plants obtain food? (e) How are the plants that have grown along the side of the dish nourished? (f) Do you detect an odor in your culture? (g) Explain your answer.

Explain a sporangium at the tip of an ascending hypha with high power. Find the thin sporangium wall, which may have burst open and released spores. Examine the spores and notice the large numbers produced. (h) What advantage is offered by the fact that the sporangia develop on top of the ascending hyphae?

Make a drawing of the bread mold on a separate piece of paper and label: **rhizoids** (descending hyphae), **stolon** (transverse hypha), and **sporangium.** Make a drawing of a sporangium as seen under high power. Label: **sporangium wall, spores, ascending hypha.**

PART 2 / BLUE-GREEN MOLDS

The drug penicillin is extracted from one species of *Penicillium*. *Penicillium* is found as a green growth upon almost any form of decaying organic matter. *Aspergillus* is a common blue-green mold found on bread, cheese, and decaying fruit.

Procedure and Observations
Using a sterile inoculating loop, transfer a loop of the *Penicillium notatum* culture to the center of the sterile gelled agar. Rotate the loop on the surface of the agar to remove the mold culture. Then, in the same manner, transfer a loop of the Aspergillus niger culture to a second Petri dish. Place the inoculated plates in a dark, cool place for a week or more. At the end of this time, use a hand lens to examine the colonies. (a) Describe the colony formed by *Penicillium*. (b) by *Aspergillus*.

Remove the lid from the *Penicillium* culture dish and place the culture on the microscope stage for examination. Focus on the edge of the colony with low power and locate the fruiting bodies (conidia), which are produced in chains at the tips of certain hyphae called conidiophores. (c) Describe the hyphae. (d) How do they differ from the hyphae produced by bread mold? (e) Describe the arrangement of the conidia.

In the same manner, examine the culture of *Aspergillus*. (f) Descibe the hyphae. (g) Are they the same in structure as *Penicillium* hyphae? (h) Explain your answer. (i) Describe the conidia. (j) Are they similar to those produced by *Penicillium*? (k) Explain your answer.

Summary
(a) What structural features enable molds to thrive in various environments?
(b) How do the reproductive characteristics of molds enhance their survival?
(c) Do you think that bread mold spores are commonly found in the air around us? Explain your answer.
(d) Discuss some of the conditions necessary for the growth of bread mold.
(e) What are the three types of hyphae found in a bread mold plant?
(f) How do bread mold hyphae differ from the hyphae of blue-green molds?

INVESTIGATIONS ON YOUR OWN

1. Investigate bread mold and blue-green mold that have formed on food products in your home. It is simple to save bread or dairy products until you notice the formation of the mold. Examine these molds and draw conclusions from your observations.
2. Are bread molds and blue-green molds dangerous to consume? Do some research into this question and design an original investigation that will give scientific proof to your hypothesis. If you are uncertain about your experiment, discuss it with your teacher before carrying out the investigation.

19-2

How Does Yeast Cause Fermentation?

OBJECTIVES
- To examine the structure of yeast cells
- To study the reproduction and nutrition of yeast cells.
- To investigate the fermentation of various sugars by yeast cells.

MATERIALS

PACKAGE OF YEAST
MICROSCOPE
SLIDES
COVER GLASSES
FERMENTATION TUBES
250 ML FLASKS
COTTON PLUGS
DROPPING PIPETTES
STIRRING ROD
10% WHITE SYRUP
METHYLENE BLUE OR IODINE STAIN
YEAST SUSPENSIONS OF:
SACCHAROMYCES CEREVISIAE,
SACCHAROMYCES ELLIPSOIDEUS (PART 2)
100-ML EACH OF THE FOLLOWING (PART 2):
MALTOSE (10% SOLUTION)
SUCROSE (10% SOLUTION)
LACTOSE (10% SOLUTION)
GLUCOSE (DEXTROSE) (10% SOLUTION)
POTATO STARCH (10% SOLUTION)
CORNSTARCH (10% SOLUTION)
BROM THYMOL BLUE SOLUTION

PART 1 / CULTURING AND OBSERVING YEAST

Yeasts differ from other fungi in that the plant body consists of an oval cell enclosed by a thin cell wall, instead of having hyphae. Yeast cells form buds by producing a bulge on the side of the cell. This bulge grows rapidly and may produce other buds while it is still attached to the mother cell. Therefore, you may observe chains of cells of various sizes in your culture.

Procedure and Observations

A yeast culture may be prepared by mixing 500 ml of 10% molasses solution (10 ml of molasses to 90 ml of water) with a half a package of yeast. Stir the culture and divide it into several flasks or bottles. Fill each flask half full and plug with cotton. If fermentation tubes are available, prepare several, as shown on page 82.

Using a pipette, place a drop of yeast culture on a slide and add a drop of methylene blue or iodine. Cover with a cover glass and examine under high power. Make a drawing of several yeast cells.

Keep the flasks or tubes in a warm place overnight. Examine the cultures the next day. (a) Is there any evidence that fermentation is taking place? If so, what is this evidence? Remove the cotton plug from one tube. (b) Describe the odor.

With a pipette, put a drop of the liquid on a microscope slide and add a small drop of methylene blue or iodine stain. Add a cover glass and examine under high power.

Make a drawing of several cells to show their general appearance. (c) How have the cells changed during fermentation?

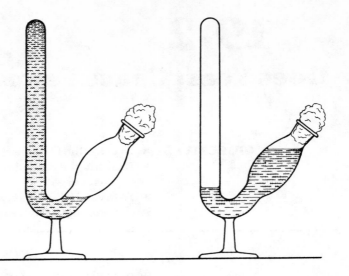

Look for cells that have buds on them. Make a drawing of these cells. Label: **bud, vacuole, cell wall, nucleus.**

PART 2 / YEAST FERMENTATION

Yeasts ferment materials more rapidly if the concentration of sugar is high and that of oxygen is low. The extent of fermentation depends on the species of yeast in the particular medium. *Saccharomyces cerevisiae* is used commercially in baking and *Saccharomyces ellipsoideus* is used in wine making. In this Part, you will determine the extent to which the species of yeast plants can ferment various sugars and starches.

Procedure and Observations
Prepare 12 fermentation tubes for the sugar and starch solutions in two series. Number one series *1A-6A* and identify each tube with the carbohydrate solution it is to receive. Number the second series *1B-6B* and identify each tube with the solution it is to receive. Fill each of the properly identified fermentation tubes with the following solutions: maltose, sucrose, lactose, glucose (dextrose), potato starch, and cornstarch. Be sure that they are filled with the solution as shown in the left tube in the figure.

Using a clean pipette, transfer 1-2 ml of the *Saccharomyces cerevisiae* suspension to each of the fermentation tubes in series *1A-6A*. Using another clean pipette, transfer 1-2 ml of the *Saccharomyces ellipsoideus* suspension to each of the fermentation tubes in series *1B-6B*. Plug the tubes with cotton and place the cultures in a warm place overnight.

Examine them the next day for evidence of fermentation and record the results in a table like the one shown opposite. DO NOT WRITE IN THIS BOOK. Use a plus (+) if fermentation occurred and a minus (−) if no fermentation occurred.

Add a few drops of brom thymol blue to the mixture in which gas was produced and observe any change that occurs. (a) What change, if any, occurred? (b) What does this indicate? Smell the fermented solutions. (c) What do you detect?

Food supplies	Fermentation	
	Saccharomyces cerevisiae	Saccharomyces ellipsoideus
Maltose		
Sucrose		
Lactose		
Glucose		
Potato starch		
Cornstarch		

Summary
(a) Why is it important that no air be left at the top of the tube in Part 1?
(b) What does iodine or methylene blue do to the yeast cells?
(c) What is an indication that fermentation has taken place in Part 1?
(d) What substances are produced during fermentation?
(e) Are there more or less yeast cells present in the day-old culture? Why is this so?
(f) What evidence was there that fermentation had taken place in Part 2?
(g) How do the two species of yeast, used in Part 2, differ in their ability to ferment various sugars and starches?

INVESTIGATIONS ON YOUR OWN

1. One of the fungi that you are probably most familiar with is the cultivated mushroom. You may be interested in dissecting a mushroom and studying its structure with a hand lens. Be sure to identify the **hyphae, stipe, annulus, cap, gills,** and **spores.**

2. Mushroom spores are often used to identify mushrooms. Spore prints of mushrooms can be made for this purpose. In order to do this, remove the cap from the stipe of a fresh mushroom. Lay it, gills down, on a piece of white paper and cover it with a dish. Leave it overnight and the next day remove the cover and gently lift the mushroom cap from the paper. Notice the outline of the gills left by the spores. What does this tell you about this mushroom?

20-1

How Do Various Algae Differ?

OBJECTIVES
- To examine representatives of various algae phyla
- To observe the structure of different species of blue-green and green algae

MATERIALS

CULTURES OF: (PART 1)
 NOSTOC
 ANABAENA
 OSCILLATORIA
 GLOEOCAPSA (ANACYSTIS)
MICROSCOPE
SLIDES
COVER GLASSES
DROPPING PIPETTE
CULTURES OF: (PART 2)
 PROTOCOCCUS (PHYTOCONIS)
 SPIROGYRA (LIVING OR PRESERVED CON-
 JUGATIVE AND VEGETATIVE FORMS)
 ULOTHRYX
 OEDOGONIUM
DISSECTING NEEDLES
SCISSORS
COLORED PENCILS
HAND LENS

In this Investigation, you will be examining a number of algae phyla. These phyla differ from one another on the basis of cell structure, photosynthetic pigments, and stored food.

PART 1 / CYANOPHYTA (BLUE-GREEN ALGAE)

Blue-green algae are characterized by the two pigments in their name. The green pigment is chlorophyll and a blue pigment is called phycocyanin. Blue-green algae are usually found in fresh water but may also be found as masses on rocks, stones, tree trunks, damp ground, and salt water.

Procedure and Observations

Examine a ball of *Nostoc* with a hand lens. (a) Describe what you see.

Cut a section of the ball of *Nostoc* and mount it on a slide in a drop of water. Add a cover glass and tap lightly to flatten the material. Examine under low power. Notice the many curved and twisting filaments embedded in the *Nostoc* jellylike matrix.

Study the filaments under high power. See if you can find swollen, empty cells called heterocysts. (b) Are heterocysts at the end of the filament or in the middle? (c) Are they present in all the filaments? (d) Is more than one present in a filament?

Draw several filaments as they appear under high power. Label: **matrix, heterocyst, filament.**

Anabaena is another filamentous blue-green alga. The filaments of *Anabaena* are solitary and never appear in colonies. Put a small quantity of *Anabaena* culture on a slide. Spread the filaments apart and add a cover glass. Examine under low and high power. (e) In what ways does *Anabaena* resemble *Nostoc*?

Try to locate the enlarged oval cells or *spores* in a filament. (f) How are these spores protected? (g) What do they contain? (h) Are the spores on the ends or middle of the filaments?

Spores separate from the filament and germinate a new cell, which eventually forms a new filament through fission. Draw a filament of *Anabaena* and label: **spore, heterocyst.**

Oscillatoria is another common blue-green alga. It is found as a floating or submerged mass of filaments in stagnant water. Different species of *Oscillatoria* vary greatly in size and range in color from bright blue-green to nearly black.

Put a small amount of *Oscillatoria* in a drop of water on a slide. Spread the filaments apart with dissecting needles and add a cover glass. Examine with lower power, then high power.

If your *Oscillatoria* is living, watch for a slight swaying motion, especially near the ends of the filaments. The cell on the end of the filament is called the apical cell. Various species of *Oscillatoria* differ in the shape of this cell. Study your slide and determine whether you have more than one species. (k) If so, how do they differ?

Draw several filaments of *Oscillatoria*. Label: **apical cell, starch grain, concave cell** (if present).

Gloeocapsa (Anacystis) is a primitive blue-green alga. It is often found on moist flowerpots and wet rocks. A cell of *Gloeocapsa* secretes a slimy sheath in which it is encased. As cells divide, each new cell secretes a sheath within the old one. Put a drop of *Gloeocapsa* culture on a slide with a cover glass. Examine under low and high power. Reduce the amount of light entering the objective and study the colony.

(l) List the ways in which *Gloeocapsa* is similar to bacteria. (m) different from bacteria.

Draw a colony of *Gloeocapsa* and label: **cell, sheath.**

PART 2 / CHLOROPHYTA (GREEN ALGAE)

Green algae are the most widely distributed of all the algae. They are found nearly everywhere there is moisture. They vary in complexity from single-celled organisms to many-celled branching filaments.

Procedure and Observations
Protococcus (Phytoconis) is one of the most common of the unicellular forms. It can be found as a green film on damp walls, rocks, fence posts, and the bark of trees. Examine the growth of *Protococcus* on a piece of bark with a hand lens. Scrape some of the algae from the bark into a drop of water on a slide. Avoid getting pieces of bark on the slide.

Spread the cells through the water and add a cover glass. Examine with low power and high power. Find a single cell and draw it under high power. Also draw several colonies. Label: **cell wall, chloroplast, nucleus.** Shade the chloroplast green.

Examine your slide to find colonies. (a) Describe the walls between the cells that are joined.

Spirogyra is a common unbranched filamentous alga which forms a green growth on the surface of quiet ponds and streams. Mount several filaments in a drop of water on a slide. Add a cover glass. Examine the cells under low and high power. (b) Are the cells in a filament all the same shape and size? (c) How many cells constitute a *Spirogyra* organism?

Examine the spiral ribbonlike chloroplast. (d) Do all of the chloroplasts spiral in the same direction in the cells of a filament?

Some species have more than one chloroplast. Examine the slide and determine whether you have more than one species. (e) If so, in what way other than the number of chloroplasts do they differ?

Locate the rounded bodies of stored food on the chloroplasts. These are the pyrenoids. Study several cells and count the pyrenoids. (f) Is the number uniform for each cell of a filament?

The cytoplasm lies in a dense layer around the wall and extends through the cell in strands. The nucleus is embedded in strands of cytoplasm. The large cavities you see in the cell are vacuoles. Locate the gelatinous sheath surrounding the filament. (g) How would the sheath aid in the identification of *Spirogyra* if you were collecting it in a pond or stream?

Make a drawing of three cells in a filament showing how the cells are joined. Label: **sheath, cytoplasm, vacuole, chloroplast, pyrenoid,** and **nucleus.**

Look for filaments of conjugating *Spirogyra*. During conjugation, the entire content of one cell passes through the *conjugation tube* and unites with the content of another cell. These contents are referred to as *gametes*. The fusion body resulting from the union of two gametes is a *zygote*. Locate two filaments in the process of conjugation. (h) How can you tell they are conjugating?

(i) Is the movement of the cell content all in one direction? (j) Do all the cells in the two filaments complete conjugation? (k) Describe the zygote.

Make a drawing and label: **conjugation tube, gamete,** and **zygote.**

Ulothrix is a filamentous green alga whose basal cell may be modified into a *holdfast* cell. These algae may be attached to rocks or be free-floating like *Spirogyra*. Mount a few strands of *Ulothrix* in a drop of water and add a cover glass. Examine under low power and high power. Study the filament carefully. (l) Can you find the holdfast cell? (m) If so, how does it differ from the other cells of the filament? (n) Describe the chloroplast.

Making a drawing of a *Ulothrix* filament and label: **chloroplast, nucleus,** and **pyrenoid.**

Oedogonium is a filamentous green alga which is usually attached by a holdfast cell when young, but is free-floating when mature. Mount a few strands of *Oedogonium* in a drop of water. Separate them gently with a dissecting needle and add a cover glass. Study the filament under low power and high power. (o) Are all the cells in a filament identical? (p) If not, how do they differ?

The large rounded cells are the **oogonial** cells, which produce the egg cell. The small, short cells are the **antheridial** cells, which produce the sperm cells. (q) How does reproduction in *Oedogonium* differ from that in *Spirogyra*?

Draw a filament of *Oedogonium* and label completely.

Summary

On a separate piece of paper, copy the terms on the left. After each term, write the names of the algal forms that apply:

(a) blue-green algae   1. *Nostoc*
(b) chlorophyta   2. *Anabaena*
(c) heterocysts   3. *Gleocapsa*
(d) gelatinous matrix   4. *Oscillatoria*
(e) filamentous   5. *Protococcus*
(f) swaying motion   6. *Ulothrix*
(g) concentric sheaths   7. *Spirogyra*
(h) damp tree bark   8. *Oedogonium*
(i) spiral chloroplasts
(j) pyrenoids
(k) conjugation
(l) holdfast cell

INVESTIGATIONS ON YOUR OWN

1. You may be interested in studying diatoms found in fresh and salt water. Diatoms occur singly or in colonies and have a wide range of shapes and colors. Prepare a wet mount of a diatom culture and examine the structure, forms, and colonies of these organisms. What colors do you observe?

2. You may also be interested in studying marine algae. These algae are usually brown and red. The brown algae have multicellular sex organs and a complex vegetative body. The red algae lack flagellated cells and contain a red pigment. The thallus is often multicellular and may be simple or branched.

Your culture of marine algae may be fresh or preserved. It should include *Fucus* and *Chondrus Crispus*. Examine both of these specimens and locate the **holdfast, stipe,** and **frond.**

3. Collect pond water from various sources. Try to obtain samples from different depths and conditions. Place samples on slides and view under low and high power. Attempt to identify the algae you have studied in this Investigation. A key may be used to identify other species.

21-1

How Can Plants Reproduce Without Seeds?

OBJECTIVES
- **To understand how mosses and ferns reproduce without seeds**
- **To learn the meaning of alternation of generations**

MATERIALS

Moss Plants with Female Sex Organs
Moss Plants with Male Sex Organs
Fresh Clump of Living Moss Plants
Dissecting Microscope or Hand Lens
Textbook or Charts
Microscope
Slide, Cover Glass
Dissecting Needle
Fresh Fern Frond Bearing Sori
   (Part 2)

PART 1 / HOW DO MOSS PLANTS REPRODUCE?

Moss plants may be found growing in dense clumps on the forest floor or compact mats on a fallen log. A clump of moss plants is composed of many gametophyte plants growing close to each other for support. At certain times of the year, the sporophytes may be seen growing from certain plants.

Procedure and Observations

Examine a small portion of a clump of moss, using a hand lens. Remove a single gametophyte and examine it closely under a dissecting microscope. The rootlike structures at the base of the leafy stem are *rhizoids* which function to absorb water and minerals. Examine a *leafy shoot*. (a) Of what adaptive value is the arrangement of the leaves on the stem axis? Draw a leafy shoot and label the **rhizoids**.

Gamete-producing structures, *archegonia* and *antheridia*, are located at the tips of the leafy stems in a cluster of leaves. (b) What gamete is produced by the archegonia? (c) by the antheridia?

These gamete-producing structures may be observed by squeezing them from the tip of the stem. Roll the tip of the stem between the thumb and the forefinger as you bring the tip in contact with a large drop of water on a slide. Use a dissecting needle to remove the fragments of the tip. Some of these pieces will be either antheridia or archegonia depending on the sex of the plants used. Use pictures in your textbook or charts as reference.

Repeat the procedure for a plant of the opposite sex. Observe the slide under the low power of the microscope. (d) Describe the structure of an antheridium. (e) Describe the structure of an archegonium.

(f) How does a sperm reach an egg for fertilization? (g) Explain why mosses are not found growing in locations having little or no moisture. (h) What cell is produced when the sperm fertilizes the egg? (i) Where is the zygote formed?

Draw and label the microscopic view of the **antheridium** and **archegonium**.

Examine a gametophyte bearing a stalk and *capsule*. (j) Why is it known as the sporophyte generation? (k) From what cell did the sporophyte develop? (l) Explain why the sporophyte is present only on certain gametophyte plants.

Locate the *capsule* at the tip of the seta. Examine the capsule using a hand lens. Determine if a tiny lid, the *operculum*, is present. As spores mature within the capsule, the operculum will fall away. Under favor-able conditions a spore germinates into a threadlike structure, the *protonema*. The protonema eventually develops into a mature gametophyte. (m) What have you observed about the sporophyte that indicates it is nutritionally dependent on the gametophyte? (n) Explain how moss plants exhibit alternation of generations.

Make a drawing of the capsule. Label: **operculum** and **spores**.

Examine the stages in the life cycle of the moss plant in the drawing below.

(o) Which structures are seen in the gametophyte generation? (p) in the sporophyte generation?

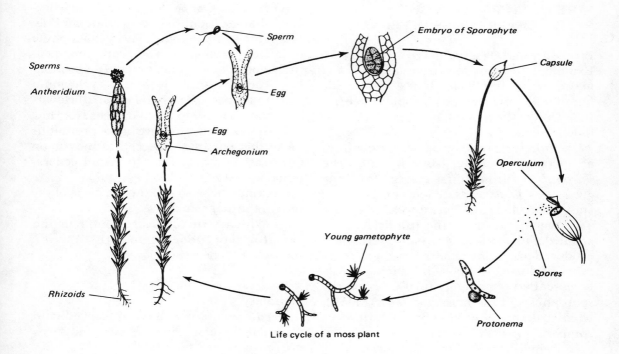

Life cycle of a moss plant

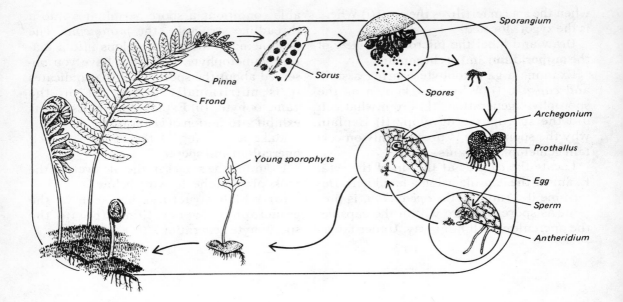

Labels in figure: Sporangium, Pinna, Frond, Sorus, Spores, Archegonium, Prothallus, Egg, Sperm, Antheridium, Young sporophyte

PART 2 / ALTERNATION OF GENERATIONS IN FERNS

Procedure and Observations

Examine the living fern frond or study the figure in the life cycle shown above. The familiar fern plant is the sporophyte generation. Unlike the mosses, it is free living and independent.

The *fronds* (leaves) of the fern grow from a horizontal, underground stem, the *rhizome*. The fronds first emerge from the ground as *fiddleheads*. Each consists of a stalk and a blade divided into leaflets or *pinnae*. When certain of the fronds mature, small dots known as *sori* (sing. sorus) are produced on the lower surface. A sorus contains a cluster of spore-producing structures called *sporangia*. (a) Compare the sporophytes of the moss and fern. (b) With what structure of a moss does a fern sorus compare?

Examine a single pinna with sori under a dissecting microscope. (c) Describe the number and position of the sori.

Draw and label: **fronds, rhizome, fiddlehead, pinna, blade,** and **sorus.**

When spores are released and land in a favorable location, they germinate and develop into gametophytes. This gametophyte is called a *prothallus*. The prothallus measures about 1 cm in diameter. The prothallus produces antheridia and archegonia which produce sperms and eggs. (d) How is fertilization accomplished in ferns? (e) How does the size and structure of the prothallus make this possible? The cell formed upon fertilization is the zygote. (f) What generation does the zygote develop into?

Examine the stages in the life cycle of the fern in the diagram above.

(g) Which structures are found in the gametophyte generation? (h) in the sporophyte generation?

Summary

(a) From what you have observed and studied, relate how mosses and ferns reproduce without seeds.

(b) Summarize your observations of mosses and ferns by constructing and filling in a chart like the one opposite. DO NOT WRITE IN THIS BOOK.

	Mosses	Ferns
1. Produces eggs		
2. Produces sperm		
3. Sporophyte Independent- (Yes/No)		
4. Structure Producing Spores		
5. Spores Germinate into:		
6. Inconspicuous Generation		
7. Conspicuous Generation		
8. Medium for Fertilization		
9. Agent for Spore Dispersal		
10. First Cell of Sporophyte		
11. First Cell of Gametophyte		
12. General Habitat		

INVESTIGATIONS ON YOUR OWN

1. To become acquainted with the mosses in your region and to determine their various habitats, make a collection of mosses. Look in any environment where there is moisture and reduced light. Collect shoots bearing stalks and capsules. Place the specimens in different envelopes and record the location, date, and habitat in your notebook. Use identification keys to trace your specimens to their particular genus. Leaf and capsule structure are used for identification purposes. The characteristic size and shape of spores are often used for identification.

2. Make a collection of fern fronds. Before beginning your collection, you should become familiar with the characteristics used in their identification. These include: general form and structure, distribution of the sori, the sporangia, and the indusia, and the form of the frond. Collect a portion of a frond and put it in a book or magazine. Assign a collection number to the specimen and record this number in your field notebook along with other data such as the location, date, and habitat. When you return to the laboratory, identify your specimens. The fronds can be pressed and saved for later study by drying them between several layers of newspaper.

22·1

How Do Plants Grow?

OBJECTIVES
- To examine the vegetative organs of a seed plant
- To measure the growth rate of the vegetative organs

MATERIALS

1 VIGOROUSLY GROWING BEAN PLANT IN AN INDIVIDUAL CONTAINER

2 BEAN SEEDS (PART 2)

1 FLOWER POT (7 TO 10 CM) OR SUITABLE CONTAINER (PART 2)

MIXTURE OF SAND AND LOAM (1:1) (PART 2)

METRIC RULER (DIVIDED INTO MILLIMETERS) (PART 2)

THREAD (PART 2)

INDIA INK (PART 2)

PART 1 / OBSERVING VEGETATIVE ORGANS

Procedure and Observations

Obtain a bean plant growing in an individual container. The plant should be about 15-18 cm tall. Turn over the container to empty the entire mass of soil and roots. Wash the soil from the roots to expose the root system. You are now able to observe all of the vegetative organs of a seed plant. (a) What parts of the plant can you observe? (b) What does it mean for an organ to be vegetative?

(c) Examine the root system closely, and describe what you see. (d) What characteristic may be observed which indicates the *anchoring* function of the roots in the

soil? (e) What are some other functions of roots?

Examine the stem. (f) What obvious plant organ is attached to the stem? (g) On the basis of your answer to (f), what is one of the functions of the stem? (h) What color is the stem? (i) What pigment is present? (j) Name another function that may be carried out in the stem. (k) How do water and minerals get to the leaves from the roots? (l) How do materials move from the leaves to the roots? (m) On the basis of your answers in (k) and (l), and what function is being performed?

Like the root, the stem often functions in the *storage* of food. Examine the leaves. (n) What color are they? (o) What is the principal function of the leaves? As you may study later, the leaf has other functions.

On a separate piece of paper, sketch the entire plant. Include the details of the branching pattern of the roots, and the shape and venation of the leaves. Label: **roots, stem,** and **leaf.** Summarize the functions of each vegetative organ.

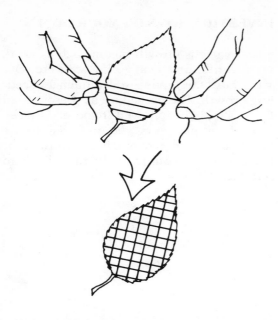

ink bottle. Carefully place the moistened thread on the leaf to make a straight line across the leaf. Repeat the procedure and make the next line approximately 3 mm from the first.

Continue until the leaf is marked as shown in the figure. In the same manner, mark the stem from the soil surface to the tip of the stem. (a) What will the markings help you to observe?

As the leaf expands, record your observations in a series of drawings by accurately representing the regions of expansion. (b) How will you be able to determine where the leaf and stem grew?

On a separate piece of paper, construct a table like the one below. Use a metric ruler to obtain actual growth measurements. Measure in millimeters the length of the stem from the soil level to the growing tip. Record the measurement in your table. DO NOT WRITE IN THIS BOOK.

Count and record the number of leaves. Determine the surface area of each leaf by multiplying the length of the leaf (base to tip) by the average width (measure in three places) of the blade. Record the total surface area of all leaves. Repeat the measurement at 2-3 day intervals for a period of two weeks. Record all data in the table you have made.

After the last measurements are recorded, carefully remove the plant from the soil. Wash the soil from the roots. Measure each root and record the total length of the root system.

Base your answers on the markings and the measurements taken. (c) Was the rate of

PART 2 / HOW FAST DO PLANT PARTS GROW?

Procedure and Observations

Plant a bean seed in a pot containing equal parts of sand and loam. Plant it just below the soil surface. Water the soil well and pour off the excess. Place the pot in a light source and keep the soil moist. Once the true leaves of the plant are formed, your observations and determination of the rate of growth may begin.

To observe where the leaf expands in its growth, mark a small leaf in the following manner: Draw a piece of thread (15-20 cm) tightly between the forefinger and thumb of each hand. Have your partner moisten the thread with the applicator from an India

Date of Measurement	Interval Between Measurements	Length of Stem	Number of Leaves	Total Leaf Area	Total Length of Roots (Last Measurements)

growth uniform in the stems and leaves during the growth period? (d) If not, when is the rate of growth most rapid? (e) Compare the total length of the stem with that of the root. (f) Did the leaf blades continue growth at a uniform rate? (g) If not, what variation occurred? (h) Where were new leaves produced? (i) How does the area of the plant above and below ground compare?

Summary

(a) Using a suitable scale of numerical value, prepare a graph with separate lines for length of stem, number of leaves, and total leaf area. Explain any observable relationship. Your graph should plot the growth per day.

On another piece of paper, complete each sentence with the names of the vegetative organ(s) of the plant which performs the function indicated.

(b) __?__ conduct water and minerals to upper plant parts.
(c) __?__ are the principal organs of photosynthesis.
(d) __?__ serve to anchor the plant.
(e) __?__ produce leaves.
(f) __?__ store food substances.
(g) __?__ exchange gases between the plant and atmosphere.
(h) __?__ absorb water and minerals.
(i) __?__ have a secondary function of photosynthesis.
(j) __?__ conduct water and minerals up and down the plant.
(k) __?__ display leaves to light.
(l) __?__ function in the process of transpiration.

INVESTIGATIONS ON YOUR OWN

Select various growth media such as sand, vermiculite, and heavy clay soil, etc. Observe how the type of soil influences seedling growth. The procedure as presented in Part 2 should be followed. To observe the effects of soil nutrients, you may wish to use laboratory prepared nutrient solutions or those prepared commercially in addition to selected soil types.

23-1

How Does Leaf Structure Relate to Its Function?

OBJECTIVES

• To observe how internal leaf structure makes a leaf the primary photosynthetic organ

MATERIALS

PREPARED SLIDE OF LEAF CROSS SECTION (*LIGUSTRUM*)
MICROSCOPE

INTERNAL LEAF STRUCTURE AND PHOTOSYNTHESIS

Procedure and Observations

Examine a prepared slide of a leaf cross section under low power of your microscope. Be sure to observe the top to the lower surface and from one margin to the other. Observe that the leaf is composed of three tissues: epidermis, mesophyll, and conducting tissue. Study the *upper epidermis*. (a) How many cells thick is it? (b) Are any chloroplasts present?

The cells of the epidermis are covered by a waxy layer called a *cuticle*. (c) Suggest its function.

The *mesophyll* is the largest area of the leaf and is composed of two regions. The first of these is made up of *palisade cells* which lie just below the upper epidermis. Study this area under high power. (d) Describe the cells and their orientation to the upper epidermis.

Locate some *chloroplasts* in the palisade cells. (e) Suggest a function of the palisade layer. (f) Why is the shape of the palisade cells important?

Study the second region of the mesophyll. Locate the *spongy layer* of cells below the palisade cells. (g) Of the two, which layer is more compact? (h) Are chloroplasts as numerous in the spongy cells as they are in the palisade cells? (i) Account for any difference you find.

Note the numerous spaces among the spongy cells. These are the *air spaces*. (j) On the basis of their relationship to other tissues in the leaf, what do you think their function is?

The spongy layer is penetrated by numerous *veins*. Move the slide until you are able to locate a vein. (k) How can you tell a vein from other structures in a leaf?

Examine the vein closely. Locate empty cells with thick walls in the upper parts of the section. These are the *xylem cells*. (l) Suggest two functions of the xylem cells.

The thin-walled cells that form a cluster below the xylem cells are the *phloem cells*. (m) What is the function of the phloem cells?

Find a small vein in your section near the leaf margin. (n) Which kind of cell composes the small vein?

Examine the *lower epidermis*. (o) How many cell layers compose it? Closely examine the lower epidermis. Try to find

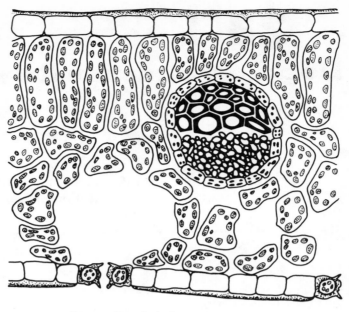

Cross section of a leaf

tiny pores with small, rounded cells on either side. The pores are the stomata and the rounded cells are the guard cells. (p) Determine the relationship between the stomata and the air spaces of the spongy tissue. (q) Suggest a function of the stomata.

On the above diagram, try to find: **cuticle, upper epidermis, palisade cells, chloroplasts, spongy cells, vein, xylem cells, phloem cells, lower epidermis, air space, stoma, guard cells.**

On a separate piece of paper, draw a cross section of the leaf that you observed. Label all of the parts listed above.

Summary

(a) Write a brief paragraph discussing how the internal structure of a leaf adapts it to the process of photosynthesis and the movement of water through the plant.

Review what you have learned by completing the following statements. Write the completed sentences on a separate piece of paper.

(b) The layer of cells which lacks chloroplasts is the ____?____.

(c) The ____?____ is the largest area of a leaf.

(d) The ____?____ layer is composed of cells which are oriented at right angles to the epidermis.

(e) The presence of ____?____ is typical of the spongy layer.

(f) The ____?____ is a waxy layer which prevents the loss of water from leaf tissues.

(g) ____?____ are composed of tissues which carry materials to and from leaf tissues.

(h) Pores found on the underside of leaves are known as ____?____.

(i) Conducting tissues in a leaf are ____?____ and ____?____.

(j) The only cells that contain chloroplasts in the epidermis are ____?____.

(k) The three basic tissues of a leaf are ____?____, ____?____, and ____?____.

INVESTIGATIONS ON YOUR OWN

Select fresh leaves (tulip, geranium, or *Tradescantia* are good). Remove a small area of the lower epidermis by tearing through the blade, twisting slightly as you tear. The epidermis will appear as a thin, transparent skin. Using a razor blade, cut off a small portion of this skin. Mount it in a drop of water and add a cover glass. Examine it under low power. Compare the epidermal cells, guard cells, and stomata of several kinds of leaves. Make drawings of each. Label the drawings where appropriate.

23-2
What Makes Leaves Green?

OBJECTIVES
- **To extract leaf pigments**
- **To determine which pigments are present in a leaf**

MATERIALS

FRESH OR THAWED LEAVES OF SPINACH
DROPPERS
TEST-TUBE RACK
FILTER PAPER
ETHYL ALCOHOL
SOLVENT (1 PART DIETHYL ETHER TO 3
 PARTS PETROLEUM ETHER — CAUTION:
 FLAMMABLE)
HOT WATER BATH
300-ML BEAKER
FORCEPS
CORK
15-CM TEST TUBE
PIN OR TACK
PAPER TOWELING
GLASS STIRRING ROD

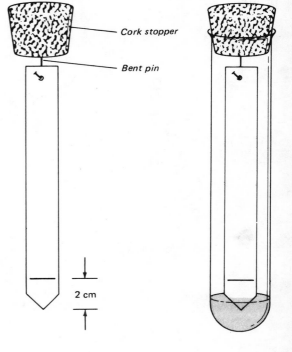

Cork stopper

Bent pin

2 cm

EXTRACTION OF LEAF PIGMENTS

Procedure and Observations

Place a large spinach leaf in a beaker of boiling water. Allow it to boil for about 1 minute. Remove the leaf with forceps and pat dry with a paper towel. Tear the leaf into pieces. Insert the pieces in a 15-cm test tube about one third full with ethyl alcohol. Place the test tube with the leaves in a hot water bath until the alcohol begins to turn green.

Remove the test tube from the water bath. Crush the leaves with a glass stirring rod. (a) Did the leaf pigments dissolve better in the water or in the alcohol? Continue heating and crushing until the solution becomes a dark green color.

Cut a strip of filter paper to just fit in a 15-cm test tube. Cut a point at the end of the strip. Draw a faint pencil line 2 cm from the point. Attach the filter paper to a cork stopper as in the figure. Use a glass rod to trace a line of the extract over the pencil line 2 cm from the pointed end of the filter paper. Allow the extract to dry. To build up a quantity of pigments, repeat this procedure about 20 times. **Before proceeding, be certain all flames are extinguished.**

Place 5 ml of solvent in a test tube. Attach the filter paper strip with a pin or tack to a cork stopper. Adjust the paper strip to where the point of the filter paper just comes in contact with the solvent. Allow the solvent to ascend the chromatogram for 15 minutes. When the solvent has reached the top of the strip, remove it and allow it to dry. Notice the faint bands of color. From the top may be seen: carotenes (orange), xanthophylls (yellow), chlorophyll b (yellow-green), chlorophyll a (blue-green), and anthocyanin (red).

Summary

(a) On a separate piece of paper, trace the shape of your paper strip. Accurately sketch the bands of color as obtained on your chromatogram. Use appropriate colors to indicate the color of pigments and identify each band.

(b) Why did separation occur as it did?

(c) What pigments seemed to be present in the greatest amounts?

(d) Would you expect similar results if leaves other than spinach had been used? Explain.

(e) Why are leaves green even though other pigments are present?

INVESTIGATIONS ON YOUR OWN

Obtain leaves from other plants, particularly those having an obvious red pigmentation. Repeat the procedure and determine what pigments are present. Summarize your findings in a series of labeled drawings.

24-1

How Do Roots Grow?

OBJECTIVES
- To examine the roots of seedlings
- To examine the structure of root tips
- To determine how roots grow

MATERIALS

RADISH, BEAN, PEA, OR CORN SEEDS
PETRI DISHES
FILTER PAPER
HAND LENS
MICROSCOPE (PART 2)
DISSECTING NEEDLES (PART 2)
DISSECTING MICROSCOPE (PART 2)
PREPARED SLIDE:
  LONGITUDINAL SECTION OF ROOT TIP
  (ALLIUM) (PART 2)
COLORED PENCILS (PART 2)

PART 1 / ORIGIN OF THE ROOT SYSTEM

A Week in Advance

To study the origin of roots, it is necessary to begin with a germinating seed from which the first root of a plant emerges. To observe the emergence of the primary root, trim a piece of filter paper to fit snugly in the bottom of a Petri dish. Flood the dish with water and drain off the excess. Lay 3 or 4 radish seeds at equal distances from each other on the filter paper and set aside until the roots have developed to a length of at least 2 cm. Repeat the procedure with other available seeds to note any differences in the primary root development.

Procedure and Observations

When the roots have developed, remove the cover from the dish and examine the seedlings with a hand lens. Locate the *primary*

root. (a) Describe its structure. (b) Where are the secondary roots developing? The fuzzy outgrowths are *root hairs*. (c) Locate and describe their growth. (d) What function do root hairs perform? (e) Describe the relationship of the base of the shoot and the base of the root.

Make an accurate drawing of the seedling. Show the branching roots and root hairs. Take note of the number and arrangement of leaves. On your figure, label: **primary root, secondary root, root hair, seed coat,** and **shoot.**

PART 2 / HOW IS GROWTH ACCOMPLISHED IN A ROOT TIP?

Procedure and Observations

Remove a germinated seed from the Petri dish prepared in Part 1. Cut a section of the portion of the root bearing root hairs and place this in a drop of water on a slide. Examine under a dissecting microscope and carefully, with dissecting needles, remove a portion of the tissue bearing the root hairs. In order to see the detail of the cells, add a drop of iodine to the preparation and examine it under low power. Observe the root hairs. (a) Are the root hairs composed of cells? (b) Explain your answer. (c) From what cells do the root hairs project? (d) Suggest how the root hairs absorb water.

Examine a prepared slide of a longitudinal section of the young root tip under low power. Use your text or charts to locate the various regions of the root tip. Move the slide and examine all areas. (e) Are root hairs present? (f) If not, explain their absence.

Locate the *root cap* at the tip. (g) What function does it serve? Cells on the surface of the root cap are worn off as it pushes through the soil. (h) Why doesn't the root tip cap disappear entirely in time? (i) Where are the smallest cells of the root tip located? Examine these cells closely. (j) What important activity is carried on in this region? (k) Why is this activity important to the root?

Move the slide from the tip toward the older regions. (l) What noticeable changes occur in the size of the cells? (m) What term applies to this region of the root? (n) Why is the activity of this region important to a root? (o) Why are the regions of the root not clearly defined? (p) From what region do the root hairs originate?

This is the region from which root hairs develop. On a piece of paper, trace the outline of the root tip. Locate with brackets the **root cap, meristematic region, elongation region, maturation region.** Accurately draw several rows of cells in each region.

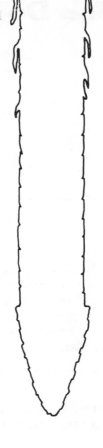

Summary

(a) On the basis of your observations of the root tip, explain how the roots grow longer.

On your paper, list the tissues given below and write the correct function after each.

(b) maturation region	(1) produces new root cells
(c) epidermis	(2) function in the absorption of water
(d) root hairs	
(e) elongation region	(3) protects the growing root tip
(f) root cap	(4) activity in this region serves to push a root tip through the soil
	(5) region producing root hairs

INVESTIGATIONS ON YOUR OWN

1. The secondary growth of a root may be studied through the examination of a carrot or similar root. Consult you text to determine what becomes of the primary tissues as the root increases in diameter. Make drawings of the longitudinal and cross sections and label the tissues you observe.

2. Make a collection of root modifications as they are found on different plants. (i.e., adventitious roots of corn, English Ivy, tap roots of Dandelion, and turnip, etc.) Give the name of the plant and tell how the modification serves the plant.

24-2

How Do Monocot Stems Differ from Dicot Stems?

OBJECTIVES
- To study the structure of a woody dicot stem
- To study the structure of a monocot stem
- To compare the structure of a monocot stem to a dicot stem

MATERIALS

CROSS SECTION OF A WOODY DICOT STEM, 10-15 YEARS OLD OR OLDER
PREPARED SLIDE OF: HERBACEOUS MONOCOT STEM (ZEA MAYS) (PART 2)
TEXTBOOK OR CHARTS
MICROSCOPE (PART 2)

PART 1 / MICROSCOPIC EXAMINATION OF A WOODY DICOT STEM

Dicot stems can be both herbaceous and woody. Herbaceous dicot stems usually live for only a single growing season. When compared to a year-old woody stem, close similarities may be observed in the tissues which compose the stem. In this Part, you will examine only a woody dicot stem.

Procedure and Observations

Examine the cross section of a woody stem. You commonly hear the terms *bark* and *wood*. (a) Where is the bark located? (b) Where is the wood in relation to the bark? (c) What tissue occupies the center of the stem? (d) Summarize the tissues that can be observed in a cross section of a woody stem.

Bark and wood are both composed of specialized tissues which can only be observed with a microscope. Without the microscope, it can be seen that bark is divided into the *outer bark* and *inner bark*. The outer bark is composed of *cork tissue*. (e) What are some functions of the cork? (f) What tissue composes the inner bark? (g) What is the function of the phloem?

(h) Although you are unable to see it, what layer of cells separates the bark from the wood? (i) What is the function of the vascular cambium? (j) What tissue composes wood?

(k) Estimate the amount of wood in proportion to the amount of bark. (l) What evidence is there that the stem has lived for more than a single growing season? (m) What are these rings commonly called? (n) Are all of the rings of equal thickness? (o) Account for your answer. (p) What is the function of the xylem?

On a separate piece of paper, construct a chart like the following one.

In your chart, summarize your observations of the woody dicot stem. Give the function of the tissue where it applies.

	Location	Function
1. Outer Covering		
2. Vascular Tissue		
3. Phloem		
4. Xylem		
5. Vascular Cambium		
6. Pith		

Copy the figure below of the cross section of a woody stem. On your copy, label: **cork tissue, phloem, bark, vascular cambium, xylem tissue, wood, pith, annual ring.**

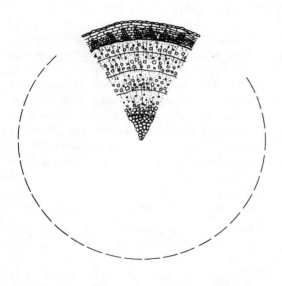

PART 2 / EXAMINATION OF A MONOCOT STEM

Procedure and Observations

Examine the prepared slide of a cross section of the monocot stem with your microscope under low power. The outer layer of cells is the *epidermis*. (a) Describe the appearance of these cells.

Note that just under the epidermis are additional thick-walled cells. These cells, along with those of the epidermis, compose the *rind* of the mature stem. (b) What tissue occupies most of the stem? (c) Describe the cells which compose this tissue.

Look for the fibrovascular bundles. Count the bundles in an estimated quarter of the stem. (d) How many do you find? (e) Where in the stem are they most numerous? (f) Of what significance is this observation?

Select a fibrovascular bundle toward the center of the stem. Examine it under high power. Note that the bundle has the appearance of a face with distinct facial regions. Large *xylem vessels* are found in the position of the "eyes" and "nose" of the face. The *phloem* occupies the position of the forehead. Locate and distinguish the *sieve tubes* and *companion cells* which compose the phloem. (g) Is a vascular cambium present? (h) What effect does its presence or absence have on a monocot stem?

Locate the thick-walled *sclerenchyma fibers* surrounding the bundle. (i) What function might they serve? The position of the "mouth" is an irregular intercellular space. (j) What can you observe to confirm that it is a space and not a large cell? (k) Suggest how this space might be formed.

Monocot stem
(cross section)

Fibrovascular bundle

On a separate piece of paper, copy the above view of a corn stem. Label: **epidermis, rind, pith, fibrovascular bundle.** On your drawing of the fibrovascular bundle and surrounding tissue, label: **xylem vessels, phloem, intercellular space, pith, sclerenchyma fibers.**

Summary

Make a chart to compare the characteristics of dicot stems and monocot stems. In the first column of your chart, list various characteristics. The following are seven characteristics which should be included:

1. Herbaceous or Woody
2. Type of Vascular Tissue Present
3. Arrangement of Vascular Tissue
4. Presence of Vascular Cambium
5. Location of Pith
6. Means of Support
7. Probable Life Duration of Stem

INVESTIGATIONS ON YOUR OWN

1. Obtain a prepared slide of a 3-year-old dicot stem (Tilia) and examine it under the microscope. You should observe that the tissues in a woody stem are much more complex than what you observe with the naked eye. Consult your textbook or a botany text for descriptions of the cells which compose the outer and inner bark and the xylem. Make a detailed sketch of a pie-shaped section and label the cells and tissues which you observe.

2. Examine a prepared slide of an herbaceous dicot stem (*Helianthus*) and locate the tissues studied in the woody dicot stem. Note the similarities and differences. Make a detailed sketch of a pie-shaped section and label the cells and tissues you observe.

3. Make a collection of cross sections of woody stems 3-4 cm in thickness and 5-8 cm in diameter. Identify each with its scientific and family name. The sanding and sealing of the cross sections will help to preserve them for future use.

25-1
How Does Water Move Through a Plant?

OBJECTIVES
- **To observe the functioning of stomata**
- **To demonstrate water loss through transpiration**
- **To observe the pathway of water through a stem**

MATERIALS

TULIP, *TRADESCANTIA*, OR GERANIUM
  LEAVES (PARTS 1, 2)
6 COLEUS OR PERIWINKLE CUTTINGS
  15-20 CM IN LENGTH (PART 3)
1 HEALTHY GERANIUM PLANT (PART 4)
SLIDE, COVER GLASS
MICROSCOPE
PAPER TOWELING
10% SALT SOLUTION
2 SANDWICH BAGS (PART 2)
COBALT PAPER (PART 2)
PAPER CLIPS (PART 2)
CELLOPHANE TAPE (PART 2)
250-ML BEAKER (PARTS 2, 3)
EOSIN POWDER OR RED INK (PART 3)
SINGLE-EDGE RAZOR BLADE (PART 3)

PART 1 / THE STRUCTURE OF THE STOMATA

In addition to providing for the movement of gases in and out of a leaf, the stomata have the function of regulating the movement of water through the plant.

Procedure and Observations
Remove a small piece of the lower epidermis from a tulip or geranium leaf by tearing the blade, twisting as you tear. The epidermis appears as a thin, transparent skin. Prepare a wet mount of a piece of the epidermis. Be careful not to wrinkle the tissue. Examine the tissue under low power. Note the shape and arrangement of the *epidermal cells* and the number and arrangement of the *stomata* (sing. *stoma*).

(a) Are chloroplasts present in the epidermal cells?

Locate the bean-shaped *guard cells* on either side of the stoma. Study the walls of the *guard cells* under low power.

(b) What variation in thickness can be observed in the inner and outer walls? (c) What structures can you observe in the guard cells?

The *stoma* is a pore opening into the air spaces of the leaf. Only a small percentage of the water absorbed by a plant is used in photosynthesis and other plant processes. The remainder is lost from the tissues of the leaf through the stomata. The guard cells regulate the size of the stomata by changing shape. (d) Why is this important to the leaf and the plant?

To observe the opening and closing of the stoma, prepare a fresh wet mount of the lower epidermis and examine under low power. (e) Are the stomata open?

Remove the water from the preparation by placing paper toweling at the left edge of the cover glass to soak up the water. Add a 10% salt solution to the right side of the cover glass. *Observe quickly.*

(f) Describe what happened to the guard cells and stoma.

(g) How can you explain the changes that occurred?

(h) Explain what natural activity of a leaf might cause the stomata to close.

Draw the lower leaf epidermis. Label: **stoma, guard cells, chloroplasts, epidermal cells.**

PART 2 / TRANSPIRATION

Transpiration is essentially the loss of water from a plant through evaporation from leaf tissues.

Procedure and Observations

Remove a leaf from a vigorously growing geranium plant. Fasten a strip of blue cobalt paper to the lower surface and upper surface by clipping the paper at both ends to the leaf. Do not damage the leaf unnecessarily. Blue cobalt paper turns pink in the presence of moisture. Place the leaf in a small plastic sandwich bag and seal it with tape. Place a strip of cobalt paper in a bag by itself and seal it. (a) What is the purpose of this second bag?

Observe the leaf after 10 minutes. (b) What is the color of the cobalt paper on the upper surface? (c) the color on the lower surface? (d) What is the color of the cobalt paper in the empty bag? (e) How do you account for the difference in the color of the cobalt paper? (f) Why is it necessary to seal the bag?

(g) Are the leaves wet? (h) From what part of the leaf did the moisture come? (i) Why is a control bag needed? (j) Originally, how did the water get to the leaf?

PART 3 / THE PATH OF RISING WATER IN A STEM

Procedure and Observations

In the examination of the structure of roots and stems, it may be observed that certain tissues are responsible for the conduction of substances up and down the stem.

(a) Which tissue is responsible for the conduction of water?

Fill a 250-ml flask about one third full of water which has been colored with powdered eosin or red ink. Place a *freshly* cut stem of coleus in the flask. Leave the stem in the solution at least 30 minutes. Remove the stem and split it lengthwise with a razor blade.

(b) What evidence do you see of the rise of dye in the stem?

(c) In the stem, locate where the water seems to have risen.

Make a cross section of a lower portion of the stem and prepare a wet mount. Examine the stem under low power of the microscope.

(d) In what tissue of the stem is there evidence that water has risen?

Summary

(a) On the basis of what you have learned about transpiration, account for the fact that leaves often wilt on a hot summer day, but return to normal at night.

(b) List as many factors as you can think of that might affect the loss of water from a plant.

(c) The following 12 events trace the movement of water from the soil, through a plant, to the atmosphere. Using your knowledge of plant structure, unscramble the pathway and write the events in order of occurrence. The first and last are done for you.

WATER
1. **water in the soil**
2. enters the petiole of the leaf
3. moves across the cortex of the root
4. absorbed by mesophyll cells
5. enters vascular cylinder
6. enters veins of leaf
7. absorbed by root hairs
8. leaves leaf through stomata
9. moves into xylem cells of stem
10. evaporates to air spaces of leaf
11. moves up xylem of stem
12. **water escapes to atmosphere**

26-1

How Do Plants Respond to Stimuli?

OBJECTIVES
- To observe the effect of light on plant growth
- To observe the effect of gravity on plant growth

MATERIALS

2 BEAN SEEDLINGS GROWN WITH LIGHT ON ONE SIDE
2 BEAN SEEDLINGS GROWN WITH LIGHT OVERHEAD
2 BEAN SEEDLINGS GROWN IN DARKNESS
RUBBER BANDS (PART 2)
BLOTTER PAPER (PART 2)
2 PETRI DISHES (PART 2)
CORN GRAINS (PART 2)
BEAN SEEDS (PART 2)
HALF-GALLON MILK CONTAINER (PART 2)

PART 1 / EXPLAINING PLANT RESPONSE TO LIGHT — PHOTOTROPISM

Procedure and Observations

Obtain two bean seedlings that have been grown under each of these conditions:

(1) Light received only from one side
(2) Darkness
(3) Light received from overhead

(a) How have the seedlings responded to light received from one side? (b) How are the leaves oriented? (c) Describe the growth of the stem. (d) Describe the growth of these seedlings.

Examine the seedlings grown in the dark. (e) How does their growth compare to those grown in the presence of light? (f) Are the seedlings grown in light "seeking" light?

(g) Consult your textbook and explain the growth response of each of the 3 types of seedling observed on the basis of auxin content.

Exchange the plants that grew directly under light with those illuminated from one side. Observe the plants periodically for several days and observe the changes that occur in the leaves and stems. Record your observations in a chart. Include the changes in the stems and the changes in the leaves for each day they were observed. (h) Explain the changes which occurred in the two sets of plants after you finish your observations.

PART 2 / GEOTROPISM AND THE GERMINATING SEED

Procedure and Observations

Cut a piece of blotter paper to fit snugly into the top of a Petri dish. Place 3 beans on a line across the center. Now, place the bottom of the Petri dish so that it pushes against the beans and holds them in place. Use a small amount of tape at the sides to hold the two halves securely together. Prepare another dish in the same manner with 3 corn grains.

Place both Petri dishes in the cut bottom quarter of a half-gallon milk carton filled one third full of water. Use rubber bands going around the carton on the front and back sides to hold each dish upright, as shown on the next page. Allow germination to occur.

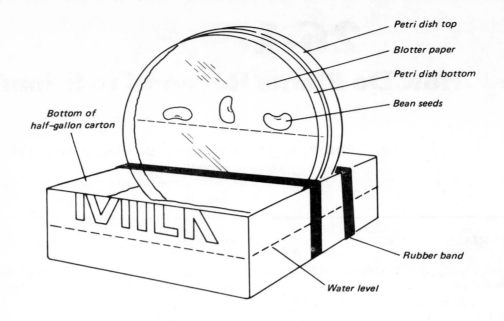

Bottom of
half-gallon carton

Petri dish top

Blotter paper

Petri dish bottom

Bean seeds

Rubber band

Water level

Observe the direction of root and shoot growth from each of the seeds. (a) Describe the root and shoot growth of the bean placed with the concave side down. (b) with the concave side up. (c) with the concave side to the right.

(d) Describe any similarities and differences in the germination of the beans and the corn grains. (e) Does the position of the seed have any effect on the growth of the root and shoot? Account for your answer. (f) Do roots show a positive or negative response to gravity? (g) Does the shoot? (h) What have you observed to support your answer?

Summary

(a) What is a tropism?
(b) How does unequal growth cause the bending of stems?
(c) When a potted plant is on its side, the stem curves upward away from gravity. Explain why most of the curvature occurs near the tip.
(d) In a natural situation, what value do tropisms have for plants?

INVESTIGATIONS ON YOUR OWN

1. To observe phototropic responses further, examine the arrangement of the leaves on plants. See if you can locate a plant in which the blade of a leaf completely shades the blade of another. Leaf orientation allowing each blade to receive a maximum amount of light is known as leaf mosaic. Write up your findings of the plants observed.

2. To observe hydrotropism, the positive response of roots to water, set up the following demonstration. Fit a piece of blotting paper snugly in a Petri dish. Cut out a 1 cm strip from the center. Moisten one half of the blotter paper with water but do not leave it soaked. Leave the remaining half dry. Lay 4-5 corn grains in the space between the blotter halves, replace the cover, and set aside. Observe the germination of the grains daily and write up your observations of the hydrotropic response.

27-1

How Does the Flower Function in Reproduction?

OBJECTIVES

- To identify the parts of the flower
- To examine the floral parts microscopically
- To understand the reproductive function of the flower parts
- To observe germination of pollen grain

MATERIALS

- GLADIOLUS FLOWER (TULIP, LILY, OR SNAPDRAGONS WILL SUFFICE)
- SINGLE-EDGE RAZOR BLADE (PARTS 2, 3)
- MICROSCOPE (PARTS 2, 3)
- PREPARED SLIDE OF CROSS SECTION OF LILY ANTHER
- SLIDE (PARTS 2 AND 3)
- COVER SLIP (PARTS 2, 3, 4)
- HAND LENS OR STEREOSCOPIC MICROSCOPE (PARTS 2, 3)
- DROPPER (PARTS 2, 3, 4)
- FORCEPS (PARTS 2, 3)
- COLLECTION OF ANTHERS FROM A VARIETY OF FLOWERS (PART 4)
- DEPRESSION SLIDES (PART 4)
- TOOTHPICK (PART 4)
- DISSECTING NEEDLE (PART 4)
- PETROLEUM JELLY (PART 4)
- 10% SUCROSE SOLUTION (PART 4)
- DISTILLED WATER (PART 4)

PART 1 / WHAT ARE THE PARTS OF A FLOWER?

Flowers must develop before there can be fruits and seeds. Seeds are contained in the fruits which develop after pollination and fertilization.

Procedure and Observations

Examine a complete flower and note that it has 4 kinds of floral parts. These parts are arranged in circles or whorls. The parts are supported on a stalk, the *pedicel*. The parts are attached to the swollen tip of the pedicel known as the *receptacle*. The outermost circle of parts is the *sepals* which may be green. In some species, the sepals appear as petals. Collectively the sepals make up the *calyx*, which serves to protect young flower parts in the bud stage. (a) Describe the sepals and their number.

The *petals* are within the calyx and collectively known as the *corolla*. (b) Describe the number and appearance of the petals.

The male and female organs make up the remaining circles of flower parts. (c) Why are they known as essential parts?

The male parts are the *stamens*. Each stamen consists of a slender stalk, the *filament*, and a knoblike mass, the *anther*. (d) How does the number of stamens compare with the parts already observed? (e) What seems to be the number plan of the flower? (f) Of what group of flowering plants is this characteristic?

The female organ, the *pistil*, occupies the center of the flower. Examine it closely and you will see that it is composed of 3 parts. The top portion is the *stigma* on which pollen lands. (g) Why is it necessary that it be sticky?

The stalk supporting the stigma is the *style*. At the base is a swollen green portion known as the *ovary*. (h) What is produced within the ovary?

Draw a flower showing all of the parts mentioned above. Label: **pedicel, receptacle, sepal, calyx, petal, stamen,** and **pistil.**

PART 2 / THE STAMEN

Procedure and Observations

Remove a stamen with forceps and examine it under a hand lens. (a) Describe what you observe.

Draw the stamen and label: **filament** and **anther.**

Prepare a wet mount of some pollen grains by dusting the *anther* on a slide. Examine them under low power and high power of the microscope. (b) Describe the surface of the pollen grains.

Examine a prepared slide of the cross section of a lily anther under low power. (c) How many cavities or pollen sacs are seen? (d) When the anther matures, how is pollen released? (e) What becomes of the pollen as it is released?

The pollen grains contain the male sex cells produced as a result of meiosis from special cells within the anther. Draw a cross section of the anther, label: **wall of anther, pollen sac, pollen grains.**

PART 3 / STRUCTURE AND FUNCTION OF THE PISTIL

Procedure and Observations

Carefully remove the *pistil* from the flower and examine it closely under a stereoscopic microscope. (a) In relation to pollination, suggest a reason for the stigma being supported as it is by the style.

Draw the pistil and label: **stigma, style,** and **ovary.**

Using a sharp, single-edged razor blade, make a wet mount of a cross section of the ovary. Examine it under a stereoscopic microscope. Notice that the ovary is divided into sections, known as *carpels*. Each carpel contains several *ovules*. (b) How do the ovules appear?

The ovules extend into a cavity known as a *locule*. (c) How many cavities or carpels make up the ovary? (d) Explain the significance of the number.

Each ovule contains an egg which is not visible. Observe that an ovule is attached to the ovary wall through a tiny stalk. (e) Why must the ovules be attached as they are?

Draw a cross section of the ovary, label: **ovary wall, carpel, ovule, locule.**

PART 4 / OBSERVING GERMINATING POLLEN GRAINS

Once pollen of a particular species has landed on the stigma of the same or closely related species, a pollen tube will begin to germinate. This phenomenon can be observed under laboratory conditions.

Procedure and Observations

Obtain a dropper of a 10% sucrose solution from a prepared stock solution. Place a drop of the solution in the center of a cover glass. Transfer some pollen grains to the drop with a dissecting needle or small brush. Use a toothpick to apply a thin ring of petroleum jelly around the depression. The slide should be deep enough to prevent the drop from touching it. Turn the slide over and line up the depression with the drop of sucrose solution with the pollen. Gently allow the slide to come in contact with the cover glass. Turn the slide upright and examine under low power of the microscope.

Pollen tubes should emerge within 20 minutes. Certain pollen requires one or two days to produce pollen tubes. Periodically check the preparation to determine the extent of germination. (a) What is the function of the pollen tube? (b) Through what structures does it grow? (c) Toward what structure does it grow?

Examine a pollen tube to see if you can find the 2 sperm nuclei. (d) What becomes of these 2 nuclei?

Draw the pollen grain at the start of the observation and several stages in the growth of the pollen tube. Label: **pollen tube, sperm nuclei.**

Summary
Briefly relate how each of the following flower parts contributes to the function of reproduction: sepal, petal, filament, anther, stigma, style, and ovary.

INVESTIGATIONS ON YOUR OWN

Collect several flowers of varying structure and examine them to determine differences and similarities. Summarize in a chart the number of each of the floral parts and any unusual features that may be observed. Determine whether they are monocots or dicots.

27-2

How Do Seed Parts Develop into Young Plants?

OBJECTIVES
- **To observe the structures of dicot and monocot seeds**
- **To recognize the basis for distinguishing monocots from dicots**
- **To observe germination and growth of seeds**

MATERIALS

DRY AND SOAKED LIMA BEANS
DRIED EAR OF CORN (PART 2)
INDIVIDUAL GRAINS OF CORN (PARTS 2, 3)
KNIFE OR SINGLE-EDGED RAZOR BLADE
HAND LENS
IODINE SOLUTION
250-ML BEAKER (PART 3)
PAPER TOWELING (PART 3)
BLOTTER OR FILTER PAPER (PART 3)
COTTON (PART 3)
COLORED PENCILS (PART 3)

PART 1 / A DICOT SEED — THE BEAN

The seed is a matured ovule and the final product of angiosperm reproduction. The new plant is provided with stored food and special coverings. Under the proper conditions vegetative growth begins. This is known as seed germination.

Procedure and Observations

Obtain one dry lima bean and one that has been soaked overnight. Examine the dry seed and note its external markings. Locate a scarlike structure, the *hilum*. (a) What does it represent? ,

Locate the *micropyle*, a tiny opening close to the hilum. (b) What is the significance of the micropyle? (c) Would you expect all seeds to have a hilum and a micropyle? Explain your answer.

Examine a seed which has been soaked overnight. Compare this seed to a dry seed. (d) What changes have occurred? (e) Offer an explanation for what you observe.

Remove the thin outer seed coat, the *testa*. (f) Describe the cotyledons which are now visible. (g) What is their function?

Separate the cotyledons allowing the embryo plant to remain attached to one of them. The *epicotyl*, often called the plumule, consists of two, tiny leaves which enclose the *terminal bud* of the future plant. Below the epicotyl is the *hypocotyl*, the embryonic stem. Locate the radicle at the base of the hypocotyl. The *radicle* is the embryonic root.

Add a drop of iodine to the testa, cotyledon, epicotyl, and hypocotyl. Remember that starch turns purple or blue-black in the presence of iodine. (h) Which contains the greatest amount of starch? (i) Suggest an explanation for what you have observed.

On a piece of paper, trace the figure of the external view of the bean. Label: **hilum, micropyle.** Also trace the figure of the internal view, label: **cotyledons, epicotyl, hypocotyl, radicle.**

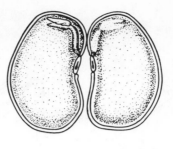

External   **Internal**

PART 2 / A MONOCOT SEED — CORN GRAIN

Procedure and Observations

Examine an ear of corn. (a) Is this the product of a single flower or a group of flowers? Explain your answer.

Remove a single grain. Locate the silk scar as a projection near the top of the grain. (b) Account for the location of the silk scar.

A corn silk represents a greatly elongated style ending in the stigma. It is attached to an individual ovary. (c) If an ear of corn had 250 grains, how many corn silks would there have been? Explain your answer. (d) Would you expect to find a hilum and micropyle in the corn grain? Explain what you are able to locate.

Locate the prominent dent on one side of the grain marking the location of the cotyledon and the embryo plant. In corn, the *point of attachment* corresponds to the stalk of the bean's flower. The grain receives nourishment through this point.

Trace the figure of the external view of a corn kernel. On your drawing, label: **point of attachment, silk scar.**

Position a soaked kernel "dent" side up. Using a sharp razor blade, cut lengthwise at right angles to the broadside of the grain. Observe the embryo and its parts in longitudinal view. The outer covering is the *ovary wall*. The lower portion contains the embryo and *cotyledon*. The upper part of the embryo is the *epicotyl sheath*, directly below is the *hypocotyl*. The cotyledon is attached to the epicotyl and hypocotyl. The bulk of the grain is *endosperm* tissue which supplies food to the embryo plant.

Add a drop of iodine to the endosperm. (e) What color appears? (f) In what form is food stored in the corn grain?

Trace the internal view of the corn kernel as shown below. Label: **embryo, cotyledon, epicotyl sheath, hypocotyl, endosperm.**

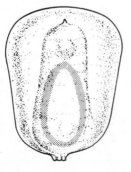

External   **Cross section**

113

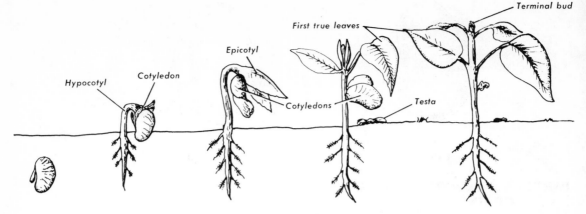

Steps in the germination of a bean seed

PART 3 / FROM SEED TO SEEDLING

Procedure and Observations

Prepare a germination jar by cutting a piece of blotter paper to line a 250-ml beaker. Tightly pack cotton on the inside to give support to the blotter. Place several bean seeds and corn grains in a row between the blotter and the glass about one half the distance from the top of the beaker. Moisten the cotton so that it is damp and avoid excess water. Put the beaker in a warm location. Allow the seeds to germinate until the young seedling plants are well formed. Observe the plants daily and make the following observations.

Bean Seeds:
(a) What embryonic structure emerges first from the seed coat? (b) Why is this important to the seedling?

Observe the growth of the hypocotyl. (c) How does it appear? (d) Of what advantage could this be to a seedling growing in the soil? (e) Describe the position of the cotyledons. (f) As germination progresses, what becomes of the cotyledons?

Study the drawings representing stages in the germination of a bean seed. Follow the changes in each part of the embryo. On a separate piece of paper, trace the steps of the germination of a bean seed. On your tracing, use colored pencils to indicate each part of the embryo in the earliest stage. With the same colors, shade in those structures in later stages.

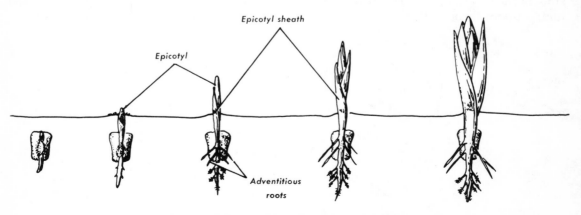

Steps in the germination of a corn seed

Corn Grain:

Observe a germinated corn grain. Note the direction of development of the emerging root and shoot. (a) How are you able to distinguish each? (b) What type of tropism does each exhibit?

Examine a seedling that has "emerged" above ground level. Look for a colorless structure known as the *epicotyl sheath*, which surrounds and encloses the developing shoot. A similar structure is at the root tip. (c) What function would these structures have for the developing seedling? (d) What becomes of the epicotyl sheath as the foliage develops?

On another piece of paper, copy the figure of the steps in the germination of a corn seed. On your drawing, use colored pencils to indicate each part of the embryo in the earliest stage. Use the same color for each structure in the later stages.

Summary

Review what you have learned about seed structure and germination by writing the following as complete sentences. The words you need are given.

(a) The ___?___ of the seed becomes the first true leaves of the newly emerged dicot plant.

(b) The radicle of the seed becomes the ___?___ of the new seedling.

(c) The ___?___ of a dicot seed supply food to the developing embryo.

(d) The ___?___ in the bean marks the point at which the ovule was attached to the fruit.

(e) The ___?___ of the corn grain contains starch.

(f) The point at which the pollen tube entered the embryo sac is marked by the ___?___.

(g) The arching over of an emerging bean plant serves for protection of delicate tissues. In a corn seedling this function is served by the ___?___.

(h) The ___?___ of a corn grain is likened to the pedicel on the ovary of a bean plant.

ANSWERS

cotyledons	hilum
epicotyl sheath	point of attachment
epicotyl	micropyle
radicle	primary root
hypocotyl	endosperm
silk scar	

INVESTIGATIONS ON YOUR OWN

Seed viability is the capability of seeds to germinate. Select 100 seeds of several species to test for their viability. Wet a piece of muslin or burlap and lay it out. Place 100 seeds of the same species in well spaced rows on the wet cloth. Wet another piece of cloth and lay it over the seeds carefully. Roll the two pieces together, loosely. This device is known as a "rag-doll tester." Prepare such a device for each species of seed. Keep the seeds moist for several days to a week. Check regularly to see if the seeds have germinated.

When germination has occurred, unroll the cloths and count the number of germinated seeds. Summarize your results in a bar graph indicating percent of seeds germinated for each species. Discuss why some seeds were unable to germinate and differences you observed when compared to the predicted viability of the seeds.

28-1

How Is the Sponge Adapted for a Sessile Life?

OBJECTIVES
- To observe the structure of a simple sponge
- To determine how the structure of a sponge relates to its life functions

MATERIALS

SPECIMEN OF *GRANTIA* (*SCYPHA*)
HAND LENS
DISSECTING MICROSCOPE (OPTIONAL)
METRIC RULER
SCISSORS
PROBE OR DISSECTING NEEDLE
WATCH GLASS

PART 1 / WHAT IS A SIMPLE SPONGE?

Grantia (*Scypha*) is a simple marine sponge. You will not see the cells, but you can observe many of its structures that adapt it to a sessile way of life.

Procedure and Observations

Examine the outer surface of the animal with the aid of a hand lens or dissecting microscope. (a) What feature places it in the phylum Porifera? (b) Does it resemble any of the types of sponges in diagram A, B, or C (opposite)? (c) What is the size of your sponge specimen? (length and width in mm)

Carefully insert a probe or dissecting needle into one of the small holes. (d) Does it enter the center of the animal?

In the living animal, water flows into the sponge through these tiny holes called *in-current pores*. Carefully insert a probe or dissecting needle into the larger hole. (e) Does it appear to also enter the center of the animal? This larger pore is the *osculum* or *excurrent pore*.

PART 2 / INSIDE A SIMPLE SPONGE

Procedure and Observations

Insert the point of the scissors into the osculum of your specimen and carefully cut the animal lengthwise. (This can also be done by placing the specimen on a glass slide and then slicing through it with a razor blade.) Use a hand lens or a dissecting microscope to examine the inside of the sponge. (a) Can you identify the two layers of cells?

Locate several *canals* passing through the body wall. You won't be able to see the *flagella* lining these canals, but three arrangements are shown in diagrams D, E, and F. (b) What is the function of the flagella? (c) How does the function of the flagella in the sponge differ from those you have seen in some protists?

(d) Does your sponge specimen resemble any of those in diagrams D, E, or F?

Your text describes the method by which a sponge obtains its food. (e) In your specimen of the sponge, where is the food trapped?

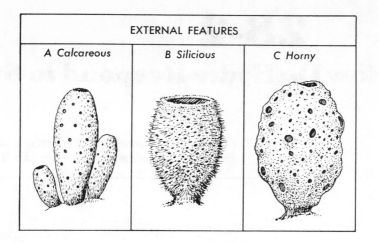

EXTERNAL FEATURES		
A Calcareous	B Silicious	C Horny

Summary

(a) What observations indicate the "division of labor" among the cells making up a sponge?

(b) How is a sponge adapted for a sessile life?

(c) What is the main difference between calcareous, silicious, and horney sponges?

(d) On a separate piece of paper, make a drawing of your sponge specimen. Label: **spicules, incurrent pore,** and **osculum**. Also draw arrows to indicate the direction of water flow.

INVESTIGATIONS ON YOUR OWN

1. Collect and examine other sponges. Determine whether your specimen is of the calcareous, silicious, or horny type. This is not easy to do. Use dissecting needles to separate the cells for study under a microscope. You will see many interesting spicules. The spicules of calcareous composition will be dissolved when a drop of chlorine bleach or weak hydrochloric acid is added. Silicious spicules will not dissolve.

2. Collect and examine other sponges. Make drawings of the specimens. Dissect them and make temporary slides. Look for the flagellated collar cells.

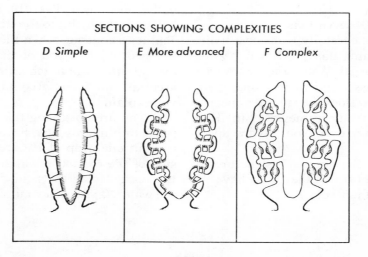

SECTIONS SHOWING COMPLEXITIES		
D Simple	E More advanced	F Complex

28-2
How Do Hydra Respond to Stimuli?

OBJECTIVES
- **To observe the structure of a living hydra**
- **To observe behavior of a living hydra**

MATERIALS

HYDRA CULTURE
DAPHNIA CULTURE
DISSECTING MICROSCOPE
SYRACUSE WATCH GLASS
DROPPING PIPETTE
METRIC RULER
PROBE
FLASHLIGHT (PENLIGHT TYPE) (PART 2)
PIECE OF BLUE CELLOPHANE PAPER
   (PART 2)
1% ACETIC ACID (PART 2)

PART 1 / LOOK AT A LIVING HYDRA

The hydra is a simple coelenterate found in fresh-water ponds and streams. This tiny animal attaches itself to plants or debris in the water.

Procedure and Observations
Using a pipette, carefully transfer a hydra to a Syracuse watch glass. Add enough water to cover the animal. Watch the hydra with the aid of a dissecting microscope, using diffused light. (a) Does the animal appear to have any supporting framework? (b) How many tentacles are on your hydra specimen?

Tentacles are characteristic structures of coelenterates. (c) Do all the hydra have the same number of tentacles?

Locate the *basal disk*, by which the animal attaches itself to a surface. A small slit at the anterior end, between the tentacles, is the *mouth*. (d) Can you locate the *gastrovascular cavity*? (e) By now you have been able to see how the hydra moves and perhaps how it can change its shape. Describe these movements. (Use your specimen for Part 2.)

PART 2 / HOW A HYDRA BEHAVES

Procedure and Observations
While observing the hydra, tap the rim of the Syracuse watch glass with a pencil. (a) Describe the reaction of the hydra to this stimulus.

Using the probe, touch the animal in various areas — such as the tentacles, mouth, body, and basal disk. (b) Record the behavior of the hydra to the stimulus of touch. Tentacles contract when they or mouth are touched. (c) Did you observe anything to indicate that the touch stimulus spread to areas distant from the contact? (d) How can you explain this?

As you are observing the hydra with the dissecting microscope, have your lab partner put *one* drop of 1% acetic acid at one side of the Syracuse watch glass. Observe the tentacles as the acid diffuses through the water. (e) Record your observations.

Rinse out the Syracuse watch glass and put in fresh water. Place several hydras in the glass. Shine a light on one side. (f) Record the reaction.

Now, shine the light through the blue cellophane on one side of the watch glass. (g) What is the reaction this time?

(Use the same specimens for Part 3.)

PART 3 / HOW A HYDRA CAPTURES PREY

Procedure and Observations
Select a few small *Daphnia*, and use a pipette to transfer them to the watch glass containing the hydras. Your dissecting microscope will allow you to observe the reaction of the hydras. (a) Describe how a hydra captures *Daphnia*. (b) What evidence indicates the use of stinging cells by the hydra? (c) How does the hydra ingest its food?

Summary
(a) What observations in the behavior of a hydra indicate coordination?
(b) Compare feeding behavior of a hydra to that of a sponge.
(c) Use the drawing at right as a reference. On a separate piece of paper, draw a hydra. On your drawing, label: **tentacles, mouth, nematocyst, gastrovascular cavity,** and **basal disc.**

INVESTIGATIONS ON YOUR OWN

Aurelia belongs to the same class of coelenterates as the large jellyfish. It is found in waters all over the world. The medusa stage in the life cycle is most obvious. If you have a preserved specimen available, examine it carefully. Make a diagram and label the major structures. Compare the medusa form of *Aurelia* to the polyp form of a hydra.

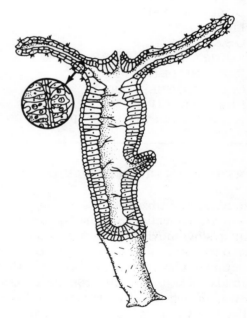

29-1

Are Planarians Able to Regenerate?

OBJECTIVES
- To observe the reaction of planarians to various stimuli
- To determine if planarians are able to regenerate

MATERIALS

LIVING PLANARIANS
PIPETTES
SYRACUSE WATCH GLASS
HAND LENS (OR DISSECTING MICROSCOPE)
PENLIGHT FLASHLIGHT
DISSECTING NEEDLE
LIVER
GLASS SLIDE
ACETIC ACID
RAZOR BLADE (PART 2)
CULTURE DISHES (PART 2)
EPSOM SALTS (PART 2)
GLASS MICROSCOPE SLIDE (PART 2)

PART 1 / PLANARIAN BEHAVIOR

Procedure and Observations

If you are collecting planarians for study, visit a slow-moving stream or pond and turn over some stones and sticks. Examine the undersides carefully because these animals look like small droplets of gray, brown, or white jelly. They can also be collected by tying a piece of liver to a string and letting the liver remain on the bottom of a quiet stream or pond for a few hours. When the planarians are transferred to the collecting jar, they will begin to crawl along the sides and bottom.

In the laboratory, remove a planarian from the collecting jar with a pipette. Then place the planarian in a Syracuse watch glass with some pond water. Examine the animal with a hand lens. (a) Briefly describe the dorsal surface. (b) Describe the way in which the animal moves.

Create a current in the water in the watch glass by using a pipette. (c) How does the animal react?

The projections on each side of the head are called *auricles*. Touch them lightly with the pointed end of a dissecting needle. (d) Describe the reaction. (e) Touch the animal on other areas and describe the reactions. (f) Is the anterior end or the posterior end more sensitive to touch?

(g) Shine the beam of a penlight on the anterior end and the eyespots. What is the animal's response? (h) Shine the flashlight beam on other areas and compare the responses. (By using care, you can shine the light on the sides and on the posterior end.) (i) Does the anterior end or the posterior end appear to be more sensitive to the light stimulus?

(j) Put a small piece of liver in the water and record the animal's reaction. Put a drop of acetic acid in the water near the planarian. (k) What is the reaction to this stimulus?

Transfer the animal to a glass slide and examine the ventral surface with your hand lens. Locate the mouth and the pharynx. (l) Describe the ventral surface.

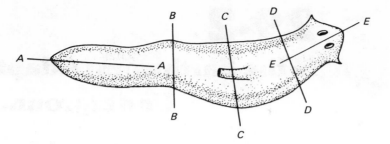

Look at the diagrams in your text showing the digestive and nervous systems. (m) Does the worm have an anus? (n) Where are indigestible waste materials eliminated?

Draw a planarian and label: **anterior**, **posterior**, **right**, **left**, **head**, **auricles**. Draw in the **eyespots**.

PART 2 / REGENERATION IN A PLANARIAN

Procedure and Observations

You already know that the sponge and hydra can develop an entire animal from a small section. Can planaria do the same? Put a planarian in a culture dish and add a few crystals of Epsom salts. In a few minutes, the worm will be anesthetized and can be transferred with a toothpick to a drop of water on a glass slide.

The diagram above shows various ways in which the animal may be sectioned. With a razor blade, cut the planarian in the desired location and transfer each section to a separate culture dish. Add fresh water and put the dishes in a dark place. Observe the animals daily, changing the water as you do so. Make drawings of your observations. Include the time of regeneration and the letter indicating the location of the cut.

Summary

In this Investigation, you saw the response of the planarian to many stimuli. See what you remember by completing the following sentences. Select your answers from the following words:

positive   ventral surface   anterior end
negative   dorsal surface   posterior end

(a) The response of a planarian to a current of water was ___?___.
(b) The response of a planarian to touch was ___?___.
(c) The response of a planarian to light was ___?___.
(d) The response of a planarian to liver was ___?___.
(e) The response of a planarian to acetic acid was ___?___.
(f) The organs for sensing the environment appear to be concentrated at the ___?___.
(g) The mouth is located in the ___?___.
(h) The ___?___ has cilia which cause the animal to have a gliding motion.
(i) The auricles are sensitive to touch and are located at the ___?___.
(j) The ___?___ did not appear to respond when the light was placed on it.

INVESTIGATIONS ON YOUR OWN

1. If your school has specimens of tapeworms available, examine one carefully to identify the structures labeled in your text. Compare the tapeworm to the planarian in the manner in which it obtains its food, digests its food, absorbs its food, respires, and moves.
2. Using reference books, compare the life histories of a tapeworm and a planarian.

29-2

Is the Earthworm Adapted for Underground Life?

OBJECTIVES
- To observe movement of a living earthworm
- To examine external adaptations of an earthworm
- To identify internal structures of an earthworm

MATERIALS

PAPER TOWELING
PROBE (PARTS 1 AND 2)
PENLIGHT FLASHLIGHT
RED LIGHT SOURCE
LOOSE, MOIST SOIL
LIVE EARTHWORM
PRESERVED EARTHWORM (PART 2)
HAND LENS OR DISSECTING MICROSCOPE
    (PARTS 1 AND 2)
CHARTS OF EARTHWORM ANATOMY
DISSECTING PAN (PART 2)
SCISSORS (PART 2)
SCALPEL (PART 2)
FORCEPS (PART 2)
DISSECTING NEEDLES (PART 2)
STRAIGHT PINS (PART 2)

PART 1 / EXTERNAL ADAPTATIONS AND BEHAVIOR OF THE EARTHWORM

Procedure and Observations
External structure of the earthworm.

Place a live earthworm on a damp paper towel. (a) Describe its movements. (b) Does it have an anterior and a posterior end? (c) What type of symmetry does the earthworm have? (d) What evidence of segmentation do you see?

Holding the animal in one hand, lightly rub your fingers along its dorsal, lateral, and ventral surfaces. (e) Describe your observations.

Now examine the animal with the hand lens or dissecting microscope. (f) Where are the bristles located? (g) How many bristles are on each segment? The bristles are called *setae*. (h) How do they function in locomotion? (i) How would the setae aid the animal in burrowing?

Observe the *dorsal blood vessel* extending along the back of the animal. (j) Does it appear to pulsate? (k) What is the direction of blood flow in this vessel? (l) How does the pulse rate in this vessel compare to your own pulse rate?

On the following observations, if your specimen is too active, you may wish to use a preserved animal. Locate the *mouth*. Above the mouth is an overhanging "lip" called the *prostomium*.

Use a hand lens or dissecting microscope to examine some of the segments. Locate the *excretory pores*. (m) How many are on each segment? (n) What is the function of the excretory pores? The thickened area encircling the body is the *clitellum*. (o) What is its function?

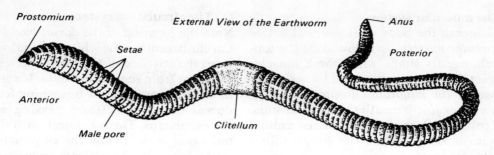

Prostomium   External View of the Earthworm   Anus

Setae   Posterior

Anterior

Male pore   Clitellum

Behavior of the earthworm.

Again, examine the living animal with the hand lens. (p) Does the earthworm have any visible sense organs?

Using a probe, touch the anterior end and then other areas of the body. (q) What kind of response did the animal make? (r) Which area or areas are most sensitive to touch?

Shine a flashlight on the anterior end of the worm. (s) Describe the reaction. (t) Explain how this behavior is related to survival. Shine the flashlight on other areas of the body. (u) Describe the reactions. Now, shine the red light on the anterior end of the worm. (v) Describe the reaction. (w) Can you explain any difference in the reaction of the animal to the white light and red light?

Put your animal on top of loose, moist soil. (x) Observe and record its behavior. (y) How is this behavior related to soil fertility?

(z) On the diagram above, locate the following: *anterior end, posterior end, mouth, prostomium, anus, setae, clitellum.*

PART 2 / INTERNAL STRUCTURES OF AN EARTHWORM

Procedure and Observations

Using a preserved earthworm, follow these instructions in dissecting the animal.

1. Read the directions carefully *before* you begin to cut.
2. Identify structures to be cut *before* you begin to cut.
3. Lift the structure to be cut.
4. Cut only when directed to do so.
5. When possible, use your fingers instead of a needle to expose structures.

6. Before you begin, be sure you understand the following terms: anterior, posterior, dorsal, ventral, median, longitudinal.
7. Labeling should be done as you investigate each structure.

Put a preserved earthworm in the dissecting pan, dorsal side up. Pin both ends of the worm to the wax at the bottom of the pan. Begin about two centimeters behind the clitellum and cut forward through the body wall slightly to the left of the dorsal blood vessel. Use the point of the scissors to make this cut. *Use care to cut through the body wall only*.

Extend this incision to the prostomium. Separate the edges of the cut and notice that there is a space between the body wall and the intestine. This is the *coelom*. Observe the partitions (*septa*) extending from the body wall to the intestine. Using forceps and dissecting needles, break the septa. Pin the sides of the body wall to the wax.

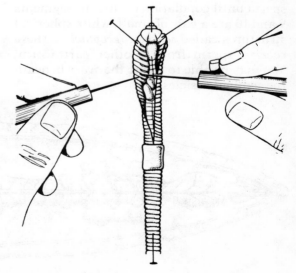

A. The muscular system

Just beneath the body wall you will notice the *circular muscles*. (a) How does the animal change its shape when these muscles contract?

Observe the *longitudinal muscles*, which form a layer just beneath the circular muscles. (b) How does the body of the animal change in shape when the longitudinal muscles contract?

B. The digestive system

This system is composed of a tube extending from the mouth to the anus. The *buccal cavity* passes from the mouth to about the third segment. The thick-walled *pharynx* is located in segments 4 and 5. (c) Why are the thick walls an adaptation to the function of the pharynx?

Follow the long, slender *esophagus* from the pharynx to segment 15. Locate the large, thin-walled *crop* posterior to the esophagus. (d) What is its function? Posterior to the crop is the thick-walled *gizzard*. (e) How does it aid in digestion? The *intestine* extends from the gizzard to the anus.

C. The reproductive system

Locate the paired, white, *seminal vesicles* in segments 10, 11, and 12. These organs store sperm until copulation occurs. In segments 9 and 10 are a pair of small, white spherical structures called *seminal receptacles*. These receive sperm from another earthworm. You may be able to locate the *ovary* beneath the seminal vesicles.

D. The circulation system

Note the location of the *dorsal blood vessel*. Carefully remove the white seminal vesicles from the left side of the body and separate the septa from segments 6 to 11. Identify the thick dark *aortic arches* branching from the dorsal blood vessel and passing around the esophagus. These connect with the *ventral blood vessel* below the esophagus. The muscular walls of the aortic arches contract and function as "hearts." (f) In which direction does the blood flow? (g) Why is it said that the earthworm has a "closed" circulatory system?

E. The excretory system

The small, white, loose tubes along each side of the digestive tract are excretory organs called *nephridia*. They are located in each segment except the first three and the last. To see these structures, you may extend the original cut posteriorly about five centimeters. Pin back the body wall, and carefully pull out the intestine. A dissecting microscope and dissecting needle will help you locate the nephridia. (h) What wastes are excreted by these organs? (i) Where do these wastes leave the body?

F. The nervous system

Examine the area dorsal to the buccal cavity in segments 2 and 3. Find the small white "brain" or *suprapharyngeal ganglion*. Two nerves arise from this ganglion and pass around either side of the esophagus. These nerves join the *subesophageal ganglion* located below the esophagus. From this ganglion, the *ventral nerve cord* extends the length of the animal.

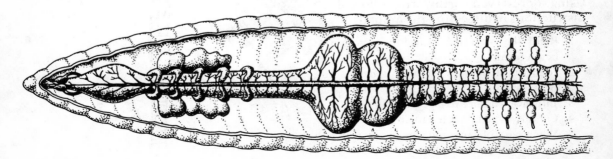

Remove part of the intestine and observe the ventral nerve cord. Notice the small ganglion in each segment. Cut the nerve cord and pull it free from the body. Notice the small nerves branching from it. (j) Where do these nerves go?

Notice that a distinct respiratory system was missing. (k) How does respiration occur in the earthworm?

On a separate piece of paper, make a drawing of the dissected earthworm. Study the structures carefully and use the figure opposite as a reference for organ position. On your drawing, label: **pharynx, esophagus, crop, gizzard, dorsal blood vessel, seminal vesicles, intestine, body cavity (coelom), nephridium, ganglion, hearts.**

Summary

(a) Compare and contrast the earthworm with other worms you have studied.

(b) Of what adaptive value is segmentation?

Test what you have learned by matching the functions with the organs listed below. On your paper, write the list of functions on the left. After each function, write the name of the organ which performs the function.

(c) relay and coordinate reflex movements

(d) push blood into the dorsal artery from the ventral part of the body

(e) stores food

(f) carries food

(g) remove nitrogenous wastes

(h) holds food until swallowed

(i) motor function — carries impulses to muscles for movement; sensory function — carries impulses to brain from parts of the body

(j) store sperm from another individual until such time as they are needed for the fertilization of eggs

(k) carries blood forward

(l) forms the skin and serves for protection

(m) absorbs digested foods

1. aortic arches
2. crop
3. dorsal blood vessel
4. epidermis
5. esophagus
6. ganglia
7. intestine
8. kidneys
9. nephridia
10. pharynx
11. sperm vesicles
12. ventral nerve cord

INVESTIGATIONS ON YOUR OWN

1. Obtain specimens of each of the classes of Annelida. Make a drawing of each one and label the external structures that adapt each to its particular environment. List the similarities and the differences of the animals.

2. Use your library and find out how earthworms are raised. Make a narrow terrarium and fill it with loose earth. Introduce several earthworms. Make observations over a period of time and write a report on your observations.

30-1

What Are Mollusks?

OBJECTIVES
- To observe the characteristics of the phylum Mollusca
- To observe features of mollusks which separate them into classes
- To identify and label the parts of a clam

MATERIALS

SPECIMENS OF CHITON, CLAM, SNAIL, AND SQUID

CHARTS OF CHITON, CLAM, SNAIL, AND SQUID

HAND LENS (PARTS 1 AND 2)

CLAM SHELLS (PART 2)

FRESH CLAM (PART 2)

DISSECTING TRAY

PROBE (PARTS 1 AND 2)

SCREWDRIVER (PART 2)

SCALPEL (PART 2)

PART 1 / CHARACTERISTICS OF THE MOLLUSKS

Procedure and Observations

Examine the specimens, or use charts or diagrams in this Investigation. Compare the various mollusks. (a) Which ones have an external shell? (b) What symmetry does each have? (c) Do you observe any evidence of segmentation on the specimens?

Carefully examine each specimen for a muscular structure called a *foot*. (d) Compare the foot of the clam, snail, and chiton. (e) What structures form the foot of the squid? (f) Are jointed appendages present on any of your specimens?

(g) From your observations, what characteristics do all the mollusks possess? (h) What features are different enough to separate the mollusks you have observed into three classes? (i) To which class does each of the following organisms belong?

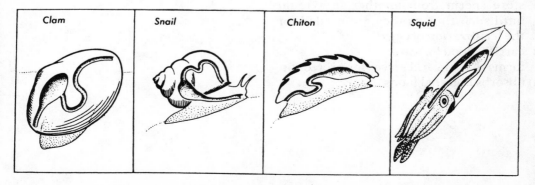

Clam   Snail   Chiton   Squid

PART 2 / ANATOMY OF A MOLLUSK

Procedure and Observations

Place your clam specimen in a dissecting tray and examine it. (a) How many shells (or *valves*) are present?

The shells are fastened together by an elastic ligament at the *dorsal* surface. Near the anterior end of the ligament is a hump on the shell. This is the *umbo* and is the oldest part of the shell. (b) Can you now determine the right and the left shell?

As the clam grows, it secretes layers, each one extending beyond the last. This makes a series of concentric *growth rings*. Find the growth rings on the clam's shell.

Now, look at the empty clam shell and notice the thin outside layer. This is the *horny layer*. (c) Describe its appearance.

Examine a broken piece of the clam shell with your hand lens. Observe the middle or *prismatic layer*. (d) Describe its appearance.

The inner layer is the *pearly layer*. (e) Describe its appearance.

Now, take the clam specimen and open the shells with a screwdriver. With a scalpel, cut the two large muscles that hold the shell closed. Open the shell and lay it back on the dissecting tray. Examine the muscles and identify them: the *anterior* and *posterior adductor muscles*. Notice the *scars* that are left on the shell by the removal of these muscles.

Examine the dorsal edge of the shell and notice the toothlike projections that fit into the grooves in the opposite shell. (f) What purpose does this arrangement serve?

Notice the *mantle* that surrounds the animal and lines the shell. The space between the two parts of the mantle is the *mantle cavity*. You can examine the organs in the mantle cavity by removing part of the mantle with a scalpel. (g) Where is the *muscular foot* located?

Observe the sheetlike *gills* also located in the mantle cavity. To observe how water circulates through the mantle cavity, notice two joined tubes (*siphons*) on the posterior end of the animal. The *incurrent siphon* is the ventral one and brings water into the mantle cavity. The *excurrent siphon* is the dorsal one and removes water from the mantle cavity. When water enters the mantle cavity, it flows over the gills which function in respiration. (h) What gas exchanges occur in the gills?

The gills are adapted to perform another important function. Try to find *cilia* on the gills with the aid of a hand lens or a dissecting microscope. When water passes over the gills, mucus traps particles and the cilia move them. A pair of *palps* on either side of the stomach directs the particles toward the mouth. Locate the *mouth* between the anterior end of the palps.

Using the scalpel, cut away the muscle of the foot to locate the *digestive gland* which surrounds the posterior part of the stomach. Identify the *intestine* and follow it to where it passes through the *pericardial cavity*. You will then be able to identify the *heart*.

Summary

(a) What structures of the mollusks distinguish them, as a group, from other phyla you have studied?

(b) What structures are used to distinguish classes Pelecypoda, Gastropoda, and Cephalopoda?

(c) How does a bivalve, like the clam, obtain its food?

(continued)

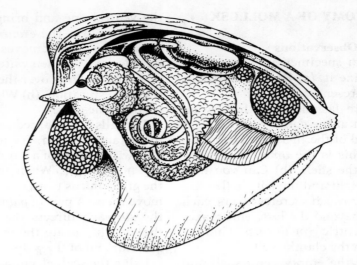

Locate the italicized structures in the diagram. Using the above figure, test your knowledge by drawing and labeling the following: **hinge, umbo, mouth, esophagus, stomach, intestine, anus, digestive gland, heart, gills, foot, anterior adductor muscle, posterior adductor muscle, incurrent siphon, excurrent siphon.**

INVESTIGATIONS ON YOUR OWN

1. Fill a narrow aquarium with sand and then add enough water to a depth of about six centimeters above the sand. (Use salt water or fresh water depending on the habitat of the animal you will use.) Place freshly collected clams on the surface and observe the method by which they dig. Once they appear to be siphoning water, add a little lamp-black or carmine to the water and observe the action of the currents. After they have siphoned water for a few hours, dissect an animal and locate the carbon or carmine particles inside the animal. Write up your observations.

2. Measure the effect of obstacles on a snail's pace. On a piece of paper, draw concentric circles at 1 cm intervals. Place the white paper under a glass container and put the snail in the center. When it starts to move, measure the distance it travels in 30 seconds. Repeated tests will allow you to obtain an average speed for "snail travel."

   Test the speed under various conditions, such as temperature, surface, and slope.

31-1

How Does a Crayfish Respond to Stimuli?

OBJECTIVES
- To examine the external adaptations of a crayfish
- To observe behavior of a crayfish

MATERIALS

LIVE CRAYFISH
SMALL AQUARIUM (OR LARGE FINGERBOWL)
SMALL ROCK
PROBE
PENLIGHT FLASHLIGHT
SATURATED SALT SOLUTION
VINEGAR
INDIA INK
DIAGRAMS OR CHARTS OF CRAYFISH
   ANATOMY

OBSERVING A LIVE CRAYFISH

Procedure and Observations

Put a living crayfish in the aquarium or a large fingerbowl and cover it with water. (a) What type of skeleton does the animal have?

The body of the crayfish is divided into two distinct regions. The anterior region is called the *cephalothorax*. The posterior region is the *abdomen*. The abdomen ends in a reduced abdominal segment, the *telson*. (b) How many segments are on the abdomen?

The cephalothorax is covered by the *carapace*. (c) How many pieces make up the carapace?

Notice the *cervical groove* that marks the division between the head and thorax. Observe that the carapace extends forward. This forms a horny beak called the *rostrum*.

(d) Where are the large compound eyes in relation to the rostrum?

The most anterior appendages are the branched *antennules*. Locate the *antennae* which are attached to the head, posterior to the antennules. (e) Describe their structure.

Now, arrange the small aquarium so you can observe the mouthparts of the crayfish. (f) How do the mouthparts move?

The thorax has eight pairs of appendages. Three pairs are *maxillipeds* and are used in handling food. Five pairs are legs. Try to identify all eight pairs. (g) How do the maxillipeds differ from the walking legs?

Notice that the first pair of legs are well-developed *chelipeds*. (h) Are these pincers the same size? Explain. The next four pairs of legs are called *walking legs*. (i) In what ways do they differ from one another?

Arrange the aquarium so you can observe the ventral surface of the abdomen. The abdominal appendages of the crayfish are called *swimmerets*. In the female, the first pair of swimmerets is small. In the male, the first two pairs are modified for transferring sperms. (j) Can you determine the sex of your specimen?

The sixth pair of swimmerets is enlarged to form the *uropods*. The uropods and the telson form the powerful tail fin used in backward swimming. Find the *anal opening* on the ventral side of the telson.

Now, place a rock in the bottom of the aquarium. (k) Observe and record the be-

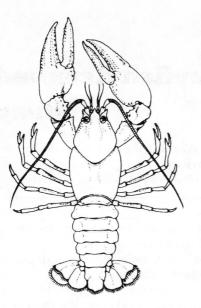

In the figure opposite, locate the terms italicized in the discussion. Using this figure as a reference, test what you learned about the external anatomy of the crayfish by drawing and labeling: **rostrum, antennule, antenna, compound eye, cephalothorax, abdomen, cheliped, telson, uropod,** and **walking leg.**

INVESTIGATIONS ON YOUR OWN

1. You may study adaptive behavior of sowbugs or pillbugs. These are common terrestrial crustaceans. Watch them walk and test their responses to various stimuli.

   Put 5 or 6 animals in two dishes. Place a piece of wet paper towel in one. Keep the dishes away from heat or strong light, and observe them for 10 or 15 minutes. Compare the results.

   Cut a piece of paper towel to fit the bottom of 2 other dishes. Moisten the paper and put 5 or more animals in each dish. Cover one half of each container with black lightproof paper. Put one container in a closed drawer or under a box. Put the other container in a well-lighted area. Compare the results after 10 or 15 minutes.

   Line the bottom of 2 dishes with black, lightproof paper. Cover the paper with a damp paper towel and place 5 or more animals in each. Now, place a light under one side of one dish. Compare the results after 10 or 15 minutes. Summarize your conclusions about the reactions of sowbugs and pillbugs to moisture, light, and heat. When do you think these animals would search for food? Do your experiments suggest the habitat of these animals?

2. Make diagrams of sowbugs and pillbugs. Compare the characteristics of these terrestrial crustaceans to the crayfish. What structural adaptations allow the sowbugs and pillbugs to live on the land?

havior of the crayfish for 5 minutes. (l) Describe the manner in which the crayfish walks. Touch a probe to an antenna. (m) Describe the reaction.

Shine the penlight flashlight on the anterior end of the crayfish. Then, shine it on the posterior end of the animal. (n) Compare the reactions and explain this behavior.

Put 5 drops of saturated salt solution in the water near the animal. (o) Describe its reaction.

Put 5 drops of vinegar near the animal. (p) Describe its response.

Clean the aquarium and add a drop of India ink just posterior to the cephalothorax. (q) What is the direction of flow of water through the gill chambers? (r) What creates these water currents?

Summary
(a) Give the functions of each of the following structures of the crayfish:
   1. Antenna
   2. Mandible
   3. Maxilla
   4. Maxilliped
   5. First walking leg
   6. Walking legs
   7. First abdominal appendage
   8. Swimmeret

32-1

What Are the Specialized Structures of a Grasshopper?

OBJECTIVES
- **To identify specialized structures in the grasshopper**
- **To examine the complex structures used in feeding**
- **To observe the complex organ-system development in the grasshopper**

MATERIALS

PRESERVED GRASSHOPPERS
CHARTS
DISSECTING PAN
SCISSORS
FORCEPS
SCALPEL
HAND LENS

PART 1 / EXTERNAL ANATOMY

Procedure and Observations

Place the grasshopper in a dissecting pan and identify the characteristics of the class Insecta. (a) State these characteristics. (b) To which order does the grasshopper be-

long? (c) What characteristics of this order can you identify?

Use your hand lens and examine your specimen carefully. Your text and charts may also be helpful.

Locate and identify the following structures on your specimen. The grasshopper is divided into three body regions: **head, thorax, abdomen**. The following structures are located on the head: **antenna, compound eye, simple eye, mouth parts**. The thorax holds the **walking legs** and **leaping legs,** and the **forewing** and **hind wing**. On the abdomen, you can find the **spiracles** and **ovipositor**.

Now, examine the mouthparts of the grasshopper to see how they are adapted to feeding on grass. Using the hand lens, care-

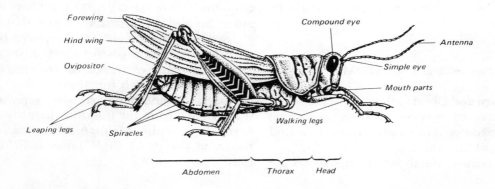

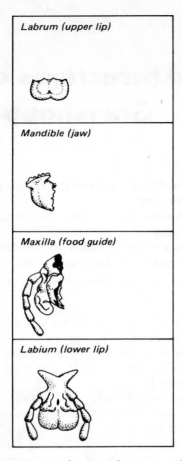

Labrum (upper lip)

Mandible (jaw)

Maxilla (food guide)

Labium (lower lip)

fully remove each mouthpart with a forceps. Compare the mouthparts to those in the figure.

(d) What is the function of the labrum? (e) How are the mandibles adapted for crushing blades of grass? (f) How are the maxillae adapted for holding and cutting food? (g) What is the function of the labium?

Notice that the maxillae and the labium have palpi. (h) How do these function in feeding?

PART 2 / INTERNAL ANATOMY

Procedure and Observations
Read the directions carefully before beginning your dissection. The organs you are to find are indicated in *italics*.

First, remove the three left legs. Insert the point of your scissors under the dorsal surface of the last abdominal segment. Being careful not to cut underlying organs, make an incision just to the left of the mid-dorsal line. Continue the cut through the thorax. Then, in front of the thorax, cut down the left side to the ventral surface. Make another lateral cut on the left side between the next-to-the-last and the last abdominal segments.

With the forceps, pull down on the left side and look for the large *dorsal blood vessel* ("heart"). Now, use your scalpel to cut the muscles close to the exoskeleton as you slowly pull down the left side of the insect. Locate the finely branched *tracheae* going to the spiracles.

Insert the point of the scissors at the back of the head and cut through the exoskeleton over the top of the head between the left antenna and left eye. Extend this incision to the *mouth*. Use the forceps and scalpel to remove the exoskeleton on the left side of the head. Locate the *dorsal ganglion* ("brain"). You may be able to identify a large, whitish nerve passing from the dorsal ganglion around the *esophagus* to the *ventral ganglion*. Follow the *ventral nerve cord* posteriorly and compare your observations to diagrams in your text or available charts. You should locate several *ganglia* in your specimen.

You have already identified the mouth and the esophagus. Cut away the tissue to expose the digestive tract all the way through the animal. From the posterior end of the esophagus, notice that the digestive tract enlarges into a *crop*. Posterior to the crop, the wall of the digestive tract becomes muscular and is the *gizzard*. Notice that the gizzard and the *stomach* are separated by a narrowing of the digestive tract. Also, observe that many *gastric caeca* are attached here. (a) What is their function?

Posteriorly another narrowing separates the stomach from the *intestine*. Identify the many long, thin, *Malpighian tubules* attached at this point. (b) What is their function?

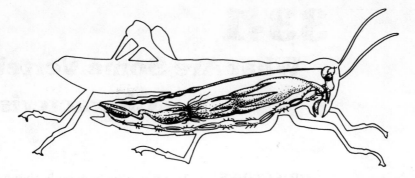

Observe the narrow *colon* posterior to the intestine. Then, the digestive tube enlarges to form the *rectum*, in which wastes are concentrated before passing out the *anus*.

In the female, the *ovary* is located above the intestines. If the specimen you are dissecting is a male, a series of whitish tubes, the *testes*, are located above the intestines.

Summary
(a) How do the structural differences of the grasshopper enable it to exhibit more complex behavior than centipedes and millipedes?
(b) In comparing the structural differences of the grasshopper and the spider, what conclusions might you state regarding the range of distribution of an individual animal and of the species?

Locate the italicized structures in the figure above. On a separate piece of paper, draw the internal anatomy of your grasshopper. On your drawing, label: **labrum, labium, esophagus, crop, gizzard, gastric caeca, stomach, Malpighian tubules, intestine, colon, rectum, anus, heart, dorsal ganglion, ventral nerve cord.**

INVESTIGATIONS ON YOUR OWN

1. Many examples of the order Orthoptera are found throughout many areas. A special collection of grasshoppers, crickets, katydids, locusts, and cockroaches can be made for your school museum. Be sure to label your specimens completely.

2. Select one order of insects. Collect and mount specimens from various stages of development for your class museum.

3. The great diversity of insects may be observed by comparing mouthparts of various specimens. Determine the type of feeding for which the mouthparts appear to be adapted. List your results in a chart. If possible, paste the various parts to a piece of paper and label them.

33-1

What Are Some Vertebrate Characteristics?

OBJECTIVES
- To determine how body shape can be adaptive
- To observe differences in vertebrate appendages
- To compare the head structures and sense organs
- To note differences in body coverings

MATERIALS

LIVING OR PRESERVED SPECIMENS OF:
    LAMPREY EEL
    DOGFISH SHARK
    FISH
    FROG
    TURTLE
    SNAKE
    BIRD
    MOUSE OR GERBIL
    (ANY OTHER AVAILABLE SPECIMENS MAY
      BE USED OR SUBSTITUTED)

PART 1 / IS BODY SHAPE AN ADAPTATION TO ENVIRONMENT?

Vertebrate evolution has progressed along lines of adaptation of the body and its structures to certain environments. Your examination will be limited to some of the more obvious adaptations. It should be noted that there will be exceptions to what you observe.

Procedure and Observations

Assemble the specimens in the order listed here. On a separate piece of paper, construct a chart like the one on the next page. Write all of your observations in the chart you have made. DO NOT WRITE IN THIS BOOK.

(a) What general environments are occupied by the specimens? Record the habitat for each representative in your chart.

Now, examine each specimen to determine its body shape. (b) What does it mean for a body to be streamlined? (c) Which animals appear to have a streamlined body? (d) Which are somewhat streamlined? (e) Which ones do not have any apparent streamlining? (f) Why is streamlining not important for the animals in (e)? (g) How does streamlining relate to the habitat of the animals?

Record the shape of the body of the animals observed in your chart.

Animal and Class	Habitat	Body Shape	Appendages	Head-Mouth Structures	Sense Organs H-hearing S-sight T-taste Sm-smell	Body Covering
Lamprey Eel Cyclostomata					H S T Sm	
Dogfish shark Chondrichthyes					H S T Sm	
Bony fish Osteichthyes					H S T Sm	
Frog Amphibia					H S T Sm	
Turtle and snake Reptilia					H S T Sm	
Bird Aves					H S T Sm	
Mouse or gerbil Mammalia					H S T Sm	

PART 2 / DO APPENDAGES ADAPT VERTEBRATES TO AN ENVIRONMENT?

Procedure and Observations

Appendages are used primarily for locomotion, although certain minor functions are performed by them. (a) What is an appendage? (b) How many appendages may be observed? (c) Do any of the specimens lack appendages? (d) Which ones? (e) How do they move? (f) What is a digit? (g) Which animals have digits on their appendages? (h) How many? (i) Which animals have claws or nails on their digits? (j) Of what use are digits and claws or nails?

Record your observations of appendages and digit structure in your chart. Indicate whether the animal has fins and appendages, and if digits are present whether they are clawed.

PART 3 / HEAD STRUCTURES AND ASSOCIATED ORGANS

Procedure and Observations

Compare the shapes of the head. (a) On what animals do the heads appear to "blend" with the rest of the body? (b) On what animals is it possible to observe a distinct head? (c) What term applies to the head region of a bilaterally symmetrical animal? (d) Why is it important to the animal that sense organs be located at this end?

Describe the head and mouth structures under the proper heading in your chart.

Examine the heads as closely as possible for the presence or absence of the following structures: eyes, eyelids, irises of the eye, ears or a structure for hearing, nostrils, mouth structures, tongue, and teeth. If you are observing living specimens, try to gather evidence for sensory development by using various devices such as food, brightly colored objects, etc. Try to make a

judgment on the apparent sensory development of each animal. Record your observations under the proper heading in your chart by using the following symbols:

(0)	— not present or unable to be determined
(+)	— present, poorly developed
(++)	— fairly well developed
(+++)	— well developed

PART 4 / THE BODY COVERING

Procedure and Observations

Closely examine the skin and body covering of each of the specimens. (a) Which specimens apparently have no outgrowths such as hair or scales? (b) Which specimens have scales?

Examine the scales of each organism closely. (c) How do the scales differ? (d) What animal has feathers? (e) For what function are feathers an adaptation? (f) Which animal has hair? (g) How can the presence of hair be considered an adaptation?

Record your observations of body covering in your chart.

Summary

Using the data obtained from comparing the animals, summarize how each of the following allows for adaptation to a particular environment:
(a) Body Shape
(b) Appendages and Digits
(c) Head and Sense Organs
(d) Body Covering

Multiple Choice: On a separate piece of paper, list the characteristics given below. After each characteristic, write the name of the class which corresponds to that characteristic. Your choices appear after each statement below.
(e) Members of this class possess a rounded mouth: Osteichthyes, Amphibia, Cyclostomata, Chondrichthyes

(f) Members of this class possess scales and clawed digits: Mammalia, Amphibia, Osteichthyes, Reptilia

(g) In what class would you find appendages modified for flight? Amphibia, Chondrichthyes, Aves, Cyclostomata

(h) Which class is characterized by having a body covering of hair? Reptilia, Mammalia, Aves, Amphibia

(i) Which one of the following classes would *not* have fins? Reptilia, Chondrichthyes, Osteichthyes, Cyclostomata

(j) Which class supports themselves entirely on their hind limbs? Aves, Osteichthyes, Reptilia, Amphibia

(k) The most highly developed sense organs could be found in the class: Osteichthyes, Reptilia, Mammalia, Amphibia

(l) A smooth body covering and the ability to live on land characterizes the class: Amphibia, Reptilia, Aves, Osteichthyes

INVESTIGATIONS ON YOUR OWN

Compare the skeletal features of four vertebrate animals. Observe the structure of the backbone, ribs, hip and shoulder girdles, limbs, skull, and jaws. Note the skeletal adaptations for locomotion, protection of the vital organs, and body shape. Summarize your observations in a table.

34-1

How Is a Bony Fish Adapted for Life in Water?

OBJECTIVES
- To examine the external structures of a fish
- To dissect and observe the fish's internal organs
- To understand how these structures adapt the fish to life in water

MATERIALS

FRESH OR PRESERVED YELLOW PERCH
(BLACK SEA BASS OR OTHER
CARNIVOROUS SPECIES MAY BE USED)
MICROSCOPE
SLIDE
COVER SLIP
DISSECTING PAN
DISSECTING MICROSCOPE (PART 2)
PROBE (PARTS 1, 2)
FORCEPS (ALL PARTS)
SCISSORS (PARTS 2, 3)

PART 1 / EXTERNAL ANATOMY OF A BONY FISH

Procedure and Observations

Lay the fish in a dissecting pan. Examine it to determine its body regions. Locate the *head*, the *trunk*, and the *tail*. Open the mouth and observe the action of the upper jaw (*maxilla*) and the lower jaw (*mandible*). Examine the jaws for the presence of teeth. (a) Describe the teeth. (b) Suggest the relationship of tooth structure to the diet of your specimen.

(c) Determine the probable use of the *tongue* based on its structure, location, and attachment.

(d) Describe the number and location of the *nostrils*. Insert a probe into one of the nostrils. (e) Does it matter which one? (f) Does the probe enter the mouth cavity? (g) Explain.

Open the mouth wide and probe into the throat cavity or *pharynx*. Raise the *operculum* covering the gills. (h) Into what structure does the pharynx lead?

Insert a probe into the opening of the *esophagus*. (i) Account for the large size and elasticity of the esophagus.

(Elasticity may not be observable on a preserved specimen.) The narrowed extension of the body attaching the head to the trunk is called the *isthmus*. (j) How is this modification in body structure important to the functioning of the gills?

Raise the dorsal fin by pulling it forward. Notice that the dorsal fin consists of a spiny portion and a soft ray portion. (k) Describe the dorsal fins. (l) Suggest a function of the spiny dorsal fin.

Examine all other fins of your specimen and determine their structure, number, location, probable function, and whether they are supported by spines, spines and rays, or rays. Summarize your observations in a table like the one opposite. DO NOT WRITE IN THIS BOOK.

Name of Fin	Number	Location	Support	Function
Pectoral				
Pelvic				
Dorsal				
Anal				
Caudal				

The *lateral line* is believed to be a pressure-sensitive organ. (m) Locate and describe the lateral line.

Examine the scales on your specimen. (n) Describe the arrangement of the scales.

Using forceps, remove several scales. Rinse a scale in water and make a wet mount of a scale using a cover glass to keep it flat. Examine under low power of a microscope. (o) Describe the structure of the embedded edge and the portion of the scale that overlapped it.

As a fish grows, the size rather than the number of scales increases. As the scales grow, concentric rings are formed. (p) Describe the pattern seen in the rings.

Count the regions of closely spaced concentric rings formed during winter and determine the number of winters your specimen has lived. (q) What is the approximate age of your fish?

Make a drawing of a fish scale under low power magnification.

Locate the following structures on the figure below: **maxilla, mandible, nostril, operculum, lateral line, anterior dorsal fin, posterior dorsal fin, pectoral fin, pelvic fin, anal fin, caudal fin, anus.**

On a separate piece of paper, draw your fish specimen. On your drawing, label each of the structures mentioned above.

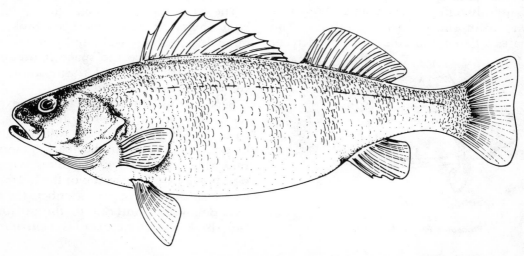

PART 2 / INTERNAL ANATOMY

Procedure and Observations

Gill Structure:

Place the fish in a dissecting pan to correspond to the figure. Raise the operculum and examine the gills. Locate the most ventral and dorsal points of attachment of the operculum. Cut along the line connecting these points and remove the operculum. (a) How many gills are exposed?

Remove a gill by cutting the upper and lower attachment of the *gill arch*. Rinse off the gill and examine it under a stereoscopic microscope. Locate the capillary *gill filaments*. (b) What function takes place in the filament?

Locate the bumpy projections on the gill arch known as *gill rakers*. (c) How do they function indirectly in the functioning of a gill?

The Organs of the Body Cavity:

Read the following directions carefully before starting. Hold the fish, ventral side up, with the head pointing away from you. Insert the point of your scissors through the body wall anterior to the anal opening. Cut forward to the space between the gill covers on the lower side of the head (cut #1).

Now lay the fish with its head to the left in the dissecting pan. Continue the incision from the isthmus to the top of the body cavity (cut #2). Make another incision close to the anal opening (cut #3).

Carefully remove the muscular body wall away from the underlying organs. This creates a flap of muscular tissue which can

be removed by using a scalpel to cut the attached edge along the top edge of the body cavity (cut #4). The organs of the body cavity should now be exposed; if not, remove any remaining tissue.

Locate the reddish-brown *liver* (cream-colored in preserved specimens) in the anterior end of the body cavity. On the lower side of the liver, locate the *gall bladder*. Cut the liver free from its attachment and remove it. This exposes the short *esophagus* and the *stomach*. Locate the *pylorus* where the stomach and *intestine* join. Find the small, pouchlike structures extending from the pylorus. These are the *pyloric caeca*. Follow the loops of the intestine to the anal opening. It may be necessary to remove masses of fat. Be sure you can identify all parts of the alimentary canal. Now, cut the alimentary canal at the esophagus and just above the anal opening and carefully remove it.

Locate the gonads. The female will have a large, yellowish *ovary* containing many eggs. The eggs are known as roe. In the male, *testes* are found in the same location. The testes are somewhat smaller than the ovary and creamy white. If you have done your dissection carefully, you should be able to locate threadlike ducts leading from the gonad and a small tube leading from the *urinary bladder*. Both join and lead to the *urogenital opening* just posterior to the anal opening.

The *air bladder* lies along the top of the body cavity. It may have been broken in removing the body wall, and you will only be able to observe the space it occupied. Locate dark masses of tissue along the spine. These are the *kidneys*.

Section the isthmus carefully to expose the *heart* lying in the *pericardial cavity*. Locate the large *cardinal vein* which carries blood from the body to the heart. It empties into a thin-walled sac, the *sinus venosus*, which is located at the top of the heart. Locate a soft-walled upper chamber, the *atrium*. Below and anterior to the atrium is the thick-walled, muscular *ventricle*. A

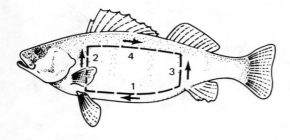

Procedure for opening body cavity

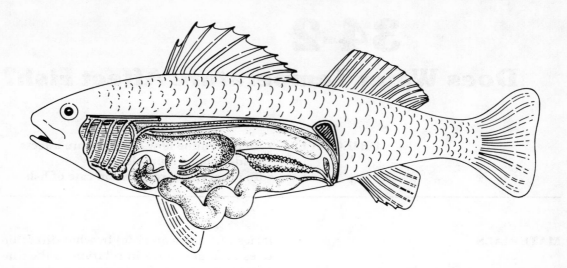

muscular enlargement, the *bulbous arteriosus*, leads from the ventricle to the ventral aorta. Arteries arise from a branch of the ventral aorta and pass into the gill arches. Make a drawing of the fish heart, label: **cardinal vein, atrium, sinus venosus, bulbus arteriosus, ventricle, ventral aorta.**

Summary

(a) What external structures have you observed that adapt a fish to life in water?

(b) Review the structures you have observed by completing the following diagram. On a separate piece of paper, draw the internal organs of your fish and label: **gill filaments, liver, gall bladder, stomach, pylorus, pyloric caeca, intestine, anus, heart, gonad** (testes or ovary), **urinary bladder, urogenital opening, air bladder, kidney.**

INVESTIGATIONS ON YOUR OWN

Carefully remove the brain of the fish. Place it in a vial with preservative. Make a drawing and, using your text as a reference, label the lobes. Associate the function of each lobe with the label.

34-2
Does Water Temperature Affect Fish?

OBJECTIVES
- To determine how temperature affects cold-blooded animals
- To observe the respiration rate of fish

MATERIALS

AQUARIA OR BATTERY JARS
GOLDFISH (COMETS ARE BEST FOR THIS EXPERIMENT)
THERMOMETER (CELSIUS)
GLASS FUNNEL
CRUSHED ICE
TIMING DEVICE
WARM WATER

THE RESPIRATION RATE OF FISH

Cold-blooded animals are literally at the mercy of their environment. Lowering the body temperature in response to reduced temperature of the environment may result in the crystallization of proteins in the blood, resulting in death. An increase in body temperature may speed up metabolism to such an extent that the tissues are literally burned up.

Procedure and Observations

Put a goldfish in an aquarium or battery jar with enough water to cover the dorsal fin. Observe the movements of the operculum and the mouth. (a) How do the movements of the mouth and operculum coordinate?

(b) As water enters the gill chambers from the mouth, what gases are being exchanged between the gill filament capillaries and the water? (c) In what direction does each gas move in relation to the filament? (d) What gas is contained in the water leaving the gill chamber? (e) Explain how the operculum movements can be used as an indication of the respiration rate of fish.

To determine the effect of water temperature on respiration rate, place a thermometer at the edge of the aquarium so that it can be read without disturbing the fish. Slowly add crushed ice to the aquarium to avoid exciting the fish and to reduce the shock factor. Reduce the water temperature to near freezing. Observe the movement of the operculum. Count the movement of the operculum for one minute at the lowest temperature. Record the rate of operculum movements in a table like the one opposite.

Remove as much ice as possible. Now, slowly add warm water through a funnel down the sides of the aquarium opposite the position of the thermometer. A siphoning system may be used to remove water so that the ice and water volume remain constant. (f) Why is it necessary to avoid exciting the fish when adding water?

Closely observe the thermometer and continue to add warm water slowly until a 3-degree rise in temperature is noted. Allow time for the fish to adjust to the temperature change, then count and record the number of operculum movements in one minute at this temperature.

Degrees Celsius	Fish #1	Fish #2	Fish #3	Fish #4	Average Rate
0					
3					
6					
9					
12					
15					
18					
21					
24					
27					
30					
33					

Continue adding and removing water and record the number of operculum movements at each 3-degree temperature interval until the temperature reaches 30° Celsius.

After the experiment, remove the goldfish and place it in a well-aerated aquarium at room temperature. Obtain data from three other members of the class. Place their data in the appropriate part of your chart. DO NOT WRITE IN THIS BOOK.

On a piece of graph paper, construct a graph showing respiration rate for each fish at each temperature. Calculate the average rate of operculum movements for all four fish and record in your table. On the same graph, plot the average respiration rate.

(g) How does the graph of the operculum movements of your fish compare to the other three? (h) Explain any differences. (i) Discuss your observations of the activity of the fish during this experiment. (j) At which temperature was the rate of operculum movements greatest? (k) What is the relationship between increase in water temperature and respiration rate in the goldfish? (l) List the factors which, in addition to water temperature, could influence the respiration rate in your fish.

Summary

Fish are adapted for an aquatic life in both warm and cold waters. In terms of your results, discuss how the respiration rates of fish in these environments could vary.

INVESTIGATIONS ON YOUR OWN

To what extent does environment affect the color pattern of a fish? To answer that question, you can perform some experiments to determine whether environmental conditions cause variations in coloration of fish. Obtain two sets of fish that differ markedly in the coloration pattern. Green sunfish and bullhead catfish are suitable specimens.

Put each fish in an individual aquarium or battery jar with the water level slightly above the dorsal fin of the fish. The shallow water causes the fish to aerate the water by its own movement. Wrap the aquaria for each fish with paper of different colors, using white, brown, black, yellow, green, and red if possible. Be sure that the sides and bottom are entirely covered. Put the aquaria on a table so that the top light is the same for all of the fish. It will probably be necessary to change the water in all of the aquaria many times in the course of the experiment. Avoid exposing the fish to daylight when this is done.

Examine the fish each day, noting any color change. Continue daily observations for three to four weeks, or longer if desir-

able. Small fish (3-6 cm) may show noticeable color changes in a few days. Larger fish may require from several weeks to a full month.

Several factors should be included in the report and analysis of your observations. To what extent did each fish change to a color resembling the background? Did some colors produce more change than others? Did color changes occur more in certain areas than in others? Did the two species differ in their reaction?

35-1
How Is a Frog Adapted for a Double Life?

OBJECTIVES
- To observe how a tadpole is adapted for an aquatic life
- To compare a tadpole to an adult bullfrog
- To observe how an adult frog is adapted for both aquatic and terrestrial habitats

MATERIALS

LIVING BULLFROG TADPOLES IN VARIOUS STAGES OF DEVELOPMENT
AQUARIA TO HOUSE THE TADPOLES
CHARTS SHOWING DEVELOPMENT OF TADPOLES
LIVING ADULT FROG (PART 2)
BATTERY JAR OR AQUARIUM (PART 2)

PART 1 / THE TADPOLE

The bullfrog tadpole spends two winters and two or three years in its various tadpole stages. This explains why you can find bullfrog tadpoles in many stages of development.

Procedure and Observations
Look at the tadpoles in the aquarium or use charts showing the metamorphosis. Observe the *caudal fin* that surrounds the tail. (a) How can you explain that the caudal fin and tail are not so large on some of the tadpoles?

(b) See if you can determine which legs are the first to appear. (c) What happens to the tail as the legs begin to develop?

(d) Examine the mouth with its *horny lip*. (e) What is the shape of the mouth? Observe the feeding behavior of the tadpoles. (f) How is the horny lip used?

Compare the mouths of young bullfrog tadpoles to those in which hind legs have developed. (g) Explain any differences.

Notice that the mouth movements continue even though the tadpoles are not feeding. They are taking in water which passes over the gills and out through a *spiracle*. (h) Where are the spiracles located?

The gills are located on either side of the head but are covered by a fleshy *operculum*. Carefully look at the area under the operculum. (i) Do any of your specimens show a budlike growth in this area?

It is here that the *forelegs* will develop after the lungs have formed. (j) What might occur if the forelegs developed before the lungs?

Compare the eyes on the younger tadpoles with those having hind legs. (k) How do

145

they differ? (l) Can you suggest an adaptive value for this difference in eye position?

On a separate piece of paper, make a drawing of a stage about midway in a tadpole's development. Label: **gills, horny lip, operculum, tail, caudal fin, eye, mouth, hind leg, foreleg.**

PART 2 / THE LIVING FROG

Procedure and Observations

Place a frog in a battery jar, aquarium, or sink with enough water so the animal can swim. (a) What part of the frog is above the surface of the water when it floats? (b) Of what advantage is this to the frog?

Touch the frog and watch it swim. (c) Describe the swimming movements.

Examine the *eyes*. (d) Are eyelids present? (e) How many? Notice that the frog cannot move its eyes as you can. Move an object close to the frog's eye or barely touch it. (f) Describe the reaction.

The thin membrane covering the eye from below is the *nictitating membrane*. (g) Of what advantage would this membrane be to the frog while under water? (h) on land?

Take the frog out of water and watch the breathing movements. (i) Describe the action of the floor of the *mouth* and muscles of the body wall. (j) When the frog breathes, does it open its mouth? (k) How does air get into the lungs?

(l) What is the function of the large eardrums (tympanic membranes) posterior to the eyes?

Examine the *forelegs* of the frogs. (m) How many fingers are present? (n) Are they webbed?

Holding the animal carefully, stretch out the *hind legs*. (o) Are the legs longer or shorter than the body? (p) How many toes are present? (q) Are they webbed?

Examine the coloration of the bullfrog on its dorsal and ventral surfaces. (r) How do the surfaces differ? (s) How is this considered to be protective coloration?

Summary

Arrange the stages of development of the bullfrog in the proper order of occurrence:
(a) tadpole with mouth, tail, and caudal fin
(b) egg
(c) complete resorption of the tail
(d) development of forelegs
(e) development of hind legs
(f) development of lungs

INVESTIGATIONS ON YOUR OWN

Observe the arrangement of the spots and the coloration of a leopard frog. (Use a preserved specimen.) Remove a section of the dorsal skin containing one of the frog's spots, and mount it on a slide in a drop of water, using a cover glass. Examine the entire section under low and high power of your microscope. Examine various sections from pigmented spots of the dorsal surface to clearer areas of the ventral surface. Make drawings of your observations and write up your findings.

35-2
What Are the Internal Organs of a Frog?

OBJECTIVES
- To study the internal organs of a frog
- To develop dissection technique
- To observe organ-systems of a representative vertebrate

MATERIALS

FRESHLY KILLED OR PRESERVED FROG
DISSECTING TRAY OR PAN
DISSECTING SCISSORS
PROBE
FORCEPS

PART 1 / MOUTH ADAPTATIONS

Before starting your dissection, carefully read and be certain you understand all directions given in the procedure. Check the locations of the structures to be observed in the diagrams of frog anatomy in your text. Color, texture, and flexibility of organs differ in preserved and freshly killed specimens.

Procedure and Observations

Cut the mouth at each hinge joint to allow opening the mouth wide. (a) Locate and describe the attachment of the *tongue*. (b) The tongue is sticky in the living specimen. What purpose does this serve?

At the back of the mouth may be found the openings to three structures. On a male frog, near the hinge of the lower jaw on either side, locate the opening to the *vocal sacs*. (c) What conclusions can be reached about which frogs make sounds?

Locate the slitlike *glottis* in the center of the rear of the mouth. (d) Use a probe to determine where the glottis leads. (e) Account for the extreme width of the gullet

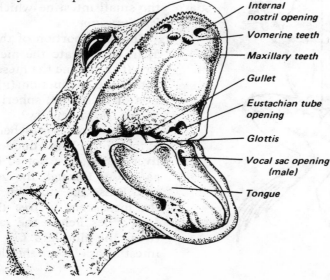

Internal nostril opening
Vomerine teeth
Maxillary teeth
Gullet
Eustachian tube opening
Glottis
Vocal sac opening (male)
Tongue

(opening of the esophagus) located above the glottis.

Locate the openings of the *Eustachian tubes* near the hinge of the upper jaw. (f) Where do they lead?

Locate the *internal nostril openings* in the roof of the mouth. (g) How can this position be considered an adaptation to a frog in the water?

(h) What is the function of the two *vomerine teeth* extending from the roof of the mouth? (i) Which of the jaws is provided with *small teeth*, upper or lower?

(j) Of what adaptive value is the positioning of the eyes?

In the figure given, locate the structures you have observed: **tongue, glottis, gullet, Eustachian tube opening, internal nostril opening, vomerine teeth, teeth.**

PART 2 / WHAT ARE SOME INTERNAL ADAPTATIONS OF THE FROG?

Procedure and Observations

Lay the frog on its dorsal side. Insert your scissors through the skin just above the anal opening and make incisions as shown in the diagram.

Fold the flaps of skin back revealing the underlying muscles. Study the ventral and lateral muscle layers now exposed by the removal of skin. Muscles can only shorten when they contract. (a) Note their pattern and explain how they might function.

Observe the large blood vessel lying along the midline under the muscle layer. This is the abdominal vein. (b) To what structure does it lead?

Repeat the same incisions as carried out on the skin, being careful not to damage underlying organs. Cut through the bones of the shoulder girdle and remove the muscle layers with forceps. The body cavity may be nearly filled with black-colored *eggs*. If so, your specimen is a female.

The Digestive System

Locate the large *liver* anterior in the body cavity. (c) How many lobes does it have? On the dorsal side of the liver, locate the greenish *gall bladder*. (d) What is its function? (e) Describe the shape of the stomach under the liver.

Observe that the anterior end of the stomach is larger than the *esophagus*. The stomach becomes smaller at the *pylorus* where it joins the *small intestine*. The *duodenum* is the short section of the small intestine leading from the pylorus. The highly coiled *ileum* is the major portion of the small intestine which widens into the *large intestine*.

Spread a portion of the coiled intestine apart and locate the membranous *mesentery*. (f) Examine the mesentery closely and determine its function. (g) What is the function of the small, spherical *spleen* located within the mesentery?

The *pancreas* is attached to the lower part of the stomach and duodenum. Remove the liver, using care not to damage other organs. Cut through the gullet at its upper end. Raise the stomach and carefully cut the mesentery to free the intestine. The *cloaca* lies below the large intestine between the hind legs. Cut through the large intestine as close to the cloaca as possible.

Lay the alimentary canal on a plain sheet of paper. Review the structures you have observed as you label the parts on the paper.

Using scissors, cut along the outer curvature of the stomach toward the pylorus. Pin the tissue of the stomach back and examine any contents which may be present. (h) Describe the lining and contents of the stomach. (i) Cut through the pylorus and account for its structure.

Remove a short piece of the small intestine and examine its lining under a dissecting microscope. (j) Describe what you observe.

The Urogenital System

Locate the cream-colored *oviducts* through which eggs pass from the anterior of the body cavity to the posterior opening, the *cloaca*.

Remove the oviducts to reveal the brownish *kidneys*. The kidneys lie along the back on either side of the spine. Notice they are covered by a thin, tough membrane, the *peritoneum*, which lines the body cavity. Locate a small twisting tube, the *ureter*, leading from each kidney to the cloaca. Attached to the cloaca is the *urinary bladder*. (k) What is its function?

Do not confuse the ureters with oviducts in the female. If your frog is an immature female, you will find two lobed, grayish ovaries lying close to the kidneys. The testes of the male are in a corresponding position.

The Circulatory System

Examine the *heart* lying in a thin sac, the *pericardium*. Use your probe to locate the great veins and arteries leading to and from the heart. (Consult your textbook to identify the larger blood vessels and chambers.) Examine the *lungs* and notice the *pulmonary veins* and *pulmonary arteries* connecting the heart and lungs.

Remove the heart, leaving as much of the blood vessels attached as possible. Examine the front side under a dissecting microscope. Locate the *right atrium*, *left atrium*, and *ventricle*. The large vessel arising from the ventricle and forming a "Y" at the top of the heart is the *conus arteriosus*. This large vessel divides into the *left* and *right truncus arteriosus*. Three major arteries arise from each branch: *carotid artery* to the head, *aortic arch* to the body, and *pulmocutaneous artery* to the lungs and skin.

Examine the dorsal side of the heart. Three branches of the *vena cava* unite in a thin-walled sac, the *sinus venosus* which opens into the right atrium.

Examine the figures of the front and back view of the heart. On the front view, locate: **ventricle, right atrium, conus arteriosus, left truncus arteriosus.**

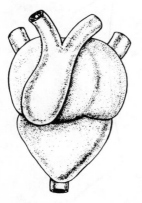

Front view

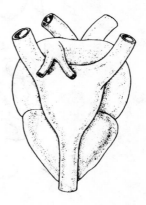

Back view

On a separate piece of paper, draw the ventral side of the heart. Label the parts named above and draw in and label: **carotid arch, aortic arch, pulmocutaneous artery.** On the dorsal view, locate: **ventricle, vena cava, sinus venosus, pulmonary veins.** Draw the dorsal view of the heart on your paper and label these parts.

Summary

(a) Briefly relate how the mouth and its structures adapt a frog to its terrestrial existence.

(b) What structures of the mouth adapt a frog to its aquatic life?

(c) Test yourself by locating the following on the diagram: **liver, gall bladder, gullet, stomach, pylorus, small intestine, mesentery, duodenum, esophagus, large intestine, pancreas, spleen, cloaca, kidney, ureter, urinary bladder, testes** (male), **ovary** (immature female). DO NOT WRITE IN THIS BOOK.

INVESTIGATIONS ON YOUR OWN

Carefully dissect the brain of a frog. To do so, remove the skin from the dorsal surface of the head. The brain is encased within a bony cranial cavity. Remove the cranium by scraping away the bone with a scapel. As you are able, break chips of bone away to reveal the brain. Expose it anteriorly, posteriorly, and to the sides as much as possible before attempting to remove it. To accompany your specimen, make a diagram showing the significant features of the frog's brain and label the parts.

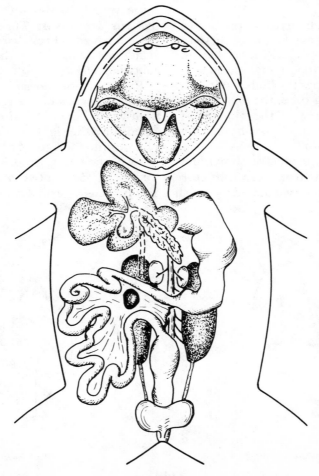

36-1

How Are Snakes and Turtles Unique Reptiles?

OBJECTIVES
- To observe external adaptations of snakes
- To study structural adaptations of the turtles
- To compare structural features of snakes and turtles

MATERIALS

LIVING LABORATORY SPECIMEN OF NON-POISONOUS SNAKE
SHED SKIN OF ANY SNAKE SPECIES
MUSEUM MOUNT OF SNAKE SKELETON
LIVING OR PRESERVED PAINTED TURTLE (DRAWING WILL SUFFICE IF NOT AVAILABLE) (PART 2)
DRIED TURTLE SHELL (PART 2)

PART 1 / CHARACTERISTICS OF SNAKES

Procedure and Observations

Examine the snake closely and observe that the skin is covered with *scales*. (a) How does this type of skin help snakes to survive on land?

Touch the skin of the snake. (b) Describe how it feels.

Locate the *vent* or *cloacal opening*. (c) What structures determine the 3 body regions of the snake?

Observe the scales with a hand lens. (d) Describe how the scales are placed. (e) Do the scales have color?

Examine the shed skin of any species of snake. (f) Compare the scales on the ventral side with those on the dorsal side. Those on the ventral side are known as *abdominal scutes*. They are internally attached through muscles to the ribs.

Closely observe a snake from the side as it moves across the surface of a table or a rough board. (g) Describe its movements. (h) How are scutes considered an adaptation for locomotion? (i) What name is given to the locomotion observed?

The head of any snake is adapted to perform a number of activities generally performed by limbs of other vertebrate animals. Using a museum-mounted skeleton, examine the skull and the *jaws*. (j) What difference can be seen in the structure of the upper and lower jaws? (k) On a living specimen, what holds the lower jaws together? (l) What structural adaptation of the jaw and gullet permits a snake to swallow prey four to five times larger than its throat? (m) Explain the orientation of the teeth on the jaws.

PART 2 / AN UNUSUAL ANIMAL — THE TURTLE

Procedure and Observations

Observe the shells of the painted turtle. (a) What body parts project from the shell? (b) How is this an adaptation for the turtle?

Examine the lower shell of *plastron* and the upper shell or *carapace*. (c) What differences may be seen? (d) Explain any adaptations that may be seen in the differences observed.

Examine a dried shell. (e) How does the covering of the *horny shields* correspond to the flat, expanded ribs beneath them? (f) What other skeletal feature fused to the dorsal side may be observed?

Examine the head of the turtle. (g) What structure has replaced the teeth normally found in other reptiles? (h) How is the location of the nostrils considered an adapta-

tion? (i) How many eyelids are present? (j) Do turtles have a nictitating membrane? (k) What reptilian characteristics may be observed in the legs and feet?

The pattern of the shields is the same on all members of a species. Thus, this pattern may be used to distinguish between species. On the carapace, locate the row of *marginal* shields extending around the edge of the shell and folding over the ribs. The single narrow shield lying just above the neck is the *precentral*. Above the base of the tail, locate the pair known as the *postcentrals*. Five large *central* shields lie in a row down the center of the carapace. To either side of these are four *lateral* shields. Draw and label the shields you have observed on a separate paper.

Observe how the plastron is joined to the carapace by a *bony bridge*. A seam running the length of the plastron divides the

SHIELDS

Dorsal and ventral views of the painted turtle.

shields into pairs. From anterior to posterior are the: *gular, humeral, pectoral, abdominal, femoral,* and *anal*. Draw and label the shields of the plastron on a separate piece of paper.

Summary

(a) It is believed that the turtle has been on earth longer than any of the present-day reptiles. Give several reasons why it has survived so well.

On a separate piece of paper, test what you have learned about snakes by completing the following sentences. The answers may be taken from the list. Some answers may not be used.

(b) The enlarged ventral scales of a snake are known as ___?___

(c) The tongue of a snake functions in the sense of ___?___

(d) The structure that holds the lower jaws together is the ___?___

(e) ___?___ are structures that adapt a poisonous snake for locating warm-blooded prey.

ANSWERS

fangs   taste
locomotion   elastic ligament
smell   poison glands
scutes   pits

37-1

How Are Birds Adapted for Varied Environments?

OBJECTIVES
- To examine modifications of beaks
- To observe adaptations of feet

MATERIALS

.MUSEUM MOUNTS OF THE FOLLOWING:
(THE DRAWINGS WILL SUFFICE IF
NONE ARE AVAILABLE)
HAWK, OWL, WOODPECKER, LOON,
QUAIL, WOODTHRUSH, PELICAN,
HUMMINGBIRD, HERON, DOVE, DUCK,
KINGFISHER

PART 1 / BEAK ADAPTATIONS OF COMMON BIRDS

Procedure and Observations

On a separate piece of paper, construct a 4-column chart of bird adaptations. In the first column, list the names of the birds being studied. In the second column, write the habitat of each bird. The third and fourth columns should be headed "beak for:" and "feet for:" respectively. You will complete this chart for each bird studied.

The habitat in which a bird lives supplies the animal with its food. For each of the birds pictured, as closely as possible determine the general habitat. List the probable habitat in your chart. Based on the habitat:

(a) What are some foods birds eat? (b) What organisms would most likely be eaten by birds living in water or marshy areas? (c) What might be the diet of birds seeking food on lawns? (d) Explain why birds of prey are often seen soaring over fields and scrubby areas. (e) Explain why dead or diseased trees serve as a food source for some species of birds.

The beaks of birds have been modified to secure a variety of foods from their habitat. Study the figures with habitat in mind. Determine which beak modification is exhibited by each bird and record it in your chart in the column headed "beak for:"

Some beak modifications:
— eat small seeds — *cracking*
— spearing fish — *stout and spear shaped*
— drilling for insects — *chisel shaped*
— to catch prey — *hooked*
— to suck nectar — *tubular*
— to scoop fish — *long and stout*
— multipurpose — *short*
— straining algae and small organisms — *flat and somewhat hooked*

Quail

Woodpecker

Owl

Thrush

Hummingbird

Hawk

Pelican

Loon

Heron

Dove

Duck

Kingfisher

PART 2 / FOOT ADAPTATIONS OF COMMON BIRDS

Procedure and Observations

Consider the modifications and adaptations of the feet of birds. It can be seen that the feet allow the species to inhabit a particular environment. Examine the specimens or pictures and determine which type of feet each bird has. Fill in the bird species below. Fill in the column "feet for:" in your chart. The numbers refer to the placement of the toes.

(a) 2 in front, 2 behind — climbing __?__

(b) 3 in front, 1 behind, long — wading __?__

(c) 3 in front, 1 behind, webbed — swimming __?__

(d) 3 in front, 1 behind, large with talons — catching prey __?__

(e) 3 in front, 1 behind — perching _____

(f) 3 in front, 1 behind — scratching __?__

(g) 3 in front, 1 behind — weak legs __?__

Summary

Review what you have learned about feet modifications by completing the sentences below. Fill in the blanks with the correct term or bird species.

(a) The __?__ and __?__ have three webbed toes.

(b) Enlarged claws on the toes of birds of prey are known as __?__.

(c) Small, weak legs are typical of __?__.

Review what you have learned about beak modifications by completing the sentence with the correct bird species. Write the complete sentence on your answer paper.

(d) A long, tubular beak is characteristic of: (1) Hawks, (2) Pelicans, (3) Hummingbirds, (4) Woodpeckers

(e) A beak adapted for spearing fish is seen in: (1) Pelicans, (2) Herons, (3) Ducks, (4) Doves

(f) Which of the following birds would have a multipurpose beak? (1) Kingfisher, (2) Thrush, (3) Woodpecker, (4) Quail

INVESTIGATIONS ON YOUR OWN

The characteristics observed in this Investigation can also be observed in a field study. Prepare a chart like the one used in this Investigation. You will also need bird identification guides, a field notebook, and binoculars.

Study the bird life of various habitats. An open field, a city street, woods, shorelines, and marshes are all inhabited by characteristic bird species. If possible, the study should run for many months. In this way, the birds of several seasons can be observed.

Once a bird has been identified, the habitat, beak modification, and foot modification should be determined. Fill in the chart for each species that you identify. Determine how each bird is adapted to its particular environment.

38-1

What Is the Anatomy of the Fetal Pig?

OBJECTIVES
- To dissect a fetal pig
- To identify the major organs of the fetal pig
- To understand characteristics of fetal life

MATERIALS

PRESERVED FETAL PIG
DISSECTING PAN OR TRAY
DISSECTING SCISSORS
SCALPEL
FORCEPS
PROBE
DISSECTING NEEDLES

PART 1 / EXAMINING EXTERNAL FEATURES OF THE FETAL PIG

Procedure and Observations

You will be examining several characteristics of an unborn mammal. The period of gestation for the pig is 112-115 days. (a) What is meant by gestation?

The age of the fetus can be estimated by measuring the body length from the tip of the snout to the attachment of the tail. Compare this length to the data given on relative sizes of a fetal pig at different times during gestation.

21 days —	11 mm
35 days —	17 mm
49 days —	28 mm
56 days —	40 mm
100 days —	220 mm
115 days —	300 mm

(b) What is the approximate age of your specimen?

Observe that the body is divided into a *head, neck, trunk,* and *tail.* The trunk itself may be divided into the *thoracic* (chest) and *abdominal* (stomach) regions. Examine the umbilical cord. Observe that it contains three blood vessels: a large vein and two smaller arteries. (c) What differences can be observed in the structure of an artery and a vein? (d) How does a fetus get rid of its waste products?

Examine the *ears*. With a probe locate the eardrum. The eyes have an upper and lower lid and a small mass of tissue in the upper corner known as the *nictitating membrane*. (e) What function does it have in the pig?

Examine the feet. (f) How many digits are present? The first digit of both the fore- and hind limb is absent and the second and fifth are reduced in size but remain functional.

Observe the paired row of *nipples* on the ventral surface of the abdomen in both sexes. The female *urogenital opening,* covered by a flap of tissue, is located just ventral to the *anus*. The male has two saclike swellings, the scrotal sacs, ventral to the anus. The male urogenital opening is just posterior to the umbilical cord.

Fetal pig ventral external view

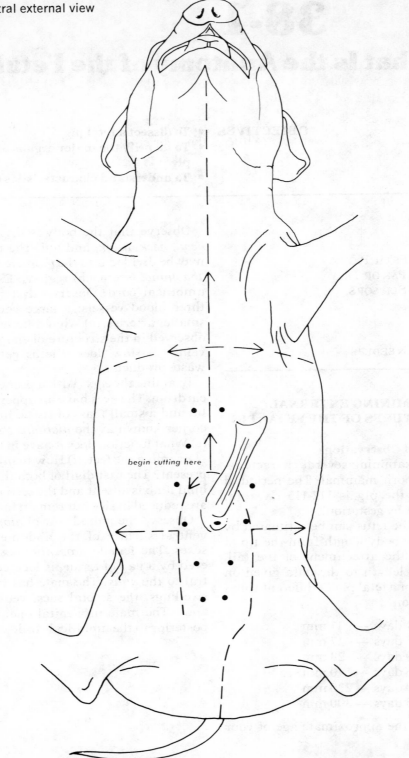

begin cutting here

PART 2 / INTERNAL ANATOMY — THE DIGESTIVE SYSTEM

In the dissection and observations of the internal organs, you will proceed by systems and *remove organs only when directed to do so*. Study and use the accompanying diagrams to aid in your observations of the internal organs. As you dissect, keep in mind the interrelationships of systems. While concentrating on a single system, use care not to damage other systems.

Procedure and Observations
Use two pieces of strong twine and tie one around a wrist and one around an ankle of the pig. Pull each under the dissecting pan and tightly tie the twine to the opposite wrist or ankle. To open the abdominal cavity, make incisions as indicated in the diagram. Cut carefully with scissors to avoid damaging the underlying organs. Pull the skin and muscle layers aside to expose the *peritoneum*, the lining of the abdominal cavity. Locate the umbilical vein. (a) To what organ does it lead?

Once determined, cut it and lay back the cord and its strip of skin. The large, brownish-red organ is the *liver*. (b) How many lobes (sections) does the liver have?

Lying beneath and to the right of the liver is the cream-white stomach. Locate where the *esophagus* joins the stomach and where the *small intestine* leaves. The first 3-4 cm of the small intestine is the *duodenum*. The remaining length is divided between the jejunum and the ileum. Observe that the small intestine is not loose in the abdominal cavity but is held in place by the *mesentery*. (c) Describe the mesentery. (d) Where is the mesentery attached?

The *large intestine* appears as a compact coil. Locate the junction of the small and large intestine. Below this junction may be found a large pouchlike structure, the *caecum*. (e) In humans, what structure is found at this junction?

The *rectum* lies in the peritoneum of the dorsal body wall. (f) What is the posterior opening of the digestive tract called?

Cut along the outer curvature of the stomach and observe the *rugae*. (g) How do these ridges within the stomach aid in mechanical digestion?

Where the stomach joins the small intestine, observe a sphincter muscle known as the *pyloric valve*. (h) What is its function?

Several organs of the abdominal cavity are associated with the process of digestion but are not a part of the digestive tract. Observe the liver more closely on its underside. (i) What saclike structure do you find? (j) Describe its appearance.

Observe the hepatic ducts leading from the liver. They connect to the cystic duct which extends to the *gall bladder*. These ducts join to become the *common bile duct*. (k) Where does the common bile duct lead?

The *pancreas* is a large white granular organ located below the stomach. The *pancreatic duct* is difficult to find in the fetal pig. It enters the duodenum posterior to the entrance of the bile duct. The red, elongated organ extending around the outer curvature of the stomach is the *spleen*. (l) Of what system is the spleen functionally a part?

Remove the organs of the digestive system that you have observed. Using your textbook, determine the function(s) each organ has in the process of digestion. On a separate piece of paper, list the organs and their functions.

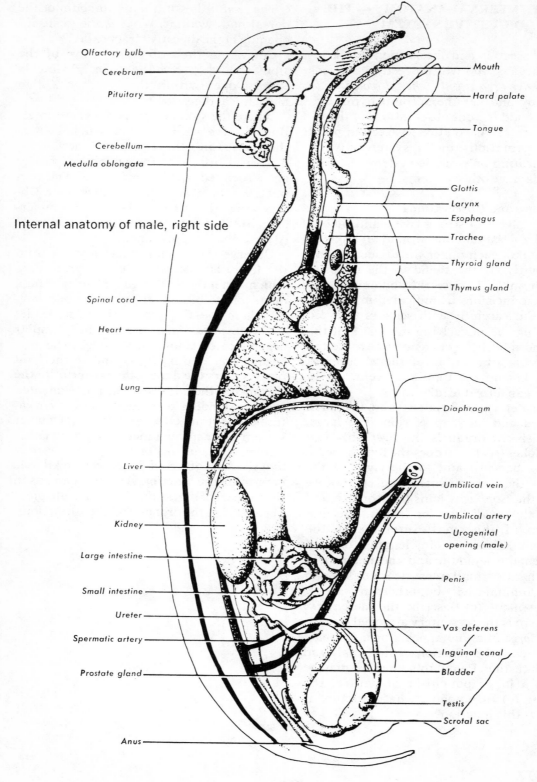

Olfactory bulb

Cerebrum

Pituitary

Cerebellum

Medulla oblongata

Internal anatomy of male, right side

Spinal cord

Heart

Lung

Liver

Kidney

Large intestine

Small intestine

Ureter

Spermatic artery

Prostate gland

Anus

Mouth

Hard palate

Tongue

Glottis

Larynx

Esophagus

Trachea

Thyroid gland

Thymus gland

Diaphragm

Umbilical vein

Umbilical artery

Urogenital opening (male)

Penis

Vas deferens

Inguinal canal

Bladder

Testis

Scrotal sac

PART 3 / ORGANS OF THE THORACIC CAVITY

Procedure and Observations

Fully expose the organs of the thoracic cavity by carefully cutting the flaps of tissue formed by your initial incision. (a) What essential organs are contained in this cavity? (b) What structure separates the thoracic cavity from the abdominal cavity? (c) Does the diaphragm function in the fetus? Explain your answer.

Locate the large blood vessel, the *posterior vena cava*, which passes through the liver and into the heart. Carefully clip the edges of the diaphragm and separate it from the body wall. Be careful not to damage the posterior vena cava. Allow the diaphragm to drop down over the liver.

Observe that the *heart* lies in a thin sac, the *pericardium*, and is partially covered by the *thymus gland*. (d) What is the function of the thymus gland?

DO NOT REMOVE THE HEART AT THIS TIME!

Locate the spongy *lungs* on either side of the heart. (e) Why do they appear collapsed?

The trachea in the neck region is easily identified by its cartilaginous rings. (f) Suggest a reason for the trachea being so constructed.

With forceps, carefully pick away some of the connective tissue holding the heart and lungs in place. Just above the lungs, observe where the trachea divides to form an inverted Y. Below the trachea in the neck and posterior to where the trachea divides to enter the lungs is the gullet or esophagus. (g) Describe the appearance of the *esophagus*.

On either side of the trachea and close to it may be seen the *carotid arteries* leading to the head and a white cordlike structure, the *vagus nerve*.

The Neck and Mouth

Continue the dissection into the neck following the trachea. Note that the thymus gland extends far into the neck. Also in the neck are the *lymph glands*. Probe between the lobes of the lymph glands and locate the reddish, bi-lobed *thyroid gland* lying over the trachea. The enlargement at the anterior end of the trachea is the *larynx* or voice box which contains the vocal cords. Leave the lungs and other organs in place.

Examine the mouth cavity containing the tongue and teeth. Notice the upper *hard* and *soft palate* forming the roof of the mouth. (h) How are these indirectly used in digestion?

To the posterior of the mouth is the *pharynx*, a common passage for food going to the esophagus and air going to the lungs. To demonstrate the latter, run a needle probe through a nostril. (i) Where does the needle appear?

Locate the epiglottis, a flaplike structure at the top of the larynx. (j) What is the function of the epiglottis?

Using your textbook, determine the function of the following organs you have observed in the thoracic, neck, and head regions. On your data sheet, list the organs and write the system and function for each.

PART 4 / CIRCULATORY SYSTEM

Procedure and Observations

The Heart

Remove the *pericardium* from the heart and observe the *ventricles*. (a) Which is larger, the right or left ventricle?

Locate the *right* and *left atria*. (b) Can any difference be noted between the right and left atria?

With your finger, touch the atria and ventricles. (c) What difference exists between these two chambers?

Locate the *anterior* and *posterior vena cava*. These carry blood from the anterior and posterior portions of the body, respectively. (d) Into what chamber of the heart do they open?

Find the *pulmonary veins* which carry blood from the lungs to the left atrium. The most noticeable artery is the *aorta*. (e) From what chamber does it arise?

The aorta curves to the left and passes posteriorly along the dorsal side of the thoracic and abdominal wall as the *dorsal aorta*. The next largest artery is the *pulmonary artery*. It arises from the anterior portion of the right ventricle and soon divides to form the *right* and *left pulmonary arteries*. (f) To what structure do the pulmonary arteries lead?

A characteristic feature of the fetal mammalian heart is the *ductus arteriosus*. This short vessel allows blood to bypass pulmonary circulation until birth, at which time there is a complete closure of the vessel. (g) Why does this occur?

To study the heart in further detail, it must be removed. Removal is accomplished by severing blood vessels which connect to it. Begin with the posterior ves-

sels and progress anteriorly. In the following order, locate and cut: the *posterior vena cava*, the *pulmonary veins*, the *anterior vena cava*, the *aorta*, and the *pulmonary arteries*. On the surface of the heart are the *coronary arteries* and *veins*. (h) What is the importance of the coronary circulation? (i) What results when coronary circulation is prevented?

Before opening the heart, be sure you are able to recognize all parts associated with its external structure.

To open the heart, make a slit along the midline of its ventral side. (This is the side you normally observe.) Identify the four chambers. Use your textbook to identify the internal features which you are able to observe. Locate the entrance and exit of the veins and arteries connected to the heart as well as the valves which prevent backflow into the heart chambers. (j) In longitudinal section how do the walls of the atria and ventricles differ?

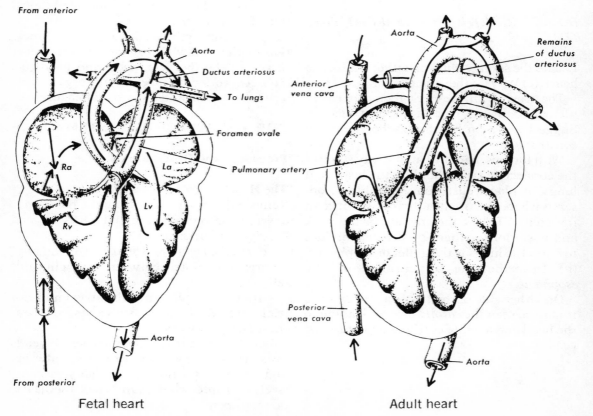

Fetal heart

Adult heart

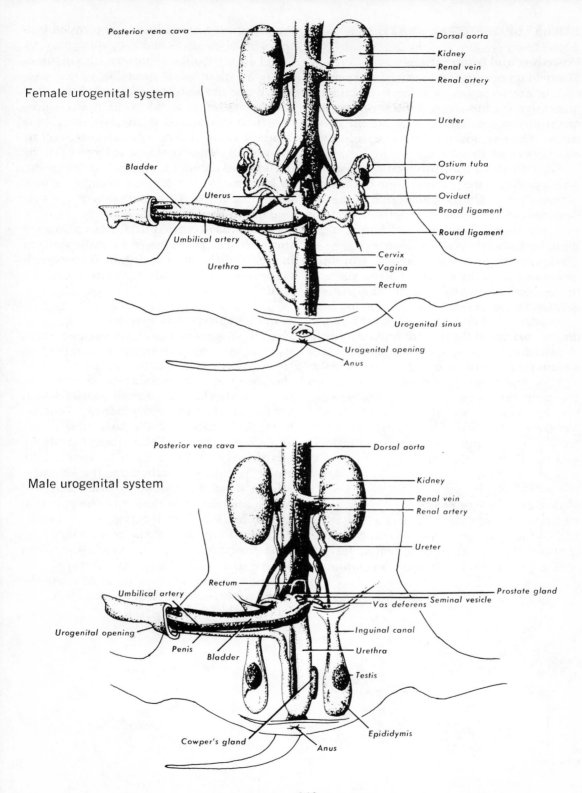

Female urogenital system

Posterior vena cava
Dorsal aorta
Kidney
Renal vein
Renal artery
Ureter
Ostium tuba
Ovary
Oviduct
Broad ligament
Round ligament
Bladder
Uterus
Umbilical artery
Cervix
Urethra
Vagina
Rectum
Urogenital sinus
Urogenital opening
Anus

Male urogenital system

Posterior vena cava
Dorsal aorta
Kidney
Renal vein
Renal artery
Ureter
Rectum
Prostate gland
Vas deferens
Seminal vesicle
Umbilical artery
Inguinal canal
Urogenital opening
Urethra
Penis
Bladder
Testis
Cowper's gland
Epididymis
Anus

PART 5 / UROGENITAL SYSTEM

Procedure and Observations

The urinary or excretory system and genital system are structurally related. Therefore, it is convenient to study them together. Recall that you are dealing with paired structures. What is observed on one side may also be seen on the other.

Using forceps, carefully remove any fat which prevents easy observation of the urogenital organs. On the dorsal side of the abdominal cavity, outside the peritoneum, are the prominent bean-shaped *kidneys*. (a) What is the function of the kidneys?

Locate the *ureter* originating from the concave side of the kidney. Follow the ureter posteriorly until it joins the *urinary bladder*. Do not remove any of these organs.

Prepare for the observation of the reproductive organs of the male or female by pulling the hind legs apart. With scissors, cut anteriorly a little to one side of the midventral line to avoid cutting the penis on the male. Press firmly on the tissue between the legs to feel the cartilaginous structure of the *pubic symphysis*. This is part of the pelvic girdle. Continue the incision anteriorly and cut through the pubic symphysis. Expose the *urethra*.

Male Reproductive System

Examine the scrotal sacs at the posterior end of the male pig. Open one sac and determine the presence of a testis. If your specimen is advanced in fetal development, the testes may have already descended into the scrotal sacs. Otherwise, they may be found in a tubelike structure, the *inguinal canal*, as small oval organs. In either case, locate one of the testes and note the coiled tubule making up the *epididymis*. Follow this tube forward as it passes through the *inguinal canal* as the *vas deferens*. Follow the vas deferens. Note how it loops over the ureters and enters the *urethra*. At this point, as in humans, the urethra becomes a urogenital duct. (b) What substances are carried in this duct?

Follow the urethra until it passes through the *penis*. The penis lies in a sheath of tissue in the ventral abdominal wall. The urogenital opening is just posterior to the umbilical cord.

Female Reproductive System

Exchange specimens to have the opportunity of examining both sexes. Spread the legs to separate the pubic symphysis and thereby expose the female reproductive system. Locate the oval-shaped *ovaries* which are found posterior to the kidneys. Leading from the ovaries are the twisted *oviducts* or *Fallopian tubes*. The oviducts continue posteriorly and are soon supported by *broad ligaments*. Further on, the oviducts join to form the *common uterus*. You will notice a slight constriction of the common uterus marking the location of the *cervix*. Posterior to the cervix, the remainder of the tube forms the *vagina*. Locate the point where the urethra joins to form the *common-urogenital sinus*. (c) In which of the previous structures would embryonic or fetal pigs be found?

Procedure and Observations

The Brain

This dissection is difficult, tedious work and requires proceeding carefully to avoid destroying important brain tissues. Position the animal so that the dorsal side is up. Remove the skin from the entire skull. To expose the brain, cut through the skull near the center. USE EXTREME CARE NOT TO INJURE THE BRAIN MEMBRANES. After the skull is opened, use forceps to break and peel away the pieces. This reveals the tough, outer membrane, the *dura mater*. Use scissors to cut this membrane and expose the brain tissue. When the brain is completely exposed down to the spinal cord, you should be able to see the two large cerebral hemispheres. Anterior to these, locate the *olfactory lobes*, which function in the sense of smell. Posterior to the cerebral hemispheres is the many folded *cerebellum*. Further posterior and below, locate the *medulla oblongata*, the enlarged anterior portion of the spinal cord.

40-1

What Happens During Muscular Activity?

OBJECTIVES
- To see that skeletal muscles work in pairs
- To understand that many systems are involved during muscular contraction
- To measure some changes that take place during muscular activity

MATERIALS

CHARTS OF MUSCLES
CLOCK OR WATCH WITH A SECOND HAND

PART 1 / MAKING BASIC OBSERVATIONS AND MEASUREMENTS

Procedure and Observations

While sitting quietly, rest your right arm on your desk with the palm of your hand up. Place your left hand lightly around your right arm as shown in the figure. Make a fist and tightly bend (flex) your right arm.

(a) Explain the changes you feel taking place in the right arm.

Now, fully straighten (extend) your right arm.

(b) Describe the changes you feel.

(c) What observations show that skeletal muscles work in pairs?

(d) With the aid of charts or your test, identify the *flexor muscle* involved in this activity.

(e) Name the *extensor muscle*. (f) Where are these muscles attached? (g) At what joint does movement take place?

(h) What must occur in the cells of the biceps when the arm is flexed? (i) What must occur in the cells of the triceps when the arm is flexed?

All body cells require energy to do their work. ATP is the energy of these active muscle cells. (j) How does the ATP get to the muscle cells?

		Immediately	2 min.	4 min.	6 min.	8 min.
SITTING POSITION	pulse rate					
	respiration rate					
WALKING	pulse rate					
	respiration rate					
RUNNING	pulse rate					
	respiration rate					

Construct a data table like the one shown above. Record your data for Parts 1 and 2 in your table. DO NOT WRITE IN THIS BOOK.

The speed at which nutrients are reaching muscles is indicated by the rate of the heartbeat. You can easily measure this by taking your pulse. Hold your fingers of one hand on the wrist of the other, as in the figure.

Count the pulse for 30 seconds. (k) What is your pulse rate per minute?

Record this "sitting position" measurement in your table.

The rate of the heartbeat also indicates the speed at which oxygen is being carried to the muscles. (l) But what other system is involved?

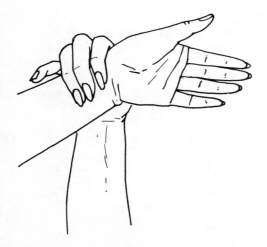

The rate of breathing is another measurement which indicates oxygen requirements of muscles. Have your laboratory partner measure your respiration rate for 1 minute. (This is done by counting the rise and fall of the chest.) (m) What is your respiration rate?

Record the "sitting position" respiration rate in your table.

PART 2 / SOME EFFECTS OF CHANGING MUSCULAR ACTIVITY

Procedure and Observations

Now, stand up and walk in place for 1 minute. In your table, record your respiration rate and your pulse rate immediately. Wait 2 minutes and record these measurements again. If necessary, repeat the measurements until the rates are back to your "sitting position" rate.

Stand up again and run in place vigorously for exactly 1 minute. Sit down and immediately make the pulse and respiration rate measurements. Repeat these measurements each 2 minutes until the "sitting position" rates are reached. Record your data.

(a) When taking your pulse after running in place, did you observe anything about the *strength*? Explain.

(b) How long did it take to "recover" from walking in place?

(c) How long did it take to "recover" from running in place?

(d) Give reasons to explain why your answers to *b* and *c* are different.

Summary

(a) Explain the statement: "Skeletal muscles that move joints work in opposite pairs."

(b) In this Investigation, why was it necessary to make the "sitting" measurements at first?

(c) Explain why your "sitting" measurements may not have been accurate resting measurements.

(d) How does this study of muscular activity indicate the coordination of several systems in your body?

Test what you have learned by completing the following sentences. Write the complete sentences on a separate piece of paper. You may select answers from the words in the list.

ANSWERS

ATP	voluntary
bends	oxygen
biceps	straightens
carbon dioxide	triceps

(e) An extensor muscle ___?___ a joint.

(f) A flexor muscle ___?___ a joint.

(g) Skeletal muscles are under our control and are said to be ___?___.

(h, i) Increasing our muscular activity will also increase the muscle's need for ___?___ and ___?___.

(j) In times of increased muscular activity, coordinated activities of the respiratory and circulatory systems serve to bring in additional nutrients. They also serve to speed up the removal of cellular wastes, including ___?___.

(k) The contraction of the ___?___ causes the elbow to bend.

(l) The contraction of the ___?___ straightens the arm at the elbow joint.

INVESTIGATIONS ON YOUR OWN

1. Many physical fitness tests include measurements like those you have made in this Investigation. Using your library, locate two or three physical fitness tests. Your physical education teacher may also have one. Compare these tests and explain how the measurements they require indicate "fitness."

2. Explain how regular exercise over a period of time might change the results you obtained in this Investigation. Can you devise an experiment which might prove your hypothesis?

41-1
How Does Starch Digestion Occur?

OBJECTIVES
- To observe activity of a digestive enzyme
- To determine why starches must be chemically changed before they can be absorbed

MATERIALS

COOKED STARCH SOLUTION (PARTS 1, 2)

PARAFFIN } (A 0.1% DIASTASE SOLUTION OR A PANCREATIN
CHEESECLOTH } SOLUTION CAN BE USED IN PLACE OF SALIVA.)

25-ML BEAKER
TEST TUBES
GLASS-MARKING PENCIL
GLASS MICROSCOPE SLIDE
IODINE SOLUTION (PARTS 1, 2)
BOILING WATER BATH
WARM WATER BATH (37° C) (PARTS 1, 2)
BENEDICT'S SOLUTION (PARTS 1, 2)
SAUSAGE SKIN OR CELLULOSE DIALYSIS TUBING (3-6 CM IN DIAMETER AND 30 CM LONG) (PART 2)
5% GLUCOSE SOLUTION (PART 2)
200-ML BEAKERS (PART 2)
SHORT PIECE OF DOWEL OR GLASS ROD (PART 2)
250-ML BEAKERS (PART 2)

PART 1 / SALIVARY DIGESTION

Saliva contains the enzyme *salivary amylase*, sometimes called *pytalin*. This enzyme acts on starches, converting them to *maltose* and *glucose*.

Procedure and Observations

Rinse out your mouth with water. Chew a piece of paraffin to stimulate the flow of saliva. Collect about 15 ml of saliva in a 25 ml beaker (covered with several layers of cheesecloth to serve as a filter). With a glass-marking pencil, divide a microscope slide into 2 sections. Place a drop of saliva in one section and a drop of cooked starch solution in the other section.

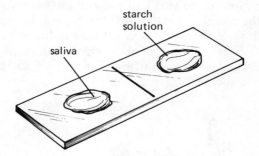

Test each with a drop of iodine solution.
(a) What do your results indicate?
Number 3 test tubes.

Into tube *1*, put 3 ml saliva.
Into tube *2*, put 3 ml cooked starch solution.
Into tube *3*, put 3 ml saliva and 3 ml cooked starch solution.

Place all 3 test tubes in a warm water bath for 5 minutes. Now add 3 ml Benedict's solution to each test tube and put them in the boiling water bath. Observe any color changes that occur, remembering that a yellow, green, or red color indicates the presence of a simple sugar, such as glucose. (b) Explain your results.

PART 2 / MUST STARCH BE DIGESTED BEFORE ABSORPTION?

Procedure and Observations

Soften the dialysis tubing by soaking it in a beaker of water for half an hour. Measure 100 ml of water into each of 3 beakers and set them in a warm water bath. Tie the ends of 3 dialysis tubings with string, and put 10 ml of 5% glucose solution in the first; 10 ml cooked starch solution in the second; and 5 ml saliva plus 5 ml cooked starch solution in the third.

Fasten the ends of the loops together and suspend each loop from the wood dowel or the glass rod on each beaker. Be sure the loop is immersed in the water, as in the diagram. After 20 minutes, test 5 ml of the water in each beaker for the presence of starch and 5 ml of water for the presence of simple sugar. (a) Did glucose pass through the membrane? (b) Did starch pass through the membrane? (c) What was indicated by the tests in the beaker where saliva plus cooked starch solution was placed in the membrane?

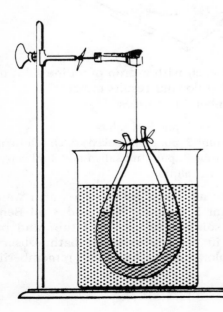

Summary

(a) What chemical changes occur when starchy foods are chewed?
(b) From your investigations on the digestion of starches, what conclusions can you make about the size of molecules that pass through membranes?
(c) Test what you have learned by writing the completed sentences on a separate sheet of paper.
1. Starch is a molecule which can be broken down by enzymes to form ___?___.
2. The large starch molecule cannot pass through ___?___.
3. Simple sugar molecules are small enough to pass through ___?___.
4. Digestion involves ___?___ large molecules.
5. Glucose is a ___?___ molecule than is a cooked starch molecule.
6. ___?___ is a solution used for testing for the presence of simple sugars.
7. ___?___ ° C was used for some of these investigations because it is the temperature of the body.
8. Saliva contains the enzyme ___?___.

INVESTIGATIONS ON YOUR OWN

1. Gastric digestion involves the enzyme pepsin and chemically changes proteins. The gastric glands also manufacture hydrochloric acid. Make a solution of artificial gastric fluid by mixing 2 g of commercial pepsin in 0.4% hydrochloric acid to make 100 ml of the fluid. Filter this and test with litmus paper. Number 6 test tubes and put them in a rack. Put a few pieces of cracker in tube *1*, a small piece of hard-cooked egg white in tube *2*, and a small piece of butter in tube *3*. Fill each tube one third full with the artificial gastric fluid that you have made. In tubes *4*, *5*, and *6*, put a piece of the same foods, but fill each tube one third full of water.

Allow the 6 test tubes to stand overnight in a warm place. Check the cloudiness of each solution and explain your results.

2. Pancreatic fluid, secreted by the pancreas into the small intestine, contains several enzymes essential to digestion. Prepare a solution of artificial pancreatic fluid by mixing 2 g of commercial pancreatin and distilled water to make 100 ml of the fluid. Add a pinch of sodium carbonate. Stir and filter to get a clear liquid. Test the solution with litmus paper. Number 3 test tubes and put them in a rack. Put a few pieces of cracker in test tube *1*, a small piece of hard-cooked egg white in test tube *2*, and a small amount of butter in test tube *3*. Fill each tube one third full with artificial pancreatic fluid. Allow these test tubes to stand in a warm place overnight. Then check the degree of digestion by noting the extent to which each of the foods has been dissolved. Explain your results.

3. Select several foods (such as lemon juice, orange juice, grapefruit juice, apples, milk, potatoes, bread, crackers, gelatin, hamburger), and test each one for simple sugars, starches, fats, and protein. Make a chart of your results, using a + to indicate a positive test and a − to indicate a negative test.

42-1

What Is Blood?

OBJECTIVES
- **To describe the cellular components of blood**
- **To observe blood circulating within a living system**

MATERIALS

PREPARED SLIDE OF BLOOD SMEARS
IF OWN SLIDES ARE TO BE PREPARED:
    STERILE LANCETS
    STERILE COTTON
    ALCOHOL
    MICROSCOPE SLIDES (PARTS 1, 2)
    COVER GLASSES
    WRIGHT'S BLOOD STAIN
LIVE GOLDFISH (PART 2)
PAPER TOWELING (PART 2)
PETRI DISH (PART 2)
MEDICINE DROPPER (PART 2)

PART 1 / LOOKING AT BLOOD CELLS

Procedure and Observations

Carefully read all of Part 1 before starting your work.

If you are not provided with prepared slides of blood smears, then use the following procedure to prepare your own:

Clean the tip of your middle finger with a swab of alcohol. Using a sterile lancet, pierce the skin near the tip to obtain a large drop of blood. CAUTION: *Do not use the same lancet more than one time.* If blood does not flow at once, stroke the finger toward the tip, pressing as you stroke.

Put a drop of blood on the slide. Use the edge of another slide to spread the blood into a thin smear. Allow the smear to dry for a few minutes. When the smear is dry, pass it quickly through a flame 3 times.

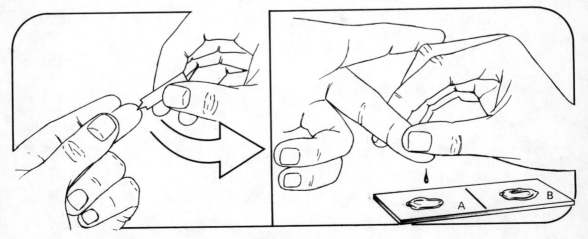

This will warm the slide and fix the blood cells in place. Add a few drops of Wright's stain to the smear. After 2 or 3 minutes, rinse the stain from the slide with water. Dry the slide. It is now ready to be studied under the microscope.

(START AT THIS POINT WITH A PRE-PARED SLIDE.)

Examine a stained human blood smear on high power of your microscope. Select an area near the end of the smear where the cells are separated and can be seen clearly. (a) What color are the red blood cells? (b) Why do they appear a lighter color near the center?

The color of stained blood cells is different from unstained red blood cells. (c) What pigment is in living red blood cells? (d) What is its function?

Locate and examine several cells that you recognize as being quite different from the red blood cells. (e) What are these? (f) Compare their size to a red blood cell. (g) What is another obvious difference? (h) What is the function of the white blood cells? (i) From studying your slide, what can you say about the number of white blood cells compared to the number of red blood cells?

Look closely at spaces between the red and white blood cells for clumps of tiny cells. These are the platelets. (j) What is their function?

Draw the different types of blood cells you see under high power of your microscope.

PART 2 / HOW BLOOD CIRCULATES

Procedure and Observations

Saturate paper toweling or cotton with water. Gently, lay a goldfish on a glass slide. Wrap the wet toweling around the middle of the fish and the slide. Leave the head of the fish and the tail fin uncovered. Place the wrapped fish in a Petri dish. Spread the tail fin and place a slide over it to hold it down. Use a dropper to keep the fish's skin moist during the Investigation. (a) Why is this important?

Place the Petri dish on your microscope stage. You may have to remove the stage clips to do this. Under low power, focus on the tail membrane. Observe the blood vessels in the tail. (b) Describe what you see. (c) Does all of the blood flow in the same direction with the same vessel? (d) within different vessels?

Observe the blood vessels under high power. Locate a blood vessel in which the cells are moving in single file. This is a capillary. (e) What is the function of the capillaries? (f) How do capillaries differ from other blood vessels?

Summary

(a) What major differences have you observed between the red blood cell, white blood cell, and platelets?

(b) Why could you easily see the white blood cells in the prepared slide, but not in unstained slides?

Test yourself by matching the words at the right with the statements. You may use a word more than once.

(c) blood cells containing nuclei
(d) disc-shaped blood cells containing hemoglobin
(e) very small blood cells
(f) function in clotting
(g) ingest bacteria and foreign matter
(h) function in respiration
(i) blood vessel

1. capillaries
2. platelets
3. red blood cells
4. white blood cells

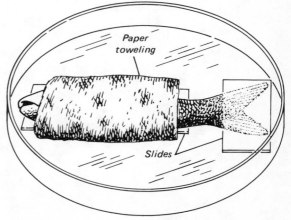

Paper toweling

Slides

173

INVESTIGATIONS ON YOUR OWN

1. You may examine red blood cells in various saline solutions to determine the salt concentration within the cells. In doing this, you may also observe what may happen to cells if there is a salt imbalance in the plasma. Try observing blood cells in the following solutions: 0.3%, 0.85%, and 1.5%.

2. You may also study temperature effects on the blood vessels by packing the fish's tail with crushed ice. Observe the blood flow. After removing the ice, allow the membrane to reach room temperature and then add warm water (about 40°C). Record your observations and write up your investigation.

42-2

How Are Blood Types Determined?

OBJECTIVES
- **To learn the technique for blood typing**
- **To understand why agglutination occurs**
- **To understand the basis for blood typing**

MATERIALS

HUMAN WHOLE BLOOD (YOUR OWN, A
    DONOR'S, OR BLOOD BANK)
STERILE LANCETS
STERILE COTTON
ALCOHOL
TOOTHPICKS
BLOOD TYPING SERA:
    ANTI-A
    ANTI-B
WAX MARKING PENCIL
MICROSCOPE SLIDE

PART 1 / DETERMINING YOUR BLOOD TYPE

Procedure and Observations

anti-A	anti-B

Use a wax pencil to divide a microscope slide in half. Label the left side "anti-A" and the right side "anti-B," as in the figure.

Put 1 drop of anti-A typing serum on the left side of your slide. Put 1 drop of anti-B typing serum on the right side of your slide.

If you are to use your own blood, review the technique for obtaining a drop of blood from your finger. Clean the tip of your middle finger with a swab of alcohol. Using a

sterile lancet, pierce the skin at the tip of the finger. If blood does not flow at once, stroke the finger toward the tip, pressing as you stroke. (**REMEMBER:** *Do not use the same lancet for more than one student or more than once.*) Put 1 drop of blood, from your finger (*or provided by your teacher*), on each side of the glass slide near the drop of typing serum. Do not dip your finger into the typing serum. Work quickly so the blood will not clot on the slide.

Use a toothpick to mix 1 drop of blood with the anti-A typing serum. *Use a different toothpick for mixing the other drop of blood with the anti-B typing serum.* After 1 minute, examine each side for clumping of cells, called *agglutination*. Clumping will appear as cells cluster together. Unclumped blood will keep a smooth, even appearance. (a) What were your results on the anti-A side? (b) What were your results on the anti-B side?

Compare your results with the possibilities in the figure on the next page. (c) What is your blood type?

If:	Anti-A	Anti B	Blood type
Agglutination in anti-A only			A
Agglutination in anti-B only			B
Agglutination in both			AB
No agglutination			O

PART 2 / WHY DOES AGGLUTINATION OCCUR?

Procedure and Observations

Read the following paragraph carefully and compare the statements to the results in the above figure.

Blood types are inherited. Agglutination comes about because of a reaction between a protein in the serum and a protein in the red blood cell. The protein in the red blood cell is called an *agglutinogen*. It is either A or B. Red blood cells of a person with type A blood contain A agglutinogen. Those of a person with type B blood contain B agglutinogen. Red blood cells from AB blood contain both A and B agglutinogen. The red blood cells from type O blood do not contain either of these agglutinogens.

The protein in serum is called an *agglutinin*. Agglutinins have been given names to indicate the types of red blood cell protein which they cause to clump. A person with type A blood, containing A red blood cell protein, would have anti-B serum protein. This anti-B serum, then, would cause a clumping of red blood cells which con-

tained the B protein. (a) With which blood types would the anti-B serum cause clumping?

You may check your answer by looking at the figure in Part 1. A person with type B blood, containing B red blood cell protein, would have anti-A serum protein. (b) With which blood types would the anti-A serum cause clumping?

Type AB blood has neither serum protein present. (c) What would happen if either anti-A or anti-B serum protein were present? Check your answer by looking at the figure in Part 1.

Type O blood has both anti-A and anti-B serum proteins present. (d) What would be the result in blood typing if anti-A typing serum were added to type O blood? (e) What would be the result in blood typing if anti-B were added to O blood? Check your answers in the figure in Part 1.

(f) What was your blood type? (g) Do you have any agglutinogens in your red blood cells? Explain your answer. (h) Do you have any agglutinins in your serum? Explain your answer.

(i) From where, do you think, the anti-A typing serum is obtained? (j) From where, do you think, the anti-B typing serum is obtained?

Blood Type	Agglutinogen Present on Red Blood Cell	Agglutinin Present in Serum
A		
B		
AB		
O		

Summary

(a) People with type O blood are said to be "universal donors." Explain.

(b) People with type AB blood are said to be "universal recipients." Explain.

(c) Construct and complete a chart like the one shown above. Do all of your work on a separate piece of paper. DO NOT WRITE IN THIS BOOK.

Test what you have learned by copying each statement given below and then indicating which blood type it describes.

(d) anti-A and anti-B serum protein present

(e) A agglutinogen in red blood cells

(f) no agglutinogen in red blood cells

(g) cells agglutinate in anti-A typing serum

(h) cells agglutinate in anti-B and anti-A typing sera

(i) no agglutination of cells in either anti-A or anti-B typing sera

(j) cells agglutinate in anti-B typing serum

(k) A and B agglutinogen in red blood cells

(l) anti-B serum protein present

(m) B agglutinogen in red blood cells

INVESTIGATIONS ON YOUR OWN

1. Make a large chart showing how the various blood types are inherited.

2. Make a study of the factors involved in the clotting time of blood. Prepare and give a demonstration to the class on the procedure of measuring clotting time. Explain factors which can cause changes in the clotting time.

177

43-1

How Can Respiration Rate Be Measured?

OBJECTIVES
- **To measure lung air capacity**
- **To determine relative amounts of CO_2 in exhaled air**
- **To compare CO_2 production at rest and after activity**

MATERIALS

TEXTBOOK
WATCH OR CLOCK WITH SECOND HAND
PHENOLPHTHALEIN SOLUTION (PART 2)
125-ML ERLENMEYER FLASK (PART 2)
DROPPER (PART 2)
6-MM DIAMETER STRAWS (PART 2)
0.04% NaOH SOLUTION IN A LABELED DROPPING BOTTLE (PART 2)
0.4% NaOH SOLUTION IN A LABELED DROPPING BOTTLE (PART 2)

PART 1 / AIR MOVEMENT AND LUNG CAPACITY

Procedure and Observations

Using your textbook, review the structures through which air passes during breathing. While sitting quietly, have your laboratory partner measure your respiration rate for one minute. (a) How many times do you inhale in one minute? (b) What happens during inspiration? (c) What happens during expiration?

The air moving in with each *inspiration* and out with each *expiration* is called *tidal air*. Observe your own breathing. At the end of normal inspiration, attempt to continue taking in air instead of expiring. (d) Describe the results. (e) Did it appear that you could take in more air than you did during normal inspiration?

The volume of air which can be inhaled above a normal inspiration is called *complemental air*.

Now, breathe normally again. (f) After a normal expiration, can you force more air out of your lungs instead of beginning inspiration? This is called *reserve air*. (g) Which volume appears to be the greater: complemental air, or reserve air?

Vital capacity is the sum of tidal, complemental, and reserve air. Some air remains in your lungs and cannot be forced out under normal conditions. This is called *residual air*.

The table here shows the *average* volumes of lung capacity.

LUNG CAPACITY	
tidal air	0.5 L
complemental air	2.5 L
reserve air	1.5 L
vital capacity	4.5 L

(h) What individual differences might account for *normal volumes* differing from the averages given in the table?

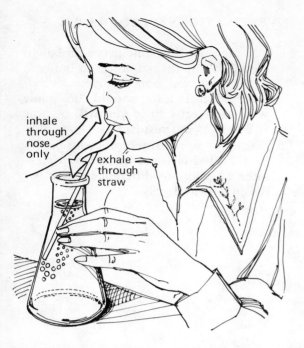

inhale through nose only

exhale through straw

PART 2 / DO WE CHANGE OUR RATE OF CO₂ PRODUCTION?

Procedures and Observations

Put 100 ml of water in the flask and add 5 drops of phenolphthalein. Add 0.04% NaOH solution drop by drop until a faint pink color remains in the solution in the flask. Put a straw into the flask and breathe *in* through your nose and *out* through the straw. Be careful to avoid sucking any solution into your mouth. The exhaled breath will bubble up through the solution.

Continue this procedure (with your normal breathing rate) for 1 minute. (a) What change do you observe in the flask?

CAUTION: NaOH can cause a burn. *Always place the dropper back in the bottle.* Now, remove the straw and add 0.4% NaOH one drop at a time. Swirl the contents of the flask after each drop. Stop when the solution remains pink for 1 minute. (b) How many drops of 0.4% NaOH did you use?

Record this as your "resting" measurement. This test not only indicates the presence of CO_2; it indicates the amount. The more drops of 0.4% NaOH required, the more CO_2 is present.

Rinse out the flask and prepare it for another test. Use the preparation described in the first paragraph. Run in place for 1 minute. Now, using a straw again, exhale into the flask for 1 minute. While you are doing this, have your laboratory partner count your respiration rate. (c) Record this rate.

Next add the 0.4% NaOH solution until the flask remains faintly pink for one minute. (d) How many drops were required?

Record this as your "running" measurement.

(e) Compare your resting respiration rate of Part 1 to the respiration rate after exercise. (f) What does the change in respiration rate indicate about the *volume* of air exchanged per minute before and after exercise?

On your data sheet, construct a chart like the one below. Determine the class average for both the "resting" measurement and the "running" measurement. Fill in your chart with the data. DO NOT WRITE IN THIS BOOK.

(g) How does your measurement compare to the average measurement for the class?

(h) What reasons can you give for any differences between your CO_2 production after exercise and the average for the class?

Number of Drops of 0.4% NaOH Needed to Neutralize		
Activity	Your Measurement	Average Measurement for the Class
Resting		
Running		

Summary

(a) What is vital capacity? Differentiate between tidal air, complemental air, and reserve air.

(b) What is the relationship between CO_2 production and respiration rate?

(c) Is the relationship of question *b* of adaptive value? Explain.

Test what you have learned by filling in the blanks of the sentences below with answers from the list. You may use an answer more than once. Some answers may not be required. Write the completed sentences on your answer sheet.

ANSWERS

alveoli	NaOH
bronchii	oxygen
capillary	red
clear	trachea
CO_2	yellow

(d) The ___?___ divides into two bronchii.

(e) In the lungs, gases are exchanged between the capillaries and the air in the ___?___ .

(f, g) The lungs function to carry ___?___ containing air to a moist membrane through which the ___?___ enters the blood.

(h) During exercise, more ___?___ passes into the lungs and is exhaled.

(i) ___?___ can be used as a test to detect the presence of carbon dioxide in exhaled air.

(j) In the presence of NaOH, phenolphthalein is a ___?___ color.

INVESTIGATIONS ON YOUR OWN

1. You may use the same procedure as in Part 2 of this Investigation to indicate CO_2 production under various activities. Several tests should be made with each activity so you will be able to average your results.

2. You may use the same procedure as in Part 2 of this Investigation to determine whether any differences occur between boys and girls.

44-1

Can We Test Taste, Smell, and Touch?

OBJECTIVES
- To determine the location of taste receptors
- To understand the role of smell receptors
- To determine the distance between touch receptors on various parts of the body

MATERIALS

10% SUGAR SOLUTION
10% VINEGAR SOLUTION
3% SALT (NaCl) SOLUTION
0.001% QUININE SULFATE SOLUTION
COTTON SWABS
VANILLA EXTRACT
APPLE
ONION
SINGLE-EDGED RAZOR BLADE (PART 2)
CORKS (PART 2)
PINS (PART 2)
METRIC RULER (PART 2)

PART 1 / IS TASTE SENSED ONLY BY THE TONGUE?

Procedures and Observations

In this Part, you will use various stimuli. (a) What is a stimulus? (b) What is a receptor? (c) What is a response?

Now, let's see if these can be measured. First, prepare a chart for recording data. Your chart should be similar to the one below. DO NOT WRITE IN THIS BOOK.

Area of the Tongue		
Substance	You	Partner
sugar		
vinegar		
salt		
quinine sulfate		

Look at the diagram of the tongue and identify the 4 areas to be tested. Rinse out your mouth with water and pat your tongue dry with a clean paper towel. Your lab partner will dip a clean cotton swab into the 10% sugar solution. Extend your tongue, and your lab partner will touch each area (one at a time) with the sugar solution. You can determine whether you perceive the "sweet" taste. **CAUTION:** *Dip the cotton swab into the 10% sugar solution only once. Use the same swab to test each area of the tongue.*

When the areas have been tested, discard the swab to prevent contamination of other solutions. In your chart, record the numbers of the areas of your tongue in which you perceived the sensation of sweetness.

Now, test your partner's tongue for the areas with "sweet" receptors. Record the

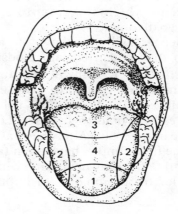

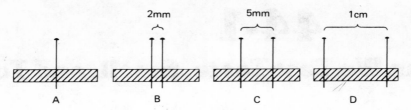

2mm   5mm   1cm

A   B   C   D

data in your chart. (d) Are the receptors for "sweetness" located in the same regions of your tongue and your partner's?

Rinse out your mouth, and wipe your tongue dry with a paper towel. With a new cotton swab, repeat the testing process with 10% vinegar. Record your results and test your partner's tongue for this substance. (e) Did you and your partner agree on the areas where the "sour" receptors are located?

Once again, rinse out your mouth, dry your tongue, and repeat the tests with salt solution. Record your results in your chart. (f) Did you and your partner have the same results?

Now, repeat your tests with quinine sulfate. (g) Do you both taste "bitter" in the same areas?

Hold your nose closed with your thumb and forefinger. Have your partner test the areas of your tongue with a swab that has been dipped into vanilla extract. (h) In what areas of the tongue do you perceive a taste? (i) What taste do you perceive?

Now, smell the vanilla extract on the swab. (j) Describe the odor. (k) Did the taste sense agree with the smell? (l) Name the basic taste which the receptors in the tongue can distinguish.

Another test will also show that it is difficult to distinguish certain foods if you cannot smell them. You will use samples of onion and apple that have been cut into small pieces. Blindfold some volunteers and have them hold their noses. Let them taste one of the foods. After they have swallowed the first sample, have them taste the other. (m) Could they determine which was the apple? (n) the onion? (o) Explain the results.

PART 2 / ANALYZING THE TOUCH RECEPTORS

Procedure and Observations

With a razor blade, cut 4 slices, about 5 mm thick, from a large cork stopper. Select one of the cork "rounds" and push a straight pin through the center until it extends from the bottom about 2 mm, as shown in figure A. Make another with the pins 2 mm apart as in figure B. Make a third "tester" as in figure C with the pins 5 mm apart. A fourth tester is made with the pins 1 cm apart as in figure D.

On a separate piece of paper, construct a chart for your results. Your chart should be similar to the one below. Record all of your results in your chart. DO NOT WRITE IN THIS BOOK.

Distance at Which 2 Points Can Be Felt		
Area Tested	You	Your Partner
cheek		
forehead		
upper lip		
back of neck		
tip of finger		
back of hand		
lower arm (front)		
upper arm (front)		

Now, with your eyes closed, your partner will test the skin of your cheek. Selecting one of the testers, your partner will touch it to your cheek. **CAUTION:** *Be certain not to break the skin or put so much pressure that* *the cork touches the skin*. You can respond by telling your lab partner whether you feel one pin or two. Then, the other testers will be used.

Your lab partner will record, in your chart, the closest distance at which you can distinguish two pins. If you cannot distinguish two pin points even when the pins are 1 cm apart, then record ">1 cm" in the table. (a) What does this test tell you about the space between touch receptors in the cheek?

Have your partner test the other areas indicated in your chart, and record your sensations. Then, exchange places, and you test your laboratory partner.

(b) Which areas did you find most sensitive? (c) Which areas did you find least sensitive? (d) Are touch receptors distributed evenly over the various areas of your body? Explain.

Summary
(a) In what area of the tongue did you find receptors for:
sweet?
sour?
salt?
bitter?
(b) Why are foods "tasteless" when you have a cold?
(c) Do all areas of the skin have the same sensitivity to touch? Explain.

Test what you have learned by completing the following statements. Write the complete sentence on your paper.
(d) A cell, or group of cells, that receives a stimulus is a ____?____.
(e) A factor or environmental change capable of producing activity in protoplasm is a ____?____.
(f) The reaction to a stimulus is called a ____?____.
(g) The concentration of touch ____?____ is not the same on all parts of the body.

INVESTIGATIONS ON YOUR OWN

Make up a series of different concentrations of solutions to determine the sensitivity of your taste buds. Select one of the substances of sweet, salt, bitter, or sour, and determine the lowest concentration at which you can detect the substance. This is a good activity for two students working together.

44-2

How Do We See?

OBJECTIVES
- To identify the major parts of the eye
- To observe and identify particular characteristics of vision

MATERIALS

TEXTBOOK OR CHARTS OF THE EYE
PENLIGHT FLASHLIGHT
INDEX CARD (PART 2)
STRAIGHT PIN (PART 2)
TEASING NEEDLE (PART 2)
METRIC RULER (PART 2)
COLORED CRAYONS: YELLOW, GREEN, RED,
    BLACK, BLUE, WHITE (PART 3)
UNLINED WHITE PAPER (PARTS 3, 4)
NEEDLE AND THREAD (PART 4)

PART 1 / THE EYE AND ITS RESPONSE TO LIGHT

Procedure and Observations
On a separate piece of paper, copy or trace the view of the eye shown below.

Using charts of the eye and your textbook, label the following structures of the eye on your diagram: **pupil, lens, iris, cornea, retina, optic nerve, fovea.**

Have your laboratory partner look closely at your eye and observe the size of your pupil. Next, your partner will shine the flashlight into your right eye while looking at the pupil. (a) What can be observed?

Now, shut your eyes and cover them lightly with your hands for 30 seconds. (b) Your lab partner will describe what happens to your pupils when you uncover your eyes.

Repeat this first part on your laboratory partner's eye. (c) Do the results agree?

PART 2 / INVERTED IMAGES

Procedure and Observations
Examine the first figure again, and you will see that the projection of the pin is inverted on the retina. However, when the receptors of the retina stimulate nerve cells and the impulse is carried to the brain, we interpret the image in its correct position. Let's play a trick on our senses. Punch a hole in an index card with the teasing needle. Hold

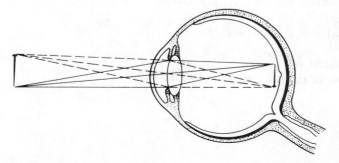

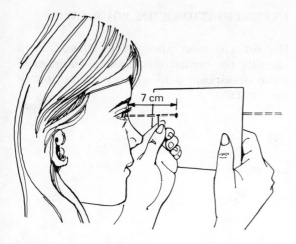

the card up toward the light about 7 cm away from your eye and look through the pin-hole. Carefully hold a straight pin (with the head up) close to your pupil. Move the pin until you see it through the pin-hole.

Draw what you see in a circle. Move the pin to the right. (a) Which way does the pin appear to move?

This impression occurs because the lens of the eye cannot make a *real image* on the retina when the head of the pin is so close. But the light passing through the pin-hole causes an *erect shadow* of the pinhead on the retina. The erect shadow is inverted by the optic nerve and the brain, so you see the pinhead upside down.

PART 3 / RETINAL FATIGUE

Procedure and Observations
Trace both of the figures below onto a separate piece of paper. Use crayons to color the sections according to the labels.

Now, stare at the dot in the center of the butterfly's body with the colored wings. After 30 seconds, stare at an unlined sheet of white paper. Observe the colors that appear. Identify these colors and compare them to the colors in the figure on the left. You may have to do this several times.

Now, in the right figure, color the sections with the colors you perceived in the *afterimage* on the white paper. Observe that the afterimage is composed of the complementary colors. For example, the receptors in the retina become fatigued for the red light, but respond to all the colors of white light *except* red. Therefore, the colors combine to produce green, the complementary color to red.

PART 4 / BINOCULAR VISION

Procedure and Observations
Roll up a piece of paper to form a tube about 3 cm in diameter. Hold the side of your right hand against the tube and look through the tube with your left eye. Keep both eyes open. (a) Do you have the impression of looking through your hand? (b) Can you think of an explanation for this?

Facing a distant corner of the room, touch your two index fingers together and hold them at arm's length. Look past your fingers at the corner of the room.

(c) How do your index fingers appear? (d) Make a sketch of what you see. (e) Explain your results.

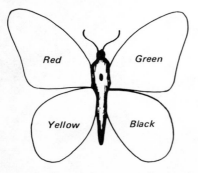

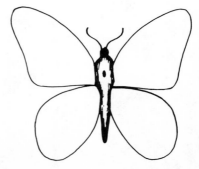

Summary

(a) Explain the function of the iris.

(b) If the retinal image is "upside down," why do we see things "right side up"?

(c) What is the advantage of binocular vision?

Test what you have learned by matching the terms with the statements below. On your paper, write the statements as they appear here. After each statement, write the term that best applies.

(d) muscles control the pupil diameter

(e) diameter decreases in bright light

(f) focuses objects on retina

(g) carries nerve impulses from retina to brain

(h) location of visual receptors

(i) complementary color of red

(j) complementary color of green

(k) complementary color of yellow

(l) complementary color of black

(m) ability to have depth perception

1. binocular vision
2. blue
3. green
4. iris
5. lens
6. optic nerve
7. pupil
8. red
9. retina
10. white

INVESTIGATIONS ON YOUR OWN

Obtain a cow or sheep eye. Dissect it to identify the structures. Make a diagram of your dissection and give the function of each part.

46-1

How Can Hormones Affect Development?

OBJECTIVES
• To observe how thyroxin influences metamorphosis in a tadpole

MATERIALS

TEXTBOOK
25 TADPOLES WITH HIND LIMB BUDS
   VISIBLE (*RANA PIPIENS* BEST)
5 FINGERBOWLS (ABOUT 9 CM DIAMETER)
POND WATER
5 PETRI DISHES
3 SHEETS OF MILLIMETER GRAPH PAPER
THYROXIN STOCK SOLUTION
IODINE STOCK SOLUTION
1 JAR STRAINED BABY FOOD
   (PLAIN SPINACH)
2 1-ML GRADUATED PIPETTES
100-ML GRADUATED CYLINDER
LABELS

TADPOLES AND THYROID HORMONE

Procedure and Observations

(a) What is the function of the thyroid hormone in the human?

Biologists have found that the thyroid hormone also affects metamorphosis in tadpoles. We can set up an experiment to see what effects will be produced when tadpoles are given an excess of thyroxin. You will do this by adding thyroxin to the water in which the tadpoles are living. (b) How will the thyroxin get into the blood stream of the tadpoles?

The thyroid gland requires iodine to produce its hormone. If the iodine supply is too low, growth and metamorphosis in the tadpole is retarded. If we were to increase the supply of iodine in the water, would the tadpoles make more thyroid hormone and would metamorphosis be advanced? Let's test the effects of added thyroxin and the effects of added iodine in our Investigation.

Number 5 fingerbowls and put 100 ml of pond water into each. Then put 5 tadpoles in each bowl. *Change the water every day and treat the bowls as follows:*

Bowl 1: Each day, add 1 ml strained baby spinach and 1 ml Thyroxin Stock Solution (containing 1 microgram of thyroxin per ml).

Bowl 2: Each day, add 1 ml strained baby spinach and 2 ml Iodine Stock Solution (containing 1 microgram of iodine per ml).

Bowl 3: Each day, add 1 ml strained baby spinach and 1 ml Iodine Stock Solution (containing 1 microgram of iodine per ml).

Bowl 4: Each day, add 1 ml strained baby spinach and 0.5 ml Iodine Stock Solution (containing 1 microgram of iodine per ml).

Bowl 5: Each day, add 1 ml strained baby spinach only.

Keep the cultures at room temperature.

Tape a piece of millimeter graph paper to the underside of each of 5 Petri dishes. Number these to correspond to the numbers of the fingerbowls. *Always use the same Petri dish for the same animals.*

187

Begin by carefully removing the 5 tadpoles from fingerbowl *1* and placing them in Petri dish *1*. Measure and record: *total length*, *body length*, and *tail length* (which will be the total length minus body length). Return the animals to their fingerbowl immediately.

Repeat the measurements with fingerbowls *2*, *3*, *4*, and *5*.

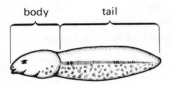

Although the medium in each of the bowls should be changed daily, these measurements can be made every 2 to 3 days. The total time for this Investigation will vary, but the average will be between 2 to 3 weeks. Be certain to observe the changes which indicate metamorphosis.

Record your measurements in a table. Then, make a graph of the mean body length of each group against the days observed.

Summary
(a) Make several conclusions which can be supported by the experimental evidence from this Investigation.
(b) If you were to repeat this Investigation, what would you do differently? State your reasons.

INVESTIGATIONS ON YOUR OWN

1. Repeat this Investigation and treat the fingerbowls as follows:
   Bowl A. 0.05 ml Thyroxin Stock Solution
   Bowl B. 0.025 ml Thyroxin Stock Solution
   Bowl C. 0.01 ml Thyroxin Stock Solution
   Bowl D. Control

2. Repeat this Investigation and treat the fingerbowls as follows:
   Bowl A. 0.02 ml Iodine Stock Solution
   Bowl B. 0.01 ml Iodine Stock Solution
   Bowl C. Control

NOTE:
The following are directions for the preparation of solutions used in this Investigation.

Thyroxin Stock Solution. First, dissolve 4 g NaOH in 1 liter of distilled water. CAUTION: NaOH will cause severe burns. Do not touch it or get it on your clothing. One liter of this solution is enough for several classes.

Dissolve 0.1 g crystalline thyroxin in 10 ml of the NaOH solution. When dissolved, add 90 ml distilled water. Next, add 1 ml of this *concentrated* thyroxin solution to 1 liter distilled water to make the *Thyroxin Stock Solution*. Put this in a 1-liter stock bottle, label it, and put it into a refrigerator. This solution will contain 1 microgram of thyroxin per milliliter.

Iodine Stock Solution. Dissolve 0.1 g iodine crystals in 5 ml ethyl alcohol. When dissolved, add 95 ml distilled water. Add 1 ml of this *concentrated* iodine solution to 1 liter distilled water to make the *Iodine Stock Solution*. This solution will contain 1 microgram of iodine per milliliter.

47-1

How Does an Embryo Develop?

OBJECTIVES
- To observe a chicken at two stages of development
- To determine the function of the extraembryonic membranes
- To relate the developing chicken embryo to the human

MATERIALS

TEXTBOOK
FERTILIZED EGG (NOT INCUBATED)
FERTILIZED EGG (60 HOURS)
FERTILIZED EGG (120 HOURS)
COTTON
SCISSORS
FORCEPS
FINGERBOWL
DISSECTING MICROSCOPE
EYE DROPPER

PART 1 / THE UNINCUBATED FERTILE EGG

Procedure and Observations

Prepare a bed of cotton in a fingerbowl and place a fertilized unincubated egg on the cotton so that the egg is held in position. Open the egg as shown in figures A and B. This will allow you to see inside.

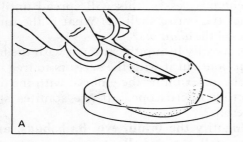

Observe the large yellow *yolk* which contains stored food for the developing embryo. On the upper surface of the yolk, observe a red "blood spot." This locates the position of the embryo which can be seen as a small white spot. The area where the embryo develops is called the *blastodisc*. Examine the blastodisc with the dissecting microscope. As cell division occurs, a plate of cells will spread out from this area. The membrane that surrounds the yolk and the developing embryo is the *vitelline membrane*.

Surrounding the yolk is the "white" of the egg. It is composed of *albumen*. Notice that the dense albumen forms an opaque cord on each side of the yolk. This is the *chalaza*. Locate the *air space* on the blunt end of the egg. At the air space, you can identify the *shell membrane* and the *inner egg membrane*.

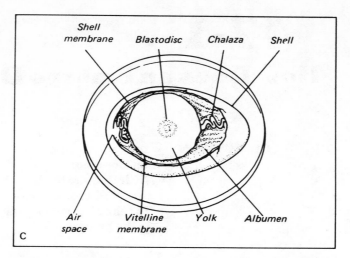

Shell
membrane   Blastodisc   Chalaza   Shell

Air
space   Vitelline   Yolk   Albumen
         membrane

C

PART 2 / THE 60-HOUR INCUBATED EGG

Procedure and Observations

Place a 60-hour incubated chicken egg on a cotton bed in a fingerbowl. As before, cut and remove a lid so you can see inside. Remove some of the fluid albumen with an eye dropper so the embryo can be clearly seen. (a) Compare the position of the embryo with the position of the blastodisc you observed in Part 1.

Now, use the dissecting microscope to examine the embryo. (b) Do you see any evidence of blood? (c) If you do, describe the direction of flow. (d) Is a beating heart present? (e) Can you identify a head?

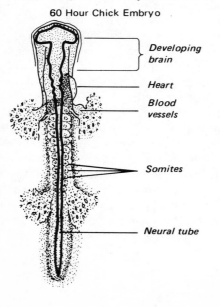

60 Hour Chick Embryo

Developing
brain

Heart

Blood
vessels

Somites

Neural tube

Identify the **developing brain,** the **neural tube** (the developing spinal cord), **somites** (the paired sections of developing muscle tissue), the **heart,** and **blood vessels.**

PART 3 / THE 120-HOUR INCUBATED EGG

Procedure and Observations

Place a 120-hour incubated chicken egg on a cotton bed in a fingerbowl. Open it carefully as before, and draw out some of the fluid albumen with the eye dropper. You will see that a clear membrane, the *amnion,* covers the embryo. It forms a fluid sac called the *amniotic sac.* (a) What is the function of this sac?

Another membrane grows from the embryo and surrounds the yolk. This is the *yolk sac.* (b) What structures do you see that identify the important function of this membrane forming the yolk sac?

Find the small sac at the hind end of the embryo. This is the *allantois.* As development progresses, this will spread until it lines the entire shell. (c) What is the function of the *allantois*?

Carefully lift up the amnion with the forceps and cut it with the scissors to free the embryo. Examine the embryo with the dissecting microscope. (d) Are somites still present?

Identify the **brain, eye, limb buds, amnion, yolk sac,** and **allantois.**

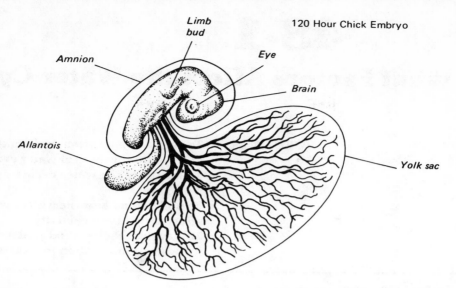

Limb bud

120 Hour Chick Embryo

Amnion

Eye

Brain

Allantois

Yolk sac

Summary

(a) How does a 120-hour incubated chicken embryo differ from a 60-hour incubated chicken embryo?

Test what you have learned by matching the terms with the statements below. On your paper, write the statements as they appear here. After each statement, write the term that best applies.

(b) grows from digestive tract and surrounds yolk

(c) form the muscles

(d) secreted by membrane and encloses embryo

(e) grows from digestive tract of embryo and functions in respiration and waste removal

(f) holds yolk and developing embryo in center of egg

(g) prevents water loss but allows gas exchange

(h) contains network of blood vessels and absorbs yolk

(i) forms the spinal column and brain

(j) rapidly dividing cells forming a plate at the surface of the yolk

1. air space
2. allantois
3. amnion
4. amniotic fluid
5. blastodisc
6. chalaza
7. chorion
8. neural tube
9. shell
10. somites
11. yolk sac

INVESTIGATIONS ON YOUR OWN

Culture frog eggs in the laboratory. If you have access to a pond where frogs breed, collect several egg masses in a bucket of pond water and bring them to the laboratory. Since the process of cell division occurs within a few hours after fertilization, various stages of development may be observed. Select eggs at an early stage of development and transfer them to a fingerbowl half filled with pond water and containing two sprigs of elodea. Place the fingerbowl in an area where the temperature will remain between 18°C and 20°C. Remove several eggs each day and examine them with the dissecting and compound microscope. Make labeled diagrams to show the changes you observe in the development of tadpoles.

Discard any eggs that become cloudy and do not develop. Hatching tadpoles may be transferred to a large bowl and fed with chopped baby food spinach as you observe their development. When you have completed your study, the young animals may then be returned to the pond from which you collected the eggs.

48-1

What Factors Affect the Water Cycle?

OBJECTIVES

- To relate evaporation and condensation of water to the natural water cycle
- To illustrate the water cycle by means of a diagram
- To understand how the water cycle can be affected by human activity
- To develop background understandings for water conservation measures

MATERIALS

WATER BATH
THERMOMETER
BEAKER
ICE
PAPER TOWELS
ELECTRIC FAN
COLORED PENCILS (PART 2)
METRIC RULER (PART 2)

PART 1 / TEMPERATURE, AN IMPORTANT FACTOR

Procedure and Observations

Heat a water bath to 100°C. Use a thermometer to check this temperature. (a) Do you notice any bubbles forming in the water? (b) What has raising the temperature done to the water molecules? (c) Do you observe any difference in the air about 10 cm above the water in the water bath?

Put a ring on a ring stand and adjust it about 10 cm above the surface of the water in the water bath. Fill a beaker about two thirds full of cool water and place on the ring. (d) Describe what occurs on the outside of the beaker.

(e) Explain what has happened to water molecules at the surface of the water in the

water bath. (f) Explain what has happened to these water molecules at the glass surface of the beaker. (g) What energy was causing the molecules of water to do this? (h) What effect would a gentle breeze have on the amount of water evaporating from the surface?

You can test your hypothesis by taking two paper towels and putting a couple of

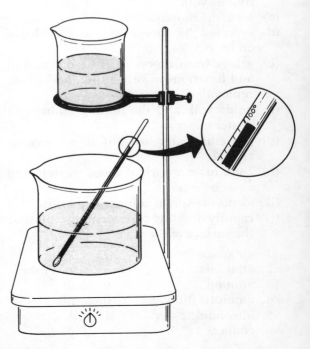

drops of water on each one. Place them on your table and let an electric fan move the air over one of the paper towels. (i) Which towel "dries" more quickly?

Something else occurs when water evaporates. Although it is more difficult to measure, you can discover what it is by another experiment. Rub a couple of drops of water on one forearm and let the electric fan blow on both forearms. (j) What do you observe? (k) Does this help you understand why water molecules can leave the surface of a lake even though the temperature of the lake is not 100°C? (l) Explain your answer.

Fill a beaker with ice and add water until it is about two thirds full. Fill another beaker with warm water. Set these beakers on the table (about a half meter apart) and observe the outsides and bottoms of the beakers. (m) Describe your observations. (n) From where did the water come that forms a puddle beneath the beaker with the ice? (o) Why did this not occur in the case of the beaker with the warm water?

(p) Can you see this water vapor in the air of the classroom? The amount of water vapor in the air is called the *humidity*. (q) What was the energy that caused this water vapor to be in the air? (r) From where did this energy come?

Your answers to *q* and *r* probably only involved a physical factor. (s) Can you name any biotic factors which contributed to the water vapor in your classroom?

PART 2 / THE WATER CYCLE

Procedure and Observations

(a) As you learned from Part 1, the process of forming water vapor is called . . . ?

(b) The return of water to the earth is . . . ?

(c) Name several forms of precipitation.

The landscape shown on the next page is a setting for the stages of the water cycle. Refer to this figure when answering the following questions.

(d) Looking at the diagram, state what can happen to precipitation.

(e) What is meant by the *water table*?

(f) What role do the plants play in the water cycle?

(g) Runoff water may cause erosion of the topsoil. How does the erosion alter the normal water cycle?

(h) Why are swamps and marshes important in a normal water cycle?

(i) How would the water cycle be altered by the cultivation of riverbanks and flood plains (bottom lands)?

(j) Why are trees and shrubs especially important in watershed regions?

(k) What influence do floods have on the water table?

(l) What role does the topsoil have in reducing floods and droughts?

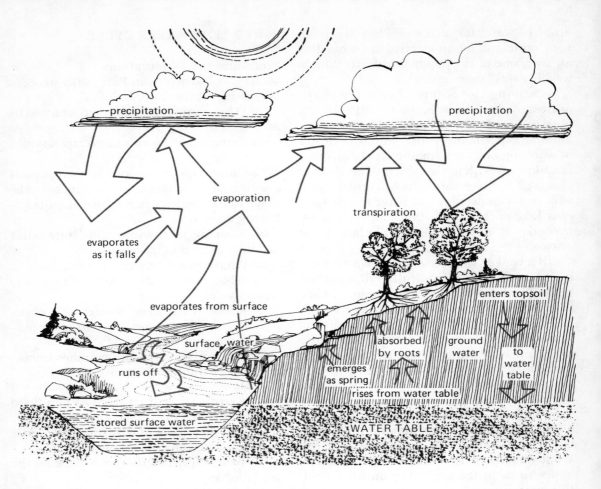

precipitation

precipitation

evaporation

transpiration

evaporates as it falls

evaporates from surface

enters topsoil

surface water

absorbed by roots

ground water

to water table

runs off

emerges as spring

rises from water table

stored surface water

WATER TABLE

Summary

(a) What are the sources of water vapor in the air?

(b) On the basis of your data, list some factors that affect the rate of water evaporation.

(c) As conservation measures, dams are often built across streams and water is allowed to pass slowly. How does this affect the water cycle?

Test what you have learned by matching the terms with the statements. On a separate piece of paper, list the statements. After each statement, write the term that best defines or describes it.

(d) water molecules go into the air

(e) a factor that increases the rate of evaporation

(f) depth at which water is standing in the ground

(g) precipitation going over the land to lakes and oceans

(h) causes water vapor to condense

(i) the amount of water vapor in the air

(j) return of water to the earth from the atmosphere

(k) water passing through plants and evaporating from them

(l) water vapor changes to water droplets

(m) is able to hold much water vapor

1. cold air	6. precipitation
2. condensation	7. runoff water
3. evaporation	8. transpiration
4. humidity	9. warm air
5. moving air	10. water table

INVESTIGATIONS ON YOUR OWN

Determine the effect of relative humidity and temperature on the rate of evaporation. Select an outdoor station where a pan of water will not be disturbed for 24 hours. The station should be away from buildings or other obstructions that would interfere with air movement. Measure exactly 500 ml of water in a graduated cylinder and pour it into a shallow pan. (In hot weather, it may be necessary to use 1,000 ml of water.) Cover the pan with a screen to prevent birds from drinking the water. After 24 hours, measure the water remaining in the pan, using the graduated cylinder. Record this amount in a table and determine the amount of water evaporated. Consult your newspaper or your local weather bureau, and find out the high and low relative humidity, high and low temperature, and high and low wind velocity during the 24-hour period. Record these data in your table also. Repeat the procedure on 5 consecutive days, if possible.

48-2

How Are Plants and Animals Interdependent?

OBJECTIVES

- To observe that both plants and animals give off CO_2 during respiration
- To observe that plants use CO_2 during photosynthesis
- To observe that plants do not use CO_2 in darkness
- To observe the interdependence of plants and animals

MATERIALS

250-ML BEAKER
STRAW
POND WATER
LIVING FRESH-WATER SNAILS
VIGOROUS TERMINAL SPRIGS OF *ANACHARIS* (ELODEA)
BROM THYMOL BLUE INDICATOR
5-ML PIPETTE
100-ML GRADUATED CYLINDER
4 CULTURE TUBES (WITH SCREW CAPS)
LABELS OR WAX PENCIL

A CLOSED ECOSYSTEM

Procedure and Observations

Put 100 ml of pond water in a beaker and add 5 ml brom thymol blue indicator. The indicator will not affect the plants or snails, but will show pH changes. In slightly alkaline solutions, it will be blue. In slightly acidic solutions (pH 6.0) that form when CO_2 is added to water, the indicator will be yellow.

Number four 15-cm culture tubes. Next, fill each tube three quarters full of the pond water with the indicator. Put a living fresh-water snail in tube *1*, a snail and one or two sprigs of *Anacharis* in tube *2*, and one or two sprigs of *Anacharis* in tubes *3* and *4*. Put the caps on the culture tubes and tighten them securely. Place tube *4* in a dark cabinet to prevent photosynthesis. Set the remaining tubes in a well-lighted place, but out of the direct sunlight.

Examine the tubes daily for 5 consecutive days and record your observations in a ta-

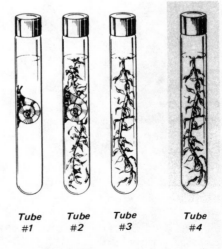

Tube #1   Tube #2   Tube #3   Tube #4

ble. Notice whether the snail is alive. If so, is it active? Is the snail in tube *2* feeding on the *Anacharis*? Does the *Anacharis* appear to be growing, healthy, or dying? Observe the condition and the color of the water.

(a) Compare the color in the tubes *1* and *4* on the fifth day. Explain the results.

(b) Compare the results in tubes *3* and *4*. Can a green plant complete a CO_2 —O_2 cycle and continue to survive without the presence of an animal? Explain your answer.

(c) Can the snail live in a closed environment without a green plant? Explain.

(d) Was there any evidence to indicate how the snail benefited from the green plant in tube *2*?

Plants and animals could survive in a small closed environment for a much longer period than the five days you conducted your investigation. Sooner or later, however, decomposition would occur. (e) Explain why this is true.

Summary

(a) What biological principles of a closed environment have you observed from this Investigation?

(b) Explain the importance of the CO_2-O_2 cycle on the earth.

Test what you have learned by completing the following statements. Write the complete statement on your paper.

(c) In the dark, plants give off ___?___

(d) In the light, plants give off ___?___

(e) In the light, animals give off ___?___

(f) If CO_2 were bubbled through water, brom thymol blue would be ___?___

(g) If CO_2 were taken out of water, brom thymol blue would be ___?___

(h) When CO_2 is bubbled through water, the water becomes more ___?___

(i) If water contains CO_2, *Anacharis* will remove it during the process of photosynthesis (when in the light) and the water becomes more ___?___

(j) Plants and animals are both required in a balanced ecosystem. This shows the ___?___ of plants and animals.

INVESTIGATIONS ON YOUR OWN

1. Prepare an aquarium in a gallon jar which can be sealed off at the top. Make a list of all the items and living things you put in the aquarium. Seal it and make daily observations. Explain how you have determined whether a balance exists or not. If you should open the aquarium to make alterations, record your reasons for doing so. When you believe your aquarium is balanced, list the numbers and kinds of plants and animals and the amount of water, sand, or rock it contains.

2. Repeat this Investigation using other organisms, such as *Chlorella* and guppies. Write up your results.

49-1

What Is an Ecosystem?

OBJECTIVES
- To view an ecosystem as a unit
- To identify the relationships of the components of an ecosystem
- To understand the pyramid of energy

MATERIALS

NO MATERIALS ARE REQUIRED

ANALYSIS OF AN ECOSYSTEM

Procedure and Observations

By now, you may be familiar with the structural adaptations and the nutritional requirements of many plants and animals. You may also be familiar with many cycles that occur between living and nonliving things. How do all of these factors fit together in an ecosystem?

On the bottom of this page is a diagram of an ecosystem. (a) Name the components of the *biotic community*. (b) How many populations are represented? (c) Name the components of the *physical environment* you can identify in the figure.

Imagine a line from the diatoms to the copepods to the sticklebacks to the duck, and to the hawk. (d) What is the relationship between these organisms? This represents a *food chain*.

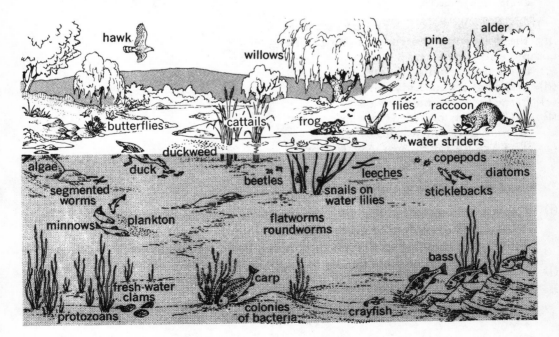

Now, determine where the diatoms get their source of energy. (e) What is it? (f) What might happen to the hawk to show that a cycle of matter exists in the ecosystem?

(g) In this food chain, which organism is considered the producer?

On a separate piece of paper, draw a pyramid like the one shown here.

Write the name of the organism at the base of your pyramid. Then, fill in the remaining layers of this pyramid with the organisms in this particular food chain. The total amount of a particular community is called the *biomass*. (h) Which level of this pyramid represents the greatest biomass? (i) Which level represents the least biomass?

This pyramid would indicate that the total weight of the diatoms would be more than the total weight of the hawks in the ecosystem. However, this may not actually be the case. Let's find out why! Imagine a line from the water lilies to the snails to the bass, to the raccoon, to the hawk. (j) This series of connections represents another . . . ? (k) What is the link between these two food chains?

(l) If we were to construct another food pyramid, then, what would be at the bottom? (m) at the top?

The hawk, then, is dependent upon more than one producer. The pyramid is also called a "pyramid of energy." (n) Why is this also a good term?

Now, consider other lines connecting organisms by nutritional relationships. (o) Are there many overlappings of relationships indicated? This is called a *food web*.

(p) In the ecosystem, what happens to the wastes and dead organisms? (q) Name the *scavengers* in the figure of the ecosystem. (r) What is their role in the ecosystem? (s) Name the *decomposers* in the figure of the ecosystem. (t) What is their role in the ecosystem?

Summary
(a) A food chain involves energy transfer. Does energy cycle? Explain.
(b) The sun is actually the base that supports the pyramid of energy. Explain this statement.

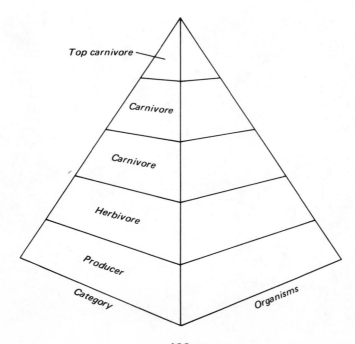

Test your understanding of the concepts learned by matching the words to the statements. You may use the words more than once, or not at all. On your paper, copy the statements given below. Write the matching word after each statement.

(c) beginning source of energy
(d) water lilies to snails to ducks
(e) represented by the drawing of the lake
(f) food chains have many interconnecting links
(g) live off energy of dead or decaying organisms
(h) all the snails in the lake
(i) carnivore communities possess less energy than the producer communities
(j) return minerals to the ecosystem
(k) water, light, temperature, sand, rocks

1. decomposers
2. ecosystem
3. food chain
4. food web
5. physical environment
6. population
7. pyramid of energy
8. scavengers
9. sun

INVESTIGATIONS ON YOUR OWN

1. Select two totally different environments near your home. Record variations in temperature, light, and air movement. Examine and classify the soil and test its pH. Collect specimens of plants and observe the various animals in the habitat. List the organisms as autotrophs, heterotrophs, and carnivores. Construct food webs to compare these two habitats.

2. Choose another ecosystem, such as a coniferous forest, the deep ocean, or tundra and construct the food chains and food webs that exist in this system.

50-1

Do Communities in an Ecosystem Change?

OBJECTIVES
- **To observe changes during succession**
- **To observe some physical changes occurring in a small ecosystem**
- **To estimate population densities during succession**

MATERIALS

POND WATER
TIMOTHY HAY
WHEAT GRAINS
REFRIGERATOR
2 1-LITER BOTTLES
5 250-ML BEAKERS
3 PETRI DISHES
WAX MARKING PENCIL
GRADUATED CYLINDER
CELSIUS THERMOMETER
COMPOUND MICROSCOPE
MICROSCOPE SLIDE AND COVER SLIP
pHYDRION PAPER
EYE DROPPER
COLORED PENCILS

MAKING AND EXAMINING HAY INFUSIONS

Procedure and Observations

Boil 2 liters of pond water. Allow it to cool, and transfer it to two 1-liter bottles. These can be stored in the refrigerator until required. Number the five 250-ml beakers *3, 6, 9, 12,* and *15.* Now measure out 200 ml of the boiled pond water and put it into beaker *15.* Add 20 pieces of timothy hay (3 cm each) and 4 wheat grains. Stir the mix-

ture and examine a drop of it with the compound microscope. (a) Do you find any organisms?

Record your findings for "0 days" in a table. Also, describe the appearance, pH, and temperature of the beginning culture. Cover the beaker with half of a Petri dish, and set the beaker in a well-lighted place in the room.

Three days later, repeat this procedure with beaker *12.* You may omit the microscopic examination of the pond water. Then, continue to make a new culture every 3 days. One or two beginning culture days will fall on a weekend, depending on the day this Investigation is started. You may start these on the day before or the day after the weekend. These cultures are called *hay infusions.* They are small ecosystems which you will observe. On the 12th day, you will begin the hay infusion in beaker *3.* On the 15th day, you will be ready to make your observations.

Observe the appearance and note any odor in each of the cultures. Using pHydrion paper, measure the pH of each culture. Measure the temperature of each culture. Record these findings in your table.

Now, stir up the contents of the 3-day old culture. Remove a drop (avoiding any solid material) and prepare a slide for microscopic examination. Use a definite pattern as you examine the slide to avoid counting the same organism twice. Keep a tally of the organisms you identify according to their specific groups. Groups easily identified are: green protists, nongreen protists, rotifers, crustaceans, and annelids. If you observe a specific organism, such as *Euglena*, or *Paramecium*, then you can add this to your list of protists. When you have covered your slide *once*, record your observations.

Clean your glass slide, cover glass, and eye dropper well before going on to the "day 6" culture. Repeat the inspection and the microscopic survey of this culture.

When you have completed inspecting the cultures, a class average count can be taken to increase the sample size. Now, using the class average counts per drop as *index of population*, plot these data to make a graph. You may use colored pencils to represent the various individuals. *Be sure to identify the color with the organism.* Use ink to plot the combined class average number of all organisms present.

(b) What were the most obvious changes you observed in the kinds of organisms present at different ages of the cultures?

(c) What were the pioneer organisms?

(d) How did these pioneers get into the culture?

(e) What organisms composed the climax community in your culture?

(f) Were any of these organisms observed in the 3-day old culture?

(g) Were any of the pioneers present in the 15-day old culture?

Summary

Test what you have learned by completing the following statements with the words from the list given. You may use a word more than once, or not at all. Write the complete sentences on your paper.

autotrophs	population
cycle	succession
dominant	sun
pioneer	timothy hay and
pond water	wheat grains

(a) A ___?___ organism is one that enters a new environment.

(b) The ___?___ organism is most abundant in a climax community.

(c) Relative numbers and species of organisms change during ___?___.

(d) The ultimate energy source of energy in a hay infusion comes from the ___?___.

(e) In setting up this Investigation, we added a food source in the form of ___?___.

(f) If any green protists appeared in the hay infusion, they would be ___?___.

(g) A sampling technique can be used to estimate the density of the ___?___.

(h) The pioneer organisms probably came from the ___?___.

INVESTIGATIONS ON YOUR OWN

1. Repeat this Investigation but maintain the cultures in the dark. Make a graph of your results.

2. Repeat this Investigation but maintain the cultures at two different temperatures. Compare the results and make graphs to show how they differ.

51-1
What Life Is Found in Soil Communities?

OBJECTIVES
- To become familiar with the life that inhabits the soil
- To compare the organisms found in different soils

MATERIALS

DISSECTING MICROSCOPE
HAND LENS
METER STICK
STRING
4 STAKES
SHOVEL
SHOE BOXES OR OTHER CONTAINERS FOR SOIL SAMPLES
BERLESE FUNNEL OR EQUIPMENT TO MAKE ONE, AS SHOWN
JAR
GOOSE-NECKED LAMP OR OTHER LIGHT SOURCE
ALCOHOL

PART 1 / COMPARATIVE STUDY OF THE FAUNA IN VARIOUS SOILS

To study the organisms that live in the soil, it is necessary to collect samples from the various areas and take them to the laboratory for examination. Since physical factors such as soil conditions influence the type of organisms found in a community, you should select two or more types of soil communities for study.

Procedure and Observations
Select soil from two or more areas such as a woods, open field, or garden for your study. The procedure will be the same for the study of the various soils. Mark off a plot 30 cm square and place stakes at the four corners. Now connect the four corners with string. This defines the area you will study.

Insert a shovel and make a cut around the square to a depth of 5 cm. Cut under the square and put it into a container to transport it to your laboratory. (a) How many square centimeters of soil are there in this sample? (b) How many cubic centimeters?

Remove a portion of the soil from this section and put it on a sheet of white paper. Separate the soil particles and examine them with a hand lens. Collect all the living organisms you can detect. Classify these as to whether they are insect larvae, pupae, or adults, worms, etc. Continue until you have examined all of the soil in each sample.

Sample Number	Type of Soil	Volume	Number of Organisms	Number of Organisms per Square Centimeter	Number of Organisms per Cubic Centimeter
1					
2					
3					

Many more organisms can be observed by setting up the apparatus shown in the diagram. Put the contents of one box into the funnel. Be sure to identify the box. If enough equipment is available, you can set up as many funnels as you have soil samples.

The heat and light from the lamp will drive the remaining organisms down where they will fall through the neck of the funnel and into the jar of alcohol. The apparatus may be left overnight. Classify as many of these organisms as you can. Prepare a table on a separate sheet of paper summarizing your soil population analysis. Tabulate those you cannot identify as *unclassified*. Construct other columns for as many groups as you can establish and identify.

Determine the type of soil for each sample, the volume, number of organisms present, number of organisms per square centimeter, and number of organisms per cubic centimeter, and record in a table like the one shown. DO NOT WRITE IN THIS BOOK.

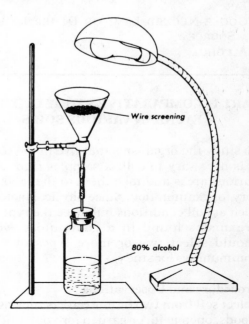

Wire screening

80% alcohol

APPENDIX

The Metric System

Most scientists working all over the world use the **metric system** of measurement. Most other people of the world also use the metric system in their daily lives. In the United States, use of the metric system is rapidly growing. You should become familiar with it.

The units of the metric system of measurement are the **meter** (for length), the **gram** (for weight), and the **liter** (for volume). Prefixes placed before the units of *meter, gram,* or *liter* will tell you the multiple of the unit. Therefore, once you have an understanding of each basic unit, this system is easy to use.

PREFIXES OF THE METRIC SYSTEM

Prefix	Scientific Notation	Decimal
KILO-	10^3	or 1000 times the unit
HECTO-	10^2	or 100 times the unit
DECA-	10	or 10 times the unit
the UNIT		
DECI-	10^{-1}	or 1/10 the unit
CENTI-	10^{-2}	or 1/100 the unit
MILLI-	10^{-3}	or 1/1000 the unit

LINEAR MEASURES

The unit of length in the metric system is the *meter* (abbreviation *m*), which is equal to 39.37 inches.

KILOmeter (km)	= 1000 meters
HECTOmeter	= 100 meters
DECAmeter	= 10 meters
meter	
DECImeter	= 1/10 meter
CENTImeter	= 1/100 meter
MILLImeter (mm)	= 1/1000 meter
MICRON (μ)—unit of measurement used in microscopic work	= 1/1,000,000 meter (10^{-6} m)
MILLImicron (mμ)	= 1/1,000,000,000 meter (10^{-9} m)
Angstrom (Å)	= 1/10,000,000,000 meter (10^{-10} m)

Note: The mμ and the Å are used as measures of the wavelengths of light. The micron, millimicron, and Angstrom units are not consistent with the system of metric prefixes.

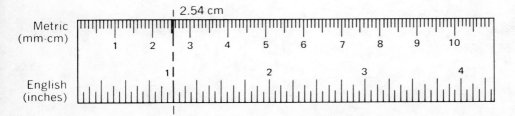

207

WEIGHT MEASURES

The unit of weight in the metric system is the *gram* (abbreviation *g*). One gram is the weight of one cubic centimeter of distilled water at 4° C.

KILOgram (kilo or kg)	= 1000 grams
HECTOgram	= 100 grams
DECAgram	= 10 grams
gram	
DECIgram	= 1/10 gram
CENTIgram (cg)	= 1/100 gram
MILLIgram (mg)	= 1/1,000 gram
MICROgram (γ)	= 1/1,000,000 gram (10^{-6} g)

VOLUME MEASURES

The unit of volume in the metric system is the *liter* (abbreviation *L*). One liter of distilled water weighs one kilogram. The most commonly used division is:

MILLIliter (mL) = 1/1000 liter

Metric-English Equivalents

1 meter = 39.37 inches
1 millimeter = approximately 1/25 inch
1 micron = approximately 1/25,000 inch
2.54 centimeters = 1 inch
1 kilogram = approximately 2.2 pounds
1 liter = approximately 1.06 quarts

Celsius and Fahrenheit Temperature Scales

Zero on the Celsius (also called centigrade) scale marks the freezing temperature of water. The equivalent on the Fahrenheit scale is 32°. Zero on the Fahrenheit scale is an arbitrary point: it marks the lowest temperature observed by the German scientist Fahrenheit during the winter of 1709. Zero degrees F corresponds to −17.77° C.

The temperature of boiling water, at sea level, is marked 100° on the Celsius scale. This is 212° on the Fahrenheit scale. There are 100 degrees between the melting point of ice and the boiling point of water on the Celsius scale. But there are 180 degrees between these two temperatures on the Fahrenheit scale. Therefore, one Fahrenheit degree is equal to 5/9 (100/180) of one Celsius degree.

The following procedure may be used to convert the temperatures of one scale to those of the other:

°F to °C: subtract 32, multiply by 5, divide by 9.

°C to °F: multiply by 9, divide by 5, add 32.

Expressed as formulae:

$°C = ⁵/₉ × (°F − 32°)$

$°F = (⁹/₅ × C°) + 32°$

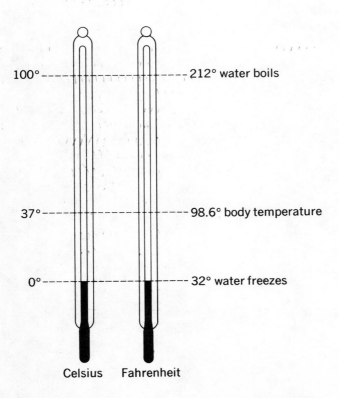

100° - - - - - - - - - - - - - - - 212° water boils

37° - - - - - - - - - - - - - - - 98.6° body temperature

0° - - - - - - - - - - - - - - - 32° water freezes

Celsius   Fahrenheit

Preparation of
Stains, Solutions, and Reagents

Preparing Solutions:

Many solutions used in this book are given in percentage concentrations. In order to prepare a solution of a given percentage, use the number of grams of material equal to the percentage and add enough solvent to equal 100 ml. For example, a 10% sodium hydroxide solution is prepared by dissolving 10 g sodium hydroxide in 90 ml water.

To reduce the concentration of an existing solution, pour the required percentage number of milliliters of the solution into a graduated cylinder. Add enough distilled water to bring the total volume in milliliters to equal the percentage of the original solution. For example, to reduce 95% alcohol to 80%, pour 80 ml of 95% alcohol into a graduated cylinder. Add enough distilled water to bring the volume to 95 ml. You now have 95 ml of 80% alcohol.

Agar, nonnutrient
15 g agar
1000 ml distilled water
> Mix and heat until agar dissolves. Stir constantly to avoid burning. To sterilize, autoclave at 15 pounds pressure for 15 minutes.

Agar, nutrient
3 g beef extract
5 g peptone
15 g agar
1000 ml distilled water
> Dissolve agar in hot water. Add peptone and beef extract. Sterilize in containers at 15 pounds pressure for 15 minutes.

Ammonium hydroxide solution, dilute
1 part conc. ammonium hydroxide
4 parts water
> Add ammonium hydroxide to water.

Benedict's solution
173 g sodium citrate
100 g anhydrous sodium carbonate
17.3 g copper sulfate
1000 ml distilled water
> Add sodium citrate and sodium carbonate to 600 ml distilled water. Heat until chemicals are dissolved. Filter this solution. Dissolve copper sulfate in 150 ml distilled water. Slowly add copper sulfate solution to the sodium citrate/sodium carbonate solution, stirring constantly. Add enough distilled water to bring the whole solution to 1 liter.

Biuret reagent
3 g copper sulfate
12 g potassium tartrate
1 liter of distilled water
600 ml 10% sodium hydroxide (*Caution: very caustic*)
> Dissolve copper sulfate and potassium tartrate in 1 liter of distilled water. Add 10% sodium hydroxide to this solution with constant stirring.

Brom thymol blue indicator

0.1 g brom thymol blue

1000 ml distilled water

Dissolve the brom thymol blue in the distilled water. If the solution appears green, add 0.4% sodium hydroxide, one drop at a time, until the indicator appears blue.

Broth, nutrient

3 g beef extract

5 g peptone

1000 ml distilled water

Dissolve beef extract and peptone in distilled water. Sterilize in the containers in which it will be used.

Carmine red

1 g carmine red

100 ml distilled water

Dissolve carmine red in distilled water.

Cobalt chloride paper

5 g cobalt chloride

100 ml distilled water

Dissolve cobalt chloride in distilled water. Soak sheets or strips of filter paper in this solution. Allow to dry until blue and store in tightly stoppered bottles. If papers turn pink, restore blue color by heating.

Congo red solution

1 g Congo red

10 ml ethyl alcohol

90 ml distilled water

Add Congo red in alcohol to distilled water.

Crystal (gentian) violet

3 g crystal violet

20 ml 95% ethyl alcohol

0.8 g ammonium

80 ml distilled water

Add alcoholic crystal violet solution (3 g crystal violet to 20 ml 95% ethyl alcohol) to 1% aqueous ammonium oxalate (0.8 g ammonium to 80 ml distilled water).

FAA (Formaldehyde, Alcohol, Acetic Acid)
10 ml 40% formaldehyde
50 ml 95% ethyl alcohol
2 ml glacial acetic acid
40 ml distilled water

Fehling's solution
34.6 g copper sulfate
500 ml distilled water
 Dissolve copper sulfate in the distilled water.

Formalin solution
1 part formaldehyde
19 parts water

Gelatin solution
1 g gelatin
100 ml water
 Stir gelatin into cold water, then heat gently.

Hydrochloric acid, 20%
20 parts conc. hydrochloric acid
16 parts water
 Carefully pour acid into water. *Never pour water into the acid.*

Iodine stock solution
5 g iodine crystals
10 g potassium iodide
1000 ml distilled water
 Place iodine crystals and potassium iodide into 1 liter flask. Add 100 ml distilled water to dissolve. Add sufficient water to make 1 liter. Refrigerate until needed.

Methyl cellulose solution
10 g methyl cellulose
90 ml water
 Dissolve methyl cellulose in water. (Methyl cellulose solution is used to slow down the movement of protozoans.)

Nitric acid, dilute
1 part conc. nitric acid
4 parts water
 Add acid to water.

Phenylthiocarbamide (PTC) solution

50 mg phenylthiocarbamide (propyl-thiouracil)

1000 ml distilled water

Dissolve PTC in 100 ml distilled water, then add distilled water to make 1 liter of solution.

Ringer's solution (Amphibian)

0.14 g potassium chloride

6.50 g sodium chloride

0.12 g calcium chloride

0.1 g sodium bicarbonate

1000 ml distilled water

Add the minerals to the distilled water and dissolve thoroughly.

Starch solution (1%)

1 g cornstarch or arrowroot starch

100 ml distilled water

Mix starch with 3 ml distilled water to form a paste. Add 97 ml boiling distilled water and stir. Cook for 2 minutes, stirring constantly. Allow to cool.

Sulfuric acid, dilute

1 part conc. sulfuric acid

5 parts water

Add acid to water. *Do not pour the water into the acid.*

Thyroid-wheat mixture

whole wheat flour
5 2-grain thyroid tablets
5 ml distilled water

On an analytical balance, weigh an amount of whole wheat flour equal in weight to five 2-grain thyroid tablets. Grind the tablets and the flour together in a mortar. Add 5 ml of distilled water to form a paste. Spread the paste on a clean glass plate. Allow the paste to dry. Then grind the dried mixture and put it in a stoppered, labeled bottle. Refrigerate until needed.

Triiodothyronine solution

0.25 g triiodothyronine crystals
400 ml distilled water

Dissolve triiodothyronine crystals in distilled water. Put in a stoppered bottle and refrigerate until needed.

Yeast suspension

1 g peptone
½ packet dry yeast
500 ml 5–10% molasses

Combine ingredients and culture for at least 12 hours at 25-30° C.